VOODOO
KILLERS

VOODOO KILLERS

Slavery, sorcery and supernatural

JOSEPH CARLSON

Futura

FUTURA

First published in Great Britain in 2011 by Futura

Copyright © Omnipress 2011

The moral right of the author has been asserted.

A CIP catalogue record for this book
is available from the British Library.

ISBN 978-0-7088-6745-7

Typeset in Great Britain by Omnipress Limited
Printed and bound in Great Britain by Cox & Wyman

Futura
An imprint of
Little, Brown Book Group
100 Victoria Embankment
London EC4Y 0DY

An Hachette UK Company
www.hachette.co.uk

www.littlebrown.co.uk

The views expressed in this publication are those of the author.
The information and the interpretation of that information are
presented in good faith. Readers are advised that where ethical
issues are involved, and often highly controversial ethical issues
at that, they have a personal responsibility for making their own
assessments and their own ethical judgements.

CONTENTS

INTRODUCTION

Wackos, fruitloops, nutjobs and freaks. Just a few of the insults that could be thrown the way of many of the people featured in this book. Most of them were responsible for heinous crimes of murder, kidnapping and slavery and many of them were marked out from the beginning of their lives as people on the fringes of society who, rejected by that society, concluded that they did not have to adhere to its strictures. Instead, they played by their own rules, indulging their basest desires or manipulating and moulding vulnerable people to their will.

In this book, however, there is also state-sanctioned killing, the kind that was often necessary, to the minds of its practitioners, for the very survival of their society and the rest of the universe. Human sacrifice, like prayer, is a form of communication with a deity, seeking gratification or special treatment from that deity. It shows a society performing the godlike act of destruction, usually in order to ensure its continued existence – from death comes life.

Sacrifice of humans was also carried out in the past for very practical reasons such as ensuring good fortune for a new a building or a bridge. Victims were sacrificed and buried in the foundations or in the walls. Children were often selected as the best victims in such circumstances and several ancient fortresses in Wales show evidence of this practice.

Strange though it sounds, it has also been suggested that ritualized human sacrifice reduced the incidence of violence in those societies in which it was practiced and helped to keep those societies together.

Of course, there were also many instances of servants or slaves being killed to accompany their master or leader into the next life and make his existence there as comfortable as it had been in this one. Excavations in Egypt and China have uncovered many examples of such sacrifices and there is evidence that prior to their death, these victims took part in elaborate ceremonies.

Often sacrifice was practiced simply to appease the gods and ensure continued existence from one year to the next. The fantastically complex Maya civilization that was at its peak in the area that is now southern Mexico and northern Central America between 250 and 900 AD, practiced human sacrifice and bloodletting, throwing victims, tied together, into a large hole in the centre of their main city, Chichen Itza. Temple sacrifices also took place when the Maya were faced with catastrophes such as pestilence, rebellion, droughts or famines.

The masters of human sacrifice, however, were the Aztecs who brought an extraordinary drama to their sacrifices. Just as in the movies, a victim was taken to the highest point of one of their stunning temples, where his still beating heart was ripped out and held aloft to the sun as the crowds below chanted and sang. The body of the hapless victim was then thrown down the steps of the temple. Tens of thousands – perhaps even hundreds of thousands – were sacrificed every year in this bloody way.

But human sacrifice has been practiced almost everywhere at every time. In Africa it was common practice until the colonial powers put a stop to it in the nineteenth century. Festivals demanded the death of humans and great events such as the death of a king demanded a great sacrifice when thousands of slaves would sometimes be ritually killed. Sadly, of course, it would appear that human sacrifice has never really gone away, as the discovery of the 'Thames Torso Boy' in London in September 2001 proves. Body parts are necessary for certain kinds of sorcery and the only way these can be obtained is through the death of a human being.

The Spanish Inquisition and the Salem Witch Trials provide further examples of state-sponsored killing. The extraordinary hysteria that gripped the small settlement of Salem in 1692 resulted in a number of executions and a community in shock for a time. The Spanish Inquisition, on the other hand, was initially about the maintenance of the power of the Catholic Church. It became a means of settling grudges and getting rid of people. It also became the vehicle of fanatics and sadists who indulged in horrific torture in order to obtain a pre-ordained result.

Sometimes, of course, people become bewitched, entranced or were just driven to kill by an inordinate desire for power. Often, however, it is nothing less than insanity that drives them to commit their horrific crimes.

Astonishing stories of sorcery can be found around the world. The dead are made to walk, the living are killed by just a glance, a whispered phrase or the apparently innocuous pointing of a stick or a bone. People frighten themselves to death in such cases, whether it be in the Australian bush, in West Africa or Haiti. The power of Voodoo is extraordinary. It has even been harnessed by governments, as in the case of Papa Doc Duvallier in Haiti who posed as the living embodiment of the Voodoo spirit, Baron Samedi.

Sorcery can be the manipulation of people's minds to make them believe they are going to die, but it can also be the manipulation of people's minds by a charismatic and powerful leader-figure who makes them believe that what he is telling them is the truth. Examples to be found here are, Ervil LeBaron, Shoko Asahara, Roch Theriault and Jeffrey Lundgren. These were men who developed a messianic hold on their followers, sometimes persuading them to carry out acts of unspeakable evil. It is uncanny how similar some of their stories are. They begin as men of religion, but often outgrow the church of which they are members. They form a splinter group, frighten their followers with a prophesy of the approach of Armageddon, become increasingly debauched and resort to murder, sometimes multiple murder. Their power over people is a kind of voodoo, a magical power that very few have.

Voodoo has mostly been effective in under-developed societies where ignorance and superstition provide an ideal breeding ground for outlandish beliefs. But real Voodoo, or similar types of witchcraft or sorcery, is also found in more advanced societies, as evidenced by the goings-on amongst Dutch and German settlers in the state of Pennsylvania in the nineteenth and early twentieth centuries. The folk religion and magic called Pow-wow, a unique blend of Christian theology and shamanistic practices, was brought over from Europe and was used by these people for healing and obtaining good fortune, but sometimes also for evil intent, as in the case of the notorious Pennsylvania Dutch Hex Murder, when John Blymire brutally murdered fellow Pow-wow hexenmeister, Nelson Rehmeyer after becoming convinced that Rehmeyer had been putting spells on him that had ruined his life.

Bad magic also resulted in murder after Raymond Fernandez learned about the religion of Vodun, or Voodoo. He wooed many women using the special powers he believed Vodun gave him, ending up with Martha Seabrook Beck, with whom he embarked on a career of murder that culminated in both being dispatched from this life via the electric chair at Sing Sing prison in 1949.

Evil has appeared in the strangest of places, places such as the sacristy of a chapel where Sister Margaret Ann Pahl was ritually murdered by priest Gerry Robinson. Or in the basement of a suburban house in Austria where Josef Fritzl kept his daughter Elizabeth captive for twenty-four years so that he could keep his eye on her and continue to rape her whenever he wanted.

The reasons for kidnapping are often complex, but invariably sexual. Men such as Gary Heidnik, Gerald Gallego and Cameron Hooker wanted to have control over women. Gallego wanted sex slaves who did his bidding for a few hours until he viciously killed them while Hooker and Heidnik kept their captives for considerable periods of time. The extraordinary story of Colleen Stan's seven years of captivity by Hooker, much of it spent in a box under Hooker and his wife's bed, beggars belief, as does the horror that to which Gary Heidnik's women captives were subjected in the basement of his Philadelphia house. This was pure evil at work, the indulgence of a human being's basest instincts.

The same can be said of Robert Bordello's activities. He was a homosexual sadist who toyed with his male captives, doing unspeakable things to them while he had them tied to a bed in his house often taking it just a little too far and killing them.

And yet, there are cases such as that of Elizabeth Smart who was abducted in 2002 by religious fanatics Brian David Mitchell and Wanda Barzee. On numerous occasions, Elizabeth had the opportunity to escape or to make it known that she was being held against her will, walking down the street in Salt lake City or left alone at a campsite. But she did not flee and even when finally found by police, it took some persuasion to get her to admit that she was Elizabeth Smart. Even then, she confirmed her identity with the odd words, 'If thou sayest, I sayest'. Colleen Stan, too, had ample opportunity to flee her captors or make it known to neighbours that she was being held prisoner. She even went out drinking with Cameron Hooker's wife. She always came back, however. Natascha Kampusch went skiing with her captor, Wolfgang Priklopil, and made numerous shopping trips with him. Perhaps these women were victims of Stockholm Syndrome, the psychological phenomenon where hostages have positive feelings towards their captors.

Satanism is a phenomenon that grew in popularity towards the end of the twentieth century, encouraged by the growth of death metal and black metal music, the lyrics of which are replete with occult messages. Often, it is emphasized by many of the musicians involved, this type of music is no more than entertainment; the lyrics, they insist, are not intended to be taken seriously. The Italian black metal group, Beasts of Satan, walked the talk, however. Beasts of Satan was a music group but it was also a Satanic cult that callously murdered three people, one because a group member thought, in his twisted mind, that she was the embodiment of the Virgin Mary.

Others were young people swept away by the fad for vampirism, happy to have found something in their shattered lives to believe in. Rod Ferrell and Natasha Cornett were lonely people who came from disturbed backgrounds in which they had been seriously let down by their parents and adults in general. Cast to the fringes of society, bullied and ostracized, they turned to murder as a means of claiming some kind of identity for themselves.

Strange cults, too, have strange rituals. The very organized mass suicide of the members of Marshall Apple white Heaven's Gate was a sacred ritual of a kind. The members bade farewell in astonishingly cheerful tapes before taking poison and pulling plastic bags over their heads. The members of the Order of the Solar Temple also carried out ritual mass suicide in three different locations. Laid out in ritual formation around an altar and garbed in robes, this was a ceremonial killing that astonished the world and as details emerged about their cult and its beliefs and practices there was more astonishment. It seemed so strange that it was thought that it must have been a con-trick, that the leaders must have persuaded everyone else to kill themselves and had then skipped off with the millions of dollars the organization had in its bank account. There was great surprise therefore, when their bodies were found amongst the dead. They had actually believed what they had been preaching.

Other murders in this book such as that of Dr Howard Appledorf and those committed by the seriously disturbed Coral Watts seem almost normal compared to the ones committed by Satanists, vampire freaks and religious maniacs. The same evil was present, however. Dr Appledorf's murderers tried and failed to make their pointless murder seem like the work of someone who was driven by the occult while Watts was driven by an insane loathing for women, believing that he was fighting and destroying their evil spirits by murdering them. His dreams were haunted by these spirits, but as he admitted to a psychiatrist, he rather enjoyed fighting them.

If anything, *Voodoo Killers* demonstrates to us what a strange world we live in. It also shows the extremes to which people can be driven by their religion, their obsessions or their mania. It is difficult not to believe that Voodoo does stalk the world around us as we go about our daily business, whether it is in the mad eyes of a kidnapper or the manipulative charm of a charismatic leader. Be careful out there!

PART ONE

HUMAN SACRIFICE

THE MAYANS AND THE AZTECS

Bloodletting and human sacrifice were practiced amongst all the cultures on pre-Columbian Mesoamerica. It first became common with the Olmec's about three thousand years ago but was passed down to the cultures that followed them, to peoples such as the Mayans. The motives for it are unclear but it is presumed that it was done in order to maintain the order of the universe.

THE MAYANS

Sacrifice was a religious act in Maya culture. Super-intended by priests, it more often than not involved bloodletting or animal sacrifice, but although human sacrifice did not take place on the scale of the Aztecs, it did happen.

Ritualized bloodletting was performed in public during one of the large number of festivals that the Mayans staged. Religious and political leaders would pierce a part of their bodies – normally the tongue, ear or foreskin and the higher the person's position in the hierarchy, the greater was the amount of blood that was expected to be given. The blood collected would be smeared directly onto the idol that was being worshipped or would be collected on paper which was then burned. In what is modern-day Nicaragua, the blood was smeared onto maize that was baked to make sacred bread. Those of the lower echelons of society could also take part in bloodletting rituals and blood from the foreskins of young men was especially prized.

Indeed, blood from the penis and the vagina was most sacred and was believed to have extraordinary fertilizing power. In one particularly gruesome ritual, like the others to do with the regeneration of the natural world, men gathered in a line, pierced a hole through their penises and passed chord through the hole, Thus strung together, their highly prized blood was collected and used to anoint the idol.

Naturally, this was all anathema to the Spanish missionaries working to convert the peoples of south and central America. One of them wrote of the difficulties they faced:

After the people had been thus instructed in religion, and the youths benefitted as we have said, they were perverted by their priests and chiefs to return to their idolatry; this they did, making sacrifices not only by incense, but also of human blood. Upon this the friars held an Inquisition, calling upon the Alcalde Mayor for aid; they held trials and celebrated an Auto, putting many on scaffolds, capped, shorn and beaten, and some in the penitential robes for a time. Some of the Indians out of grief, and deluded by the devil, hung themselves; but generally they all showed much repentance and readiness to be good Christians.

There were no domesticated farm animals in Mesoamerica. Food was obtained from hunting and deer was commonly the prey. The amount of deer parts in Classical Maya sites suggests that they were the most common animal to be sacrificed, followed in popularity by dogs and birds. Animals were commonly sacrificed before any undertaking.

Mayans were more likely to sacrifice a dog than a human, but it has become increasingly apparent that human sacrifice was practiced, especially in the city of Chichen Itza which was the Mayan capital from the late Classical period. At Chichen Itza are two large natural holes in the ground with pools at the bottom. These would have provided a good supply of drinking water for the city but the largest – Cenote Sagrado (the Well of Sacrifice) also served as a place where people were sacrificed to the rain god Chaac. Analysis of remains found in the hole has confirmed this, the wounds on the bones being consistent with human sacrifice.

It was an eleborate ceremony. A fire would be lit on an altar and the sacrificial victims would be brought forward before a crowd that would have gathered from every part of the country to witness the spectacle. A long cord was tied around each of the victims, linking them together. At the moment when the smoked stopped rising from the altar fire, they were hurled into the hole. The crowd would, meanwhile, be praying throughout the ritual and their prayers continued for some time. After the ceremony, the bodies were hauled up out of the hole and buried in a nearby grove of trees.

Around 3500 years ago, Mesoamericans began to play organized team sports centered on a bouncing rubber ball. The ball court was a feature of city centres in classical Mesoamerica and sports events drew invariably large crowds. For the winners, there was wealth, fame and prestige. For the losers, however, there was often death in the form of sacrifice to the gods, usually by decapitation, as depicted in Maya art. The Aztecs also played a version of the game. In their version, the skulls of losing team members were placed in a 'skull rack' at the side of the field, and their blood was offered as 'food for the gods'. There has even been speculation that the heads and skulls were used as balls.

Maya society was organized into independent city states, meaning that local dignitaries and religious people had the authority to initiate human sacrifices as they wished. Crop pests, political turmoil, droughts and famines were probably the most common reasons for human sacrifice. In such instances, slaves were purchased for that purpose and, following a series of rituals, were anointed with a blue dye. They were then either shot through the heart with an arrow or, in the way that film and television have always shown such sacrifice, held down on the altar to allow a priest to cut out the still-beating heart using a ceremonial knife. It would take place at the top of a pyramid or on a raised platform. No matter how the death occurred, the heart was presented to the temple idol which was smeared with the blood of the victim and then burned.

In the religious hierarchy, the head was called Ah Kin Mai ('The Highest One of the Sun') who ruled over all the priests below him called Ah Kin ('The One of the Sun'). There were two special priestly functions involved in human sacrifice: the *chac*, who were elderly men who held down the victim, and the *nacon*, who cut the living heart from the victim after skilfully making a small incision below the rib cage.

Like the Aztecs, the Mayans also used prisoners of war for sacrifice. Unlike the Aztecs, however, the Mayans did not go to war simply to find sacrificial victims.

The sacrifice of children occurred in certain circumstances such as in dedications for temples and other buildings. When a new king ascended the throne, children's hearts were also used to propitiate the gods. A mass grave of children's remains has been found in the Maya region of Comalcalco. These one-to two-year-olds were probably sacrificed when the temples of the Comalcalco acropolis were built.

THE AZTECS

In the summer of 1521, the great conquistador, Hernán Cortés, and the survivors of a disastrous battle with Aztec warriors, watched from a distance as sixty-two of their brothers-in-arms who had been captured by the enemy army were paraded in a pageant at one of the major temple-pyramids of the great Aztec capital Tenochtitlán, now Mexico City. Cortés later described the horror enacted before the Spaniards' eyes:

The dismal drum of Huichilobos sounded again,
accompanied by conches, horns, and trumpet-like
instruments. It was a terrifying sound, and when we
looked at the tall cue [temple-pyramid] from which it
came we saw our comrades who had been captured
being dragged up the steps to be sacrificed. When they
had hauled them up to a small platform in front of
the shrine where they kept their accursed idols we saw
them put plumes on the heads of many of them; and
then they made them dance with a sort of fan in front
of Huichilobos. Then after they had danced the papas
[Aztec priests] laid them down on their backs on some
narrow stones of sacrifice and, cutting open their chests,
drew out their palpitating hearts which they offered to
the idols before them.

Sacrifice played a huge part in Aztec culture. They believed in the 'Legend of the Five Suns' in which all the gods sacrificed themselves so that mankind could live. Therefore, they believed that the universe was sustained by a great ongoing sacrifice. This implied a huge indebtedness throughout society and, indeed, *nextlahhualli* (debt-payment) was a metaphor that was often used for human sacrifice.

And it was undertaken on a massive scale. When the Great Pyramid of Tenochtitlan was re-consecrated in 1487, the Aztecs are said to have sacrificed more than 80,000 prisoners over a period of four days. This may not actually have been physically possible, but there is little doubt that a huge number of sacrifices were made during that time.

One scholar has estimated that the number of people sacrificed in modern-day central Mexico in the fifteenth century was 250,000 per year and another source suggests that one in five children were killed annually.

The most common form of human sacrifice was heart-extraction. The Aztecs believed the heart to be both the seat of a person and a fragment of the sun's heat (*istli*). Heart-extraction was the means of liberating the *istli* and reuniting it with the sun. Aztec art depicts a victim's hearts flying towards the sun on a trail of blood.

The fifty-two-year cycle was fundamental to Mesoamerican cultures and the Aztecs, fearing that the universe would collapse at the end of each cycle, performed a New Fire Ceremony. All fires were extinguished and at midnight a human sacrifice was made. They would then wait until dawn, hoping that the sacrifice had been enough to placate the gods. If the sun reappeared they knew that once again the world had not come to an end and that a new cycle had begun. The body of the victim of the sacrifice was burned and the new fire from that was carried to every house and building in the city. This was a ceremony that gave the Aztecs, to their minds, a new identity. Having long been known as 'the people without face' to the enemy states that surrounded them, they became – in their own minds at least, the people who were responsible for the continued existence of the universe. They began to call themselves 'the people of the sun'.

They made many sacrifices throughout the year to specific gods. Huitzilopochtli was their tribal deity who was identified with the sun at its zenith and with war. Victims who were sacrificed to Huitzilopochtli were placed on sacrificial stone slabs and the priest would cut through the abdomen with an obsidian or flint blade to rip out the still-beating heart and hold it up to the sky. The remainder of the victim's body would be cremated or given to the warrior who had captured him. He would either cut the body into pieces that would be sent as offerings to important people or it would be eaten in ritual cannibalism.

The most powerful god of them all was Tezcatlipoca who ruled over night, sorcery and destiny. He was believed by the Aztecs to have created war to provide food and drink for him and the other gods. He was an all-seeing, omnipotent god to whom some men were sacrificed in ritual gladiatorial combat. The sacrificial victim was tied in place and given a mock weapon with which to defend himself. He was then killed in a one-sided combat with four warriors who were armed to the teeth.

In one particular ceremony the sacrifice of a young impersonator of Tezcatlipoca would be undertaken. This youth would spend the year dressed as the god and he would be treated as such, as the representative of Tezcatlipoca on earth. Four beautiful women were provided for him and he was expected to stroll through the streets of Tenochtitlan playing a flute.

On the day of the sacrifice, a great feast was held in honour of the god, at the end of which the young man would climb to the top of the pyramid-temple, break his flute in two and give his body up to the waiting priests.

Aztecs feared that if they failed to appease the fire god Huehueteotl fire would engulf their city. Therefore, a number of captives would be burned after a huge feast in the god's honour. They would then be pulled from the fire and their hearts torn out.

Meanwhile, children were sacrificed to the rain god Tláloc in order to ensure that rain would come to water their crops. Priests made the children cry as they walked to their deaths because the god required the tears of the young.

In the Aztec sacrificial ritual, the victim was taken to the top of the temple where he would be laid on a stone slab by four priests. A fifth priest then sliced open his abdomen and through the diaphragm with a ceremonial flint knife. He seized the heart and ripped it out still beating before placing it in a bowl that sat in the hands of a statue of the god being honoured. The body was then cast down the steep steps of the temple.

Meanwhile, as this was going on, priests and audience would be stabbing, piercing and cutting themselves in order to let out blood in self-sacrifice. Dances, hymns and percussive music highlighted the various phases of the ritual.

The sacrificial victim's internal organs were fed to animals while his head was put on display.

There were other forms of human sacrifice such as shooting with arrows, burning, flaying or drowning. Aztec warriors were expected to provide at least one prisoner for sacrifice and those who managed to do this would become full-time members of the warrior elite. In some instances, young warriors would band together to capture a prisoner.

But prisoners were not the only source of victims. Slaves were used, although slaves could mean Aztecs who had fallen into debt or committed a crime. Children who were sacrificed were usually from noble families, handed over for ritual slaughter by their own parents.

Whoever the victims were, however, they were expected to go to their death with dignity. If a victim showed fear or was reluctant to proceed, it was taken as a bad omen and he was taken to one side and quietly slain.

In 1521, Hernán Cortés avenged the deaths of his sixty-two soldiers when he conquered Tenochtitlan, defeating the Aztec Triple Alliance under the command of Hueyi Tlatoani Moctezuma II, marking the fall of the Aztec Empire and the end of Aztec culture.

ANCIENT GREECE AND ANCIENT ROME

ANCIENT GREECE

In Ancient Greece, human sacrifice was not as prevalent as in some other cultures mainly because people did not approve of it. Of course, it was seen as a good thing in the context of appeasing the gods, but it was still murder, no matter how it was dressed up and, generally speaking, sacrifice was mostly of domestic animals.

There were instances of it, however. For example, when a rich man died his slaves would sometimes be killed so that they might serve their master in the afterlife. There were also instances of wives being killed at their husband's funeral. The philosopher Porphyry who lived from around 234 to 305, mentions that the people of Rhodes used to sacrifice a man to the god Kronos. Later, however, in keeping with the increasing distaste for human sacrifice, a person who had been condemned to death for a crime would merely be kept in prison until the allotted date and then on the day of the festival, was led out of the gates of the city, taken to a temple, given wine and slaughtered. It was frowned upon, however, something from an uncivilized past. The Greek historian Herodotus mentions only one human sacrifice in his work, that of two Egyptian boys in order to secure favourable winds at sea. He describes it with distaste as 'an unholy act' and elsewhere in his work, he describes human sacrifice as something that only foreigners did.

Of course, Greek mythology and literature is littered with examples of human sacrifice but it was largely a discredited practice that had more or less disappeared. This can be seen in some versions of the myth of Iphigenia who was going to be sacrificed by her father Agamemnon but was replaced by a deer put there by the goddess Artemis.

One ritual that some sources have suggested was human sacrifice was the Pharmakos in which a human scapegoat was chosen – usually a slave, a cripple or a criminal – who was expelled from the community at times of disaster or turmoil, such as when a city was ravaged by plague, invasion or plague. It was believed at such time that some kind of purification was required to placate the gods

On the first day of the festival known as the Thargelia, a festival of Apollo that took place in

Athens, two men were led out. Some sources suggest the men were actually sacrificed by being burned or thrown from a cliff while others reject this and argue that they were merely subjected to beating or stoning but that the ritual stopped short of killing them.

ANCIENT ROME

Like the Ancient Greeks, the Romans of the Late Republic which is judged to have lasted from 147 until 30 BC, came to be disgusted at the idea of human sacrifice and, in fact, in 97 BC, during the consulship of Publius Licinius Crassus and Gnaeus Cornelius Lentulus, it was banned by senatorial decree. The fact that human sacrifice was proscribed became a symbol of the civilized nature of the Roman Empire, distinguishing it from other cultures.

Romans were horrified when tales began to arrive in Rome regarding the sacrificial practices of the Celts. Their victims were stabbed in the back with a sword or knife and the future was divined from the movement of their bodies and limbs as well as by the way their blood flowed as they struggled towards death.

Their disgust led the Romans to ban the practice in the various countries they conquered. Meanwhile, they turned to animal sacrifice or the notion of human sacrifice became merely a symbolic gesture.

Of course, human sacrifice had been practised on a large scale in the Roman past. Indeed, traces could be found in many of the Roman religious rituals of the time, such as the one of 15 May when the Vestal Virgins would parade and toss rush puppets from the Pons Suplicius, one of the bridges over the Tiber. It is thought to be the vestige of an older practice of sacrificing old men in this way. Similarly, in the Feriae Latinatae festival at the end of April, puppets were hung from trees, probably substituting for an earlier custom of sacrificing young boys by hanging them.

Human sacrifice is certainly thought to have occurred prior to the founding of Rome and probably also in the archaic period. There are elements of gladiatorial combat that also indicate that at one time in the distant past human sacrifice was common.

According to the Roman historian Livy, gladiatorial combat was first introduced in Rome in 246 BC, staged in honour of the dead, originally as a religious festival. Participation was in the beginning voluntary and the combat usually depicted a mythical struggle but rarely resulted in the death of any of the participants. Later, however, criminals, slaves and conquered people began to be used and their deaths became viewed as sacrifices to the souls of the dead.

There were some memorable events. In 216 BC, Marcus Ameilius Lepidus who had been a consul, was honoured by his sons following his death with three days of gladiatorial combat in the Forum Romanum, using twenty-two pairs of gladiators. In 183 BC a festival held to mark the funeral of Publius Liciniusin featured one hundred and twenty gladiators in a gloriously bloody spectacle.

In a munus – a combat in honour of a deceased person, the death of a gladiator was followed by the ritualized removal of his body from the arena, although we are unsure what form these rites took. The Christian author Tertullia, commenting on the practice in Roman Carthage, describes the removal of corpses by someone who impersonates the 'brother of Jove', Dis Pater. He struck the corpse with a mallet and another, dressed as Mercury, tested for signs of life with a heated wand.

Few gladiators survived more than ten matches or lived past the age of thirty. Most, in fact, would have died between the ages of eighteen and twenty-five.

Eventually, gladiatorial combat evolved into

an opportunity for self-promotion by rich and influential men as well as politicians trying to make a name for themselves and although many still died, there was little that was religious or sacrificial about their deaths.

From the very early days of the Roman Republic, examples can be found where criminals were given to the gods, in which case they were known as sacer. It is important to know that there was little distinction in those times between civil law and religious law – the laws were, after all, believed to have been handed down to man by the gods. Criminals, therefore, were viewed as having breached sacred rules and regulations. Those found guilty were executed in order to restore divine order and, as such, may be considered to have been sacrificial victims.

There were specific instances, however – recorded by Roman historians Livy and Plutarch – when human sacrifice was practiced at Rome. A pair of Gauls and a pair of Greeks, a man and woman in each case were buried alive in the Forum Boarium to placate the souls of the dead – the *Manes* – and the Dii Inferi – the Roman gods of the Underworld. Vestal Virgins also suffered the horrific death of being buried alive usually when they had broken their vow of chastity. In 483 BC, Vestal Oppia was buried for this reason although Livy claims that she was sacrificed, in reality, to appease the gods after a series of bad omens.

There were instances of self-sacrifice too. Roman generals are known to have sacrificed themselves to the Manes. In 340 BC, for instance, the Roman general Decius Mus offered himself to the gods in a special ritual and then charged the enemy. If he managed to survive, a larger than life statue would have been buried in his place, thus satisfying the dead. Meanwhile, captured enemy generals were ritually strangled before a statue of Mars the war god.

When the sixth Roman king, Servius Tullius, who reigned from 578 to 535 BC, expanded the Roman city walls, four individuals – an adult male aged between thirty and forty, a child, a young adult male aged sixteen to eighteen and a female – were sacrificed and buried beneath the old wall that encircled the Palatine Hill. The sacrifices were necessary because the old wall was being violated by the expansion.

Although banned, as in Ancient Greece, human sacrifice became symbolically important. In mythology, the mortal Hercules, for instance, dying on a burning wheel, achieves immortality to enter Olympus. The mortal king Osiris dies to become the divine judge of the dead.

This theme of death and subsequent resurrection into the divine became the central tenet of the mystery religions that came to Rome from the east. It can even be said that this symbolism was assimilated by Christian sects in which the crucifixion of Jesus Christ was viewed as a human sacrifice.

HUMAN SACRIFICE AND RITUAL KILLING IN AFRICA

Human sacrifice was extremely common in Africa, especially in West Africa, up to and during the nineteenth century.

Amongst the examples, one of the most notorious was the Annual Customs of Dahomey. Every year, the Kingdom of Dahomey would stage a huge festival in honour of its people's ancestors. The king would gather together his entire court along with foreign dignitaries and his people and perform sacrifices, Voodoo ceremonies, distribute gifts and – the practical part of the event – review his actions of the previous twelve months and make plans for the coming year.

It was a day when commoners could voice complaints against anyone in the kingdom, including the king himself, with the guarantee that if the complaint was upheld the person against whom it was raised would be punished.

The Voudou practitioners – *bokono* in the Fon language and *babalawo* in Yoruba – were always present and ready to determine what the divine will would be for a policy. The council of ministers would be consulted. But the 'council of dead kings' and other notable ancestors also had to be consulted to ensure that the decisions being arrived at were right and just, because the people saw the world they experienced as merely a part of a much larger universe that included the unseen world of the spirits. 'Messengers', therefore, had to be sent to the spirit world to communicate with the ancestors on these matters.

The 'messengers' numbered around five hundred men, selected from criminals or prisoners of war who would normally face a horrific death but, although they were going to die, as messengers they were at least spared that. The messages to the dead were whispered in their ears and their throats were then slit.

The answers from the dead kings were provided through divination. Cowry shells or seed pods were thrown in the air and the pattern they made on landing was plotted. From that were deduced the thoughts of the dead. Or Voudu adepts would become channels for the messages from the ancestors while they were possessed.

Sacrifices in many African states were particularly common after the death of a king or queen and on such occasions, it has been reported, hundreds or even thousands of slaves would be sacrificed. In 1727, in Dahomey, around 4,000 slaves are said to have been sacrificed on the death of the king.

Apart from in Dahomey, human sacrifice was practiced in the Benin Empire in modern-day Ghana and in the small independent states of what is now Nigeria.

To the north, human sacrifice had become rare due to the early adoption of Islam in areas such as the Hausa States between the Niger River and Lake Chad. It was banned in the remainder of the West African states only by force by the colonial powers – the British and the French – during the nineteenth century.

One important step was the success of the British in persuading the powerful Egbo secret society to come out in opposition to human sacrifice in 1850. The Egbo whose members are popularly known as Leopard Men, is a West African secret society based in Sierra Leone, Liberia and Cote d'Ivoire and that once practised cannibalism. It was devoted to paying tribute to the ancestors.

Egbo or Ekpe is a mysterious spirit that lives in the jungle and presides over the rituals and ceremonies of the society. Members are said to be messengers of the ancestors, or *ikan*. Only men can become members, boys being initiated at around the onset of puberty

Members dressed in leopard skins and would attack travellers and villagers with razor-sharp, claw-like weapons that were in the form of leopards' claws and teeth. After they had killed a victim, his or her flesh would be stripped from the body and distributed amongst members. This ritual cannibalism was supposed to strengthen not just the leopard men themselves but also the inhabitants of the villages in which they lived. Members are bound by an oath of secrecy and they have to pay for their membership.

Not only is the society a means of honouring ancestors, it also enforces the law in the region in which it operates. If someone is wronged, they inform the Ekpe-man, beat the drum in the Ekpe house or sound the Ekpe horn outside the hut of the wrong-doer. The society will then bring its influence to bear on the situation.

There are numerous instances of leopard men's activities. A German missionary, Dr Werner Jung, travelled to Liberia in 1930 to run a hospital at Bolahun in the heart of the jungle. He came face to face on many occasions with the Leopard Society and a similar organization, the Crocodile Society. He wrote about finding, on one occasion, the horribly mutilated body of a fifteen-year-old girl lying on a mat in a house. Her neck had been torn to ribbons, her intestines had been ripped out, her pelvis smashed and one thigh was missing. A part of the thigh, the flesh having been gnawed from it, and a piece of the thigh bone lay beside her body. He initially concluded that only an animal could have done such a thing, but on closer inspection noticed certain peculiarities that did not fit that conclusion. For a start, the skin at the edge of the undamaged part of her chest, seemed to have been cut regularly in gashes about an inch long. Furthermore, the girl's liver had been removed with a cut that was too straight to have been made by an animal. The intestine, too, had been cut off in a smooth, straight line and the thigh bone had been broken off by bending. None of these could have been achieved by a wild animal.

The government representative in the nearest town, Cape Mount, who claimed to have wiped out the Leopard Society in the region, was unable to discover who the perpetrators were but Junge forwarded his findings to the Minister of the Interior in Monrovia. The response from the government was that further investigation by him or any interference was undesirable in the interests of his own safety. It was only when the local chiefs were begged for help by the local population that the perpetrators were finally caught.

Astonishingly, amongst those apprehended was the head of a mission school who had reintroduced the Leopard Society to the area long after it had become extinct. The man stood trial but was not punished. He was asked by the judge merely to leave the district.

Ritual killing, known as *gboyo*, continued in Liberia into the second half of the twentieth century. Body parts such as the heart, blood, tongue, lips, genitals and fingertips are removed once the victim has been dispatched and the body is dumped. The perpetrators hope to bring wealth and power by using these body parts in sorcery. One notorious 1979 case is known as the Maryland Murders. Seven people, including a member of parliament and a senior policeman were hanged for the ritualistic murder of a musician, Moses Twe.

But it continues to happen. In March 2010, a woman and her unborn baby were killed and body parts were taken, again in Maryland County. Vials of blood were reportedly found in the nearby house of a senior county official. It has become big business now and seasoned criminals have become involved.

The exact extent of it under the presidencies of William Tubman who ruled from 1944 until 1971 and William Tolbert – 1971 to 1980 – may never be known due to the suppression of the press during those times. The fourteen-year-long Liberian Civil War, however, has provided countless reports of rape, murder and cannibalism, some of it involving men close to Charles Taylor who ruled the country from 1997 to 2003. Some sources suggest that President Taylor was himself involved in it. Ritual murder at that time became a political instrument instead of just a tribal one. Politicians used it to seek power and instead of being supposedly for the good of a community – wrong though that may be – it was for individual gain only.

In 2008, Milton Blahyi, also known as 'General Butt Naked', who had been a warlord in the long civil war, admitted to eating the hearts of children before going into battle. He would pluck out the heart and it would be divided into pieces to be eaten. Blahyi led his troops into battle totally naked except for his shoes and a gun, a practice, he claimed, that had been demanded of him by the devil. He sacrificed a child before every battle, claiming:

*Usually it was a small child, someone whose fresh
blood would satisfy the devil ... Sometimes I would
enter under the water,' he continued, 'where children
were playing. I would dive under the water, grab one,
carry him under and break his neck. Sometimes I'd
cause accidents. Sometimes I'd just slaughter them.*

Blahyi believed he had magical powers and could
become invisible. He also claimed that he met the
devil regularly and held conversations with him and
from the age of eleven to twenty-five, he participated
in monthly human sacrifices. He described a typical
battle thus:

*So, before leading my troops into battle, we would get
drunk and drugged up, sacrifice a local teenager, drink
their blood, then strip down to our shoes and go into
battle wearing colourful wigs and carrying dainty
purses we'd looted from civilians. We'd slaughter
anyone we saw, chop their heads off and use them
as soccer balls. We were nude, fearless, drunk and
homicidal. We killed hundreds of people – so many I
lost count.*

The practice of ritual killing continues into the
twenty-first century. In Tanzania, albino Africans

are being targeted because their body parts are highly prized, while in Nigeria there is an increase in the number of children disappearing and being murdered, in many cases to undergo ritual killing. People still believe that the use of charms and the performance of ritual sacrifice will strengthen them in business and politics as well as fortify them spiritually. Charms and potions will also, they believe, protect them from accidents and ill health. And in many cases, the deaths go unreported because the victims usually come from the more vulnerable sections of society. Their families and friends lack the resources and the money to seek redress and many fear the supernatural backlash if they did try to bring the perpetrators to justice.

HUMAN SACRIFICE IN THE INDIAN SUBCONTINENT

Human sacrifice in the Indian subcontinent dates back to the Indus Valley Civilization that existed during the Bronze Age, around five thousand years ago. A seal from the ancient fortified city of Harappa shows an upside-down nude female figure whose legs are outspread and from whose womb a plant is emerging. On the reverse side of the seal is depicted a man clasping a sickle and a woman seated on the ground praying. This scene has been interpreted by most scholars as a human sacrifice in honour of the Mother Goddess.

The Vedas, the oldest Hindu holy texts, written between 1500 BC and 500 BC mention human sacrifice but there is scholarly debate as to whether the references are merely symbolic. If it was practised then, however, it became less common during the post-Vedic period as the concept of *ahimsa* or non-violence entered mainstream Indian religious thinking with the emergence of religions such as Buddhism and Jainism.

In the seventh century, while describing the temple of Chandika, the Sanskrit scholar and poet Banabhatta describes a series of human sacrifices and in the ninth century, Haribhadra chronicles sacrifices to Chandika in Orissa.

Human sacrifice was, however, more common in southern India than elsewhere. An ancient Kali temple in the town of Kuknur in Karnataka, built in the eighth to ninth century, is well-known for its history of sacrifices. By the time the Hindu religious text, the Kalika Purana, was written in the eleventh century, human sacrifice was once again an accepted part of worship. The Kalika Purana states, however, that blood sacrifice is only permissible when the country is in danger and war is anticipated. The text claims that the person who performs the sacrifice will be victorious over his enemies. It contains instructions such as:

Let the head and blood of a human victim be presented on the right side of Devi (Kali), and the sacrificer address her standing in front. Let the head and blood of birds be presented on the left and the blood of a person's own body in front. Let the ambrosia proceeding from the heads of carnivorous animals and birds be presented on the left hand as also the blood of all aquatic animals.'

When the British occupied the states of Orissa and Andhra Pradesh around 1835, they uncovered the ritualistic practices of the tribe known as the Khonds who were notorious for the prevalence and the cruelty of their human sacrifices. The sacrifices were thought necessary by the pious Khonds to honour their earth goddess and persuade her fertilize the earth and allow their crops to grow.

Khonds themselves were never sacrificed. Victims had to be purchased, sometimes from traders who specialized in kidnapping people for this purpose and a high price had to be paid. Adult males were the most highly prized but small children were sometimes purchased and raised as part of a Khond family until they were old enough to be sacrificed.

Sacrificial festivities began about one month before the actual ritual and on the day itself, there was much feasting and drinking. Drugged and probably drunk, the victim was anointed with oil and turmeric and then tied to a post as everyone danced and sang around him. He was then savagely beaten by the crowd and his flesh was carved into small pieces. These were distributed and each family buried their piece in their field to ensure a good harvest and to protect them from evil.

This practice was eventually prohibited by the

British in 1845, the Khonds replacing it with the sacrifice of goats and buffaloes.

The worship of Kali, the dark god of violence and death, has been associated with human sacrifice. The Binderwurs of central India are reported to have eaten their sick and elderly in the belief that by doing so they were pleasing Kali. Cannibalism may also have been common practice amongst followers of the Shakti cults in India. The Kali sacrifice ritual is as follows:

> O man, through my good fortune thou hast appeared as a victim; therefore I salute thee ... I shall slaughter thee to-day, and slaughter as a sacrifice is no murder.' Thus meditating on the human-formed victim, a flower should be thrown on top of its head with the mantra: 'Om, Aim, Hriuh, Sriuh.' Then, thinking of one's own wishes, and referring to the Goddess, water should be sprinkled on the victim. Thereafter, the sword should be sprinkled on the victim. Thereafter, the sword should be consecrated with the mantra: 'O sword, thou art the tongue of Chandika... The sword, having thus been consecrated, should be taken up while repeating the mantra: 'Am hum phat,' and the excellent victim slaughtered with it.

Human sacrifice continues up to modern times,

however, and the victims are very often small children. A press report in 2006 stated that more than 2,500 young boys and girls had been sacrificed to the goddess Kali in India during the previous three years. In one particular case, Rama Sewak hacked his eight-year-old son to death in Delhi in broad daylight because he believed that Kali had told him that he would come back to life and bring good fortune to his family.

It was worse in the past, however, when villagers would sacrifice a child to Kali every Friday evening. However, one of the most notorious sources of sacrifices to Kali came in the shape of the wandering gangs of killers known as the Thuggee.

The Thuggee were a religious sect that worshipped the goddess, gangs of professional assassins whose membership crossed religious divides, encompassing Sikhs, Muslims and Hindus. They would roam the Indian countryside in search of victims and their methods were often subtle and painstaking. They were known to sometimes travel hundreds of miles with their victims before murdering them.

They considered it to be their religious duty to kill in the service of Kali and she had, according to the legend, created them, bringing them into existence to help decrease the population of the world. They did it by strangulation, using a rumal, a yellow silk scarf which symbolized the goddess. They were trained in the art of strangulation from an early age and killed in holy places that were known as bhils. The actual killing followed a prescribed ritual form and could only be carried out after a series of complex signs and omens had been seen. The murder happened under cover of darkness and was carried out by several men while the remainder created a distraction by singing and dancing at their camp, the raucous shouting and singing covering any noise there might be. Following the murder, sacred rights were performed in honour of the goddess and some of their plunder was always put aside for her.

The right to become a Thuggee was hereditary, passed down from generation to generation, and the leaders – Jamaadaars – also inherited their position from their fathers. If the people they murdered were accompanied by children, these were abducted and became members of the gang.

It is estimated that up to two million people died at the hands of the Thuggee over the three centuries – from the fifteen-hundreds until the mid-nineteenth century – that they operated. But the slaughter was brought to an end by one man. Captain William Sleeman, assistant to the Governor-General's agent in the Saugor and Nerbudda territories, resolved to do something about the Thuggee outrages.

He began to catalogue and map the Thuggee and the places where they killed. It was a remarkable piece of work, carried out obviously long before computers had been invented. As one Thuggee, Ameer Ali, wrote later:

The man unfolded a roll of paper written in Persian, and read a catalogue of crime, of murders, every one of which I knew to be true; a faithful record it was of my past life, with but few omissions.

With his work beginning to bear fruit, Sleeman was appointed superintendent of a new department which was the forerunner of India's Central Criminal Intelligence Department which took over the work in 1904. By that time, however, thousands of Thuggee had been imprisoned, gone into exile or been executed. Kali would have to remain thirsty for new blood.

It goes on, however. In 2006, in the remote village of Barha, a squalid collection of mud-bricked farmers' dwellings in the heart of the impoverished Khurja province of Uttar Pradesh, lived forty-three-year-old Sumitra Bushan. She had lived there for much of her life but it had never been so bad. Her husband had left her, and she was burdened with debt and facing a life of arduous labour in the sugarcane fields. Her sons, twenty-seven-year-old Satbir and twenty-three-year-old Sanjay were wastrels who never did a day's work. To make matters worse, the family, as one, began suffering from nightmarish visions of the goddess Kali.

She consulted a travelling holy man, a *tantrik*, who passed through the village. He instructed her to slaughter a chicken at the entrance to her home and offer the blood to Kali. She did as instructed but nothing changed and the nightmares kept tormenting her and her sons. She began to wake up screaming in the middle of the night.

She returned to the *tantrik* who told her this time that things were very serious and the only way she could rid herself of the dreams was to sacrifice a boy from her village.

A few nights later, she and her sons crept to their neighbour's house and abducted three-year-old Aakash Singh as he slept. They took him to their home where Satbir performed a *puja* ceremony. He recited a mantra and waved incense as his mother smeared the terrified child's body with sandalwood paste and ghee. Satbir and Sanjay then took a knife and sliced off Aakaash's nose, ears and hands before placing his bloody body in front of an image of Kali.

Next morning, Sumitra claimed to have found the boy's body outside her house but her sons confessed and the villagers attacked them. They were only just rescued before they were lynched and all three are now in prison.

It was not the only incident of its kind in the vicinity, however. In a village near Barha, a woman hacked her neighbour's three-year-old child to death after a *tantrik* told her that she would gain untold riches if she did so.

In another case, a couple who were desperate for a son, kidnapped a six-year-old and mutilated him to the accompaniment of mantras chanted by a *tantrik*. The ritual ended with the woman washing in the murdered child's blood.

While there is blind superstition and rampant illiteracy in some of India's more remote and poverty-stricken areas, human sacrifice will remain alive and well, unlike, of course, its victims.

HUMAN SACRIFICE IN EUROPE

All the people of Gaul are completely devoted to religion, and for this reason those who are greatly affected by diseases and in the dangers of battle either sacrifice human victims or vow to do so using the Druids as administrators to these sacrifices, since it is judged that unless for a man's life a man's life is given back, the will of the immortal gods cannot be placated. In public affairs they have instituted the same kind of sacrifice. Others have effigies of great size interwoven with twigs, the limbs of which are filled up with living people which are set on fire from below, and the people are deprived of life surrounded by flames. It is judged that the punishment of those who participated in theft or brigandage or other crimes are more pleasing to the immortal gods; but when the supplies of this kind fail, they even go so low as to inflict punishment on the innocent.

Julius Caesar wrote the above about the custom of human sacrifice in Britain and amongst the Celts. Romans were appalled at the barbarity of these peoples and at the notion of sacrificing human beings. They wrote incredulously about it, aghast that people could do such a thing. First century Greek historian Strabo wrote in his *Geography*:

> *The Romans put a stop both to these customs and to the ones connected with sacrifice and divination, as they were in conflict with our own ways: for example, they would strike a man who had been consecrated for sacrifice in the back with a sword, and make prophecies based on his death-spasms; and they would not sacrifice without the presence of the Druids. Other kinds of human sacrifices have been reported as well: some men they would shoot dead with arrows and impale in the temples; or they would construct a huge figure of straw and wood, and having thrown cattle and all manner of wild animals and humans into it, they would make a burnt offering of the whole thing.*

There is much debate, however, about whether the Celts actually did practice ritual killing or whether stories of it were actually no more than Roman propaganda, a justification for invading, invasion being given a veneer of respectability and responsibility by the suggestion that they were merely bringing civilized ways to barbaric societies. Examining the archaeology of the period should clarify matters, but it is sadly inconclusive.

In France, mutilated bodies have been discovered in a number of sanctuaries. Some are headless and in other cases just the head has been found. This is often used as evidence that Celts in that part of the world practiced human sacrifice but, although their deaths do appear to be cultic in nature, it has still not been proved beyond doubt that they were. In fact, where human skulls or headless bodies have been found, it is believed that in most cases, the decapitation took place after death. It is not even certain that these people were alive when they arrived at the sanctuary.

Julius Caesar mentions the practice whereby when a man died, his wife or entire family was sometimes killed so that they could accompany him in death. Whether this was done voluntarily or not is unproven. It is also debatable whether this can be considered sacrifice, suicide or, in the cases where it was involuntary, murder.

The Roman senator Cassius described how, during her rebellion against Roman occupation, the forces of the British Queen Boudica impaled Roman prisoners of war to the accompaniment of revelry and sacrifices in the sacred groves of Andate, the goddess identified with Victory in Britain.

Like much of northern Europe, the British

Isles had a tradition of human sacrifice and ritual killing. Indeed, bodies have been uncovered in the foundations of structures dating from Neolithic times right up to Roman times with injuries and in positions that suggest that they were foundation sacrifices, intended to bring good fortune to those using the building.

In Alveston, one hundred and fifty bodies were discovered that date back to the beginning of the Roman conquest of Britain and they appear to have all been killed by Druids in one single event.

Different gods required different methods of killing – victims sacrificed to Esus were hanged, those for Taranis were immolated and those killed to honour Teutates were drowned. Bodies have been uncovered in places that had special spiritual significance, such as wetlands.

One famous discovery was Lindow Man, the body of a man dug up in 1984 in a peat bog at Lindow Moss near Wilmslow in Cheshire in northwest England. Dating from probably the first century AD, Lindow Man appears to have been healthy and in his mid-twenties, a person of high status in his community judging from the fact that his body shows little or no sign of having ever been involved in heavy or rough work. He met his end, however, in a very violent manner that seems to have had ritualistic overtones. He ate a last meal consisting of charred bread and ingested a mistletoe concoction that might have sedated him, before being strangled, struck on the head and having his throat cut. One expert on Iron Age religion proposes that Lindow Man's death was an example of human sacrifice and that the triple death he suffered – bludgeoning, strangulation and having his throat cut – signified an offering to several different gods.

Other finds of bodies in France can also be considered likely human sacrifices and in Switzerland bodies have been found in lakes having been weighted with heavy timbers before being thrown into the water. At Danebury and elsewhere in Britain, the bodies of men and women have similarly been found weighted down and sometimes their bodies seem to have been savagely beaten. One grave revealed a man and a woman who had been buried alive together. Between the woman's legs was a foetus, suggesting that she had been pregnant when sacrificed and had miscarried through the sheer terror of her ordeal. Live burials have been discovered in both Ireland and across northern Europe suggesting that these deaths were indeed human sacrifices designed to appease the gods.

An excavation at Lindisfarne in 1981 revealed part of a human skull amongst swords, spears, tools and other articles that had been placed along the causeway. It was the back of a man's head. They named him Fissured Fred and soon deduced that he had been killed by a blow with a sword that had chopped out this part of his skull some 2,500 years ago. They also found several bones but that was all that remained of the man. Many believe that Fissured Fred was a human sacrifice, especially as this part of his body was found amongst so many items that themselves seemed to have been part of a sacrifice of some kind.

It is in Denmark, Germany and the Netherlands that most evidence of death by ritualistic killing has been uncovered. Many bodies have been found that were hanged or strangled, while others had died of blows to the head or had had their throats slit. They are believed to have been human sacrifices because they were found in places of spiritual significance where offerings to the gods would have been made.

Amongst Germanic peoples, human sacrifice was resorted to in exceptional circumstances such as famine, disease, war and crop failure. In Scandinavia, however, it was more institutionalized and happened frequently, some suggesting every nine years.

Roman historian Tacitus wrote how the Suebians of Germany sacrificed humans to honour their gods and Roman bureaucrat and historian Jordanes described how the Goths made human sacrifices to their god of war, hanging the severed arms of the victims from the branches of trees.

In 921, Arab traveller and writer, Ahmad ibn Fadlan, while on an embassy visit from the Baghdad Caliph to the Volga Bulgars, described the custom of the Volga Vikings of burying their warriors with slave women in the belief that these women would become their wives in Valhalla, the Viking heaven. He describes the funeral of a Scandinavian chieftain where a slave volunteered to die with him. After ten days of feasting, the woman was stabbed to death by a priestess who was described as the 'Angel of Death'. The slave's body was then burned with that of the dead chieftain on his boat. Indeed, many male warrior burials such as the ship burial at Balladoole on the Isle of Man and that of Oseberg in Norway, also show the presence of female bodies with signs of having been murdered before being put on the ship.

There were a great many human sacrifices to Odin, god of war in eleventh century Sweden, at the Temple at Uppsala. The Ynglinga Saga tells how King Domalde was sacrificed there in order to bring better harvests and victory in war. His descendent King Aun sacrificed nine of his sons to Odin in exchange for a longer life. In the Hervarar Saga, Heidrik agrees to sacrifice his son in exchange for command of more than a quarter of the men of Reidgotaland. With these men he seizes the whole kingdom and prevents the sacrifice of his son, substituting those already killed in the fighting for the boy.

Amongst the Slavic peoples of eastern Europe, too, there are signs that human sacrifice was practised, with prisoners of war being sacrificed to the Slavic god of war, Perun. Byzantine historian Leo the Deacon describes the sacrifice of prisoners by Sviatoslav I of Kiev during the Russo-Byzantine War in the tenth century.

Sacrifices were banned after the conversion to Christianity of the Kievan Rus by Prince Vladimir I in the 980s. The last known human sacrifice there was that of a young Christian, Ioann and his father Theodor who had tried to prevent the sacrifice of his son, but himself became a victim.

THE SPANISH INQUISITION

Having achieved a position of great power by the Middle Ages, the Roman Catholic Church wanted to maintain that power. To do so meant the suppression of heretics, opponents of the doctrine of the Church who publicly declared their beliefs, taught them to others and refused to denounce them.

As part of the Church's efforts to suppress heresy, Pope Gregory XI issued a papal bull – a decree – in 1231 that launched the Inquisition, a tribunal court system devised to try heretics and punish them. The Inquisition was to be conducted by the Dominican order of monks who were renowned for their knowledge of the complexities of theology.

The Spanish Inquisition was established in 1478 by the two rulers of Spain, King Ferdinand of Spain and Queen Isabella with the approval of the Pope who had been persuaded by the threat of the removal of Spanish troops from Rome where they were protecting the city from invasion by the Turks. Isabella and Ferdinand had recently succeeded in uniting their two kingdoms, Aragon and Castille and were now eager to also create religious unity in their new country. That would also contribute to the weakening of both strong family alliances in the country and local and regional political authorities.

There were also strong financial arguments for establishing the Inquisition in Spain, however. When someone was accused, all of their assets were immediately seized by the crown, their family being thrown into the street with nothing.

There had been growing concern about the religious diversity that was prevalent in Spain and non-Catholics suffered bigotry and racial violence. Jews were especially targeted, being subjected to frequent pogroms – massacres – and being isolated in ghettos. Many died in these attacks.

Following the introduction of the Spanish Inquisition, its first two inquisitors were Miguel de Morillo and Juan de San Martin. The first *auto-da-fe* – meaning literally 'act of faith', but coming to mean the burning at the stake of heretics – took place in Seville on 6 February 1481 when six people were burned alive. From that point onwards, the Inquisition rapidly grew in Castille and by 1492 tribunals had been established in eight Castilian cities – Avila, Cordoba, Jaen, medina del Campo, Segovia, Siguenza, Toledo and Valladolid.

In 1483, the man whose name is most often

associated with the Spanish Inquisition, Tomas de Torquemada was appointed Inquisitor General of Aragon, Valencia and Catalonia. Torquemada organized the process, establishing strict procedures for the Inquisition. There would be a thirty-day grace period for confessions and for evidence to be gathered.

That evidence could be something as simple as the observation of a lack of smoke coming from a chimney on Saturdays, indicating that the family living there was still secretly recognizing the Jewish Sabbath. Quantities of vegetables might be purchased by someone before the Feast of the Passover or meat might be purchased only from a butcher who has also converted to Catholicism.

Appeals were allowed to Rome, but to make such an appeal meant the death penalty and confiscation of property, as decreed by Ferdinand.

Between 1480 and 1530, it is estimated that around 2,000 people were sentenced to death by the Inquisition, a majority of them being Jews who had converted. King Ferdinand was still unhappy with the results, citing the 'great harm suffered by Christians from the contact, intercourse and communication which they have with the Jews, who always attempt in various ways to seduce faithful Christians from our Holy Catholic Faith'. In 1492, he issued the Alhambra Decree, banishing all Jews from Spain on pain of death. The only way that Jews could remain in the country was if they had converted to Catholicism. Converts such as these were known as *conversos* or sometimes the derogatory *marranos* which is Spanish for 'pig'. Many were suspicious, however, that these former Jews were still secretly practising Judaism and the Inquisition specifically targeted such people.

The number of Jews who left the country is unknown, figures ranging from 40,000 to 800,000. They went to Portugal – from which they were expelled in 1497 – and Morocco. A number also went to Italy.

The Inquisition not only sought to punish *conversos*. It also targeted Protestants, although there were not many of those in Spain, and the *Moriscos* – converts from Islam – who were mainly concentrated in the recently conquered kingdom of Granada, in Aragon and in Valencia. Their treatment was less harsh than that meted out to the Jewish *conversos*, mainly because they were mainly under the control of the nobility and their persecution would have been and insult to them as well as an assault on their economic well-being.

Offences, apart from heresy, upon which the inquisitors focussed included witchcraft, blasphemy and sodomy. Although witchcraft was pursued with a great deal less intensity than in other European countries such as France, Scotland and Germany, there were some notable cases. In Logroño, six of the witches of Zugarramurdi in Navarre were burned to death in 1610. However, the inquisitors were fairly sceptical about witchcraft, deeming it a superstition that had no basis in fact.

Blasphemy included verbal offences from taking the name of God in vain to questioning the doctrine of the Church. Also under this umbrella came issues of sexual morality and the misbehaviour of the clergy. Many people stood before a tribunal after affirming that sex between unmarried people was not a sin.

There were numerous trials for bigamy which in a time when a divorce was practically impossible to obtain, was relatively common. If convicted, men were sentenced to five years in the galley – a ship propelled by oarsmen – which was in itself a death sentence.

When the Inquisition arrived in a city, the first thing to happen was the reading of the Edict of Grace following the Sunday mass. This edict explained possible heresies and urged the members of the congregation to attend the tribunals and 'relieve their consciences'. The word 'grace' referred to the grace period within which people could reconcile themselves with the church without serious punishment. Many came forward and, having admitted their own sins, were happy to denounce others and informers, in fact, provided the main source of information for the inquisitors. After 1500, the Edicts of Faith were introduced. They dispensed with the period of grace and encouraged people to denounce their friends and neighbours.

It was made easier by the fact that the denunciations were anonymous. Defendants had no way of knowing who had denounced them. Consequently, false accusations were commonplace.

In the tribunal, the accused was required to testify but he was not provided with any legal assistance. Neither was he informed what the charges against him were. Refusal to testify was taken as an admission of guilt and anyone was permitted to testify against the accused – family members, criminals and other heretics. There would rarely be witnesses for the defence. If someone testified on behalf of an accused person suspicions were raised that they were themselves heretics.

The court, which travelled the country conducting tribunals was made up of two inquisitors who were accompanied by secretaries and other tribunal officials. The aim of the inquisitor was quite simply to extract a confession or an admission of guilt and he was specially trained in the art of interrogation, having learned how to confuse or lead an accused person or a witness. People accused of heresy were sometimes imprisoned for years until a confession was obtained.

In 1252, Pope Innocent IV issued a papal bull that permitted the use of torture to obtain a confession if all other attempts at obtaining proof of heresy had been exhausted. This task was often given to local authorities but inquisitors also participated in torture sessions. If an accused heretic confessed under torture, he had to confess again while not under torture for the confession to be valid. Torture was employed regardless of sex or age and children, the elderly and women were subjected to it, if it was deemed necessary.

Some inquisitors used starvation as a form of torture or forced the accused to drink large quantities of water or other fluids. Sometimes burning coals were placed on the body.

More effective were torture techniques such

as *strappado*, also known as *garrucha*. The hands of the accused were tied behind his back and the remainder of the rope was looped over a brace in the ceiling. The accused was then raised until he was hanging by his arms, sometimes causing the shoulders to be pulled from their sockets. To make it even more unbearable, torturers would jerk the rope and bounce the accused up and down. Weights were sometimes tied to the ankles of the victim.

The *toca* was an early form of the modern torture technique of water-boarding. Also known as *interrogatorio mejorado del agua*, it consisted of a cloth being put into the mouth of the accused and then forcing him to ingest water spilled from a jar so that he felt as if he was drowning.

The best known, of course, is the *potro* – the rack. The subject's hands and feet were tied or chained to rollers at one or at both ends of a wooden or metal frame. These rollers could be turned with a handle which pulled the chains or ropes and stretched the joints of the accused. If the handle continued to be turned too far, the victim's arms or legs could be torn off. Meanwhile, as the accused was being tortured in this way, the inquisitors could apply other tortures to his body, using heated metal pincers, thumbscrews and other devices.

A confession that was adjudged by inquisitors to be true resulted in the accused being forgiven but to completely absolve himself of all his sins, he was usually forced to perform penances, such as pilgrimages or he had to wear numerous heavy metal crosses.

A failure to confess could result in life imprisonment and repeat offenders – those who were foolish enough to confess and then return to their old habits, were handed over to the secular arm for execution. The Church did not permit itself to take life, but the secular authorities were allowed to do it. Capital punishment at that time usually meant burning at the stake.

The power of the Inquisition began eventually to decline as the Church lost ground to the state and it was definitively abolished on 15 July 1834 by a Royal Decree signed by regent Maria Christina of the Two Sicilies during the minority of Isabella II.

Centuries of persecution and fear were finally over.

THE SALEM WITCH TRIALS

For more than three hundred years, people have been speculating about the cause of the strange hysteria that afflicted the small settlement of Salem in Massachusetts in 1692. Rather than one easy answer, however, at the root of the eruption of paranoia and suspicion were various factors that included politics, religion, family feuds, economics and, of course, the fears and imaginations of simple people.

Before the momentous events of that year, Salem Village was already a settlement divided, its six hundred inhabitants split into two rival factions. Half – mostly farming families from the western part of Salem Village – wanted to separate from Salem Town while the other half – those from the eastern part – wanted to remain a part of it. They had good reason to remain part of it, their economic well-being depending on Salem Town's thriving harbours.

Those who advocated independence from the town did so because they felt that their communal Puritan way of life was threatened by the individualism of Salem Town. Among the leaders of this group was the Putnam family who were the largest landowners in Salem Village. It was their intention to create a congregation that was separate to that of Salem Town and in 1689 this came into being and began worshipping at the Salem Village Meetinghouse, led by the Reverend Samuel Parris.

Parris's appointment was controversial, his contract being viewed as exceedingly generous, providing not just salary, house and free firewood, but also the title and deed to the parsonage and the land on which it stood. The people who wanted to stay within Salem Town were infuriated. They refused to attend his services and withheld the taxes that contributed to the minister's salary.

In October 1691, an election put into office a new Salem Village Committee that consisted in the main of opponents to his appointment. They challenged the legality of his contract and Parris had to feed his family from voluntary contributions.

His family consisted of him and his wife and a nine-year-old daughter, Betty. They also looked after their twelve-year-old orphaned niece, Abigail Williams. Betty suffered from poor health and it was left to Abigail to help around the house and care for an invalid aunt.

It was a strict household and when she finished

her chores there was not a lot for Abigail to do to while away the time. Parris prohibited the girls from playing games such as hide-and-seek as he believed play to be a sign of idleness. That left reading as an improving pastime that was permitted.

At that time, books about fortune-telling and prophecy were extremely popular amongst the young girls of Essex County. They gathered in small groups to practise what they learned from the books. Betty Parris and Abigail Williams formed such a group with a couple of friends and the Pariss's slave, Tituba, often sat in with the girls. Being from the Caribbean island of Barbados, she was full of stories about witches, demons and mystic animals. Soon, other girls would come along to be frightened by Tituba and play at telling fortunes, this being done by dropping egg white into a glass and then trying to divine things from the shape it took.

For Abigail and Betty, it became very frightening and this, coupled probably with the antipathy they felt from many of their neighbours, resulted in strange behaviour. Betty became hyperactive, running wildly around the house and diving under furniture. She told her parents that she was in pain and that she was suffering from a fever.

Through the ensuing centuries, there have been

numerous attempts to explain her odd behaviour. Sources have variously suggested she was a victim of stress, asthma, guilt, abuse, epilepsy, psychosis or even just plain boredom. Another source posits convulsive ergotism as the cause. This is a condition that is brought on by eating bread made from cereal infected with ergot, a fungus that grows in grain that is kept in warm, damp conditions. Victims of this affliction experience violent fits, an uncomfortable crawling sensation on the skin, vomiting and choking. He or she may also experience hallucinations. Betty Parris experienced most of these symptoms.

Puritans, however, believed in witchcraft which they saw as the practitioner entering into a pact with the devil in exchange for certain evil powers. It was a denial of God – a crime in the eyes of Puritans – and was always thoroughly investigated.

It was not a new phenomenon. The minister of Boston's Old North Church, Cotton Mather, a believer in witchcraft, had recently published a bestselling book, *Memorable Providences*, in which he described the strange behaviour of the four children of a Boston mason, John Goodwin. Their behaviour was almost identical to that of Betty Parris and in this case Mather declared that witchcraft was the cause. He placed the blame firmly on the shoulders of an Irish washerwoman, Mary Glover. Therefore, when more girls – eleven-year-old Mary Putnam, seventeen-year-old Mercy Lewis and sixteen-year-old Mary Walcott – began to display the same kind of behaviour as Betty Parris, the suspicion that witchcraft might be behind it increased. The doctor treating the girls added to the growing hysteria by suggesting that their behaviour might have supernatural origins, a suspicion bolstered by the belief that witches were said to often target children.

Mary Sibley, a neighbour of the Parris family suggested that a 'witch cake' might make the girls reveal the source of their bewitchment. A witch cake is composed of rye meal and urine from the person who has been afflicted. This mixture is then fed to a dog and if the dog behaves in the same bizarre manner it is confirmation that the victims really have been bewitched. Sibley ordered Tituba to make a witch cake, but by this time, Tituba was the main suspect.

On 25 February 1692, she was arrested along with two other women who were named by the girls – Sarah Osborne and Sarah Good.

Sarah Osborne was an elderly lady who had taken the great risk in a Puritan community of failing to attend church for a year while Sarah Good was a homeless beggar. It was said that when she knocked on people's doors looking for alms and none was forthcoming, she would utter indecipherable words and phrases before leaving. After she had done this, people claimed, animals would sometimes suddenly die, believing that the words she uttered must surely have been curses.

An investigation was launched led by two Salem Town magistrates, John Hathorne and Jonathan Corwin who set up court in Salem Meetinghouse. It was a dramatic event during which Betty, Abigail and six other girls would frequently throw themselves writhing to the floor, screaming and kicking. Ann Putnam claimed that she could see one woman, Goodwife Cloyce, sitting on the building's roof beams. Meanwhile, Sarah Good and Sarah Osborne maintained that they were innocent.

Tituba, confessed, however, for three days spilling out a litany of red rats, talking cats and a tall man dressed in black who made her sign her name in a book. Sarah Good, Sarah Osborne and others had already signed the book. Like many facets of this story, it remains unclear why she confessed. It may have been that she thought if she did so, the magistrates would treat her with leniency.

Nonetheless, when she finished, she and the two others were taken to a jail in Boston. Two months later, the elderly Sarah Osborne died in prison of natural causes. The Salem Witch Hunt had claimed its first victim.

Back in Salem Village, however, the jailing of the three women had not prevented further accusations of witchcraft. Life in the area was becoming more difficult. There had been a smallpox epidemic and the constant fear of Indian attacks heightened the anxiety and paranoia of the locals. They began to believe that these things were being visited on them by God as punishment for the cases of witchcraft. Therefore, in order to assuage this wrath, they resolved to root out every witch.

Ann Putnam accused Martha Corey of afflicting her in March. Corey was an unpopular, outspoken woman who was the mother of an illegitimate child of mixed race that lived with her and her second husband. Next, seventy-one-year-old Rebecca Nurse was accused. An unlikely witch who was known for her kindness, she was accused by Ann Putnam and several other girls of floating into their bedrooms at night and pinching and torturing them.

The jails were filling up and new courts had to be established to deal with the sheer number of cases. Judges, inexperienced in such matters, took advice from witchcraft-believer, Cotton Mather. He told them to apply the 'touching test'. It was said that if a witch touched her victim, the victim would become cured. Witch's marks such as moles were also looked for. The accused were permitted no legal counsel and unsupported allegations and suspicions were entered as evidence. Furthermore, there was no right of appeal.

Tavern owner, Bridget Bishop was unpopular because of her criticism of her customers and her reluctance to pay bills. She was accused of turning herself into a cat and of making a part of a building collapse as she was being transported to the courthouse. She was also named by two others who had confessed – Deliverance Hobbs and Mary Warren. She was found guilty without any hesitation and sentenced to death. She was hung with four other women.

John Proctor, a sixty-year-old farmer was sceptical about the behaviour and the accusations being made by the girls. When Mary Warren, his maidservant, began displaying the same strange behaviour as them, he threatened her with a beating and the behaviour stopped immediately. He believed that discipline would soon bring the behaviour and the accusations to an end. Shortly after he began publicly expressing such opinions, he was tried, sentenced to death and hanged.

George Burroughs, who had moved to Maine, was accused of being the leader of the witches. Blamed for causing military failures on the frontier – conveniently for those in Salem who were keen to find someone else to place the blame on – he was sentenced to death. He recited the Lord's Prayer on Gallows Hill – a feat supposed to be impossible for a witch – but even that failed to save him.

As quickly as it had arrived, however, the hysteria seemed to wane by the autumn of 1692. People even began to question the actions of those who had taken part. Cotton Mather's father, Increase, said, 'it was better that ten suspected witches should escape than one innocent person should be condemned,' condemning his son's actions. He also urged that spectral evidence – evidence gleaned from dreams and visions – should not be admitted. This was done and suddenly the convictions stopped. Only five of the last thirty-three cases brought before the courts resulted in conviction. The last witch trial took place in January 1693 and the Governor of Massachusetts issued a pardon to everyone that remained accused.

Reverend Parris and his family moved from Salem in 1696. Abigail Williams died aged seventeen and Betty Parris married and had five children, dying in 1760 in Concord, Massachusetts.

Crop failures and epidemics ravaged the people of Salem for many years, proof, many argued, that God was angry with the hanging of nineteen innocent people.

KU KLUX KLAN

When the American Civil War finally ended in 1865 in victory for President Abraham Lincoln and the states of the Union, some radical members of congress attempted to destroy the white power structure of the South, the Rebel States. The Freeman's Bureau was established to protect the interests of former slaves and seventeen million dollars were spent on building four thousand schools, a hundred hospitals and on providing homes and food for the liberated slaves.

Other efforts to extend the work of the Freeman's Bureau were rejected, however, and the Civil Rights Bill of 1866 was vetoed by President Andrew Johnson. That year, however, the election brought more Radical Republicans into Congress and the first Reconstruction Act was passed. Amongst other things, it allowed for new elections to be held in each state and gave freed male slaves the right to vote.

In the midst of the surge of dissent amongst southerners, many organizations emerged in the South, determined to uphold white power, stop black people from voting and resist Republican policy. In order to achieve these aims, any means necessary were to be used, including violence. Amongst these organizations were the White Brotherhood, the Men of Justice, the Constitutional Union Guards and the Knights of the White Camelia. In Pulaski, Tennessee, in May, 1866, another was formed when six former Confederate soldiers created the first branch of the Ku Klux Klan.

The name was derived from the Greek word *kuklos*, meaning 'circle' and the organization had soon introduced a set of secret rituals and exotic names for its office-bearers. The president was known as Grand Cyclops; the vice-president was Grand Magi; the marshal was Grand Turk and the treasurer was known as the Grand Exchequer. They introduced the garb for which they would become famous – long, flowing white robes, masks to keep their identities secret and the tall, conical hats that would be forever associated with them. They were designed to inspire fear in anyone they encountered, especially those blacks superstitious enough to believe the stories that Klansmen were actually the ghosts of dead Confederate soldiers.

Their timing was perfect. The South was in turmoil following the Civil war, with bands of unemployed veteran Confederate soldiers ravaging the countryside. Lawlessness was rampant and the

Klan took advantage of the febrile atmosphere. They attacked houses belonging to former slaves, burning them to the ground and black people were often killed and left at the side of roads.

In 1867, the Klan met in Nashville, Tennessee, to attempt to bring some structure to their fledgling organization. Brian A. Scates was elected president and local chapters were established which were supposed to report to the national headquarters. In reality, however, the local branches remained ruggedly independent.

Former Confederate Brigadier General George Gordon devised the Prescript, the Klan dogma which tended towards white supremacism, asking questions of an inductee such as whether he was in favour of 'a white man's government', 'the re-enfranchisement and emancipation of the white men of the South', and 'the restitution of the Southern people to all their rights'. But the Klan represented various constituencies and extremist views, including anti-black vigilantes, poor white farmers, Democrat politicians, bootleggers, neighbours with grudges and common criminals out for whatever they could get.

Blacks also began to organize, however. They formed all-black units of the Loyal Leagues that espoused support for the policies of President

Lincoln and the Union. The Klan and the other white organizations struck at them too, with black political leaders being targeted and black farmers driven off their land. There were weekly assaults and killings in which thousands of blacks died. Masked Klansmen fired into houses and set fire to them, often with the occupants inside. In North and South Carolina alone, 197 black people were murdered and 600 assaulted between January 1866 and June 1867.

The main objective was to prevent blacks from voting. In the few weeks before the 1868 Presidential election, 2,000 people were killed or injured in Louisiana. On one occasion, 200 black voters were killed or wounded as they were hunted through woodland. The intimidation generally worked. In St. Landry Parish, there was a registered Republican majority of more than a thousand. In the election, after the murders, not one Republican voted. This happened all across the South. By this time, however, the initial explosion in membership of the Ku Klux Klan was beginning to fade. Many of the members were no more than outlaws and thugs and many influential southern Democrats began to suspect that Klan activities gave the federal government a reason to remain in tight control of the South.

As anti-Klan resistance began to spring up, the national mood swung towards cracking down on it. In 1870, a federal grand jury declared it to be a 'terrorist organization' and in 1871, the Ku Klux Klan Act was signed by President Ulysses S. Grant. Along with the 1870 Force Act, it permitted the prosecution of Klan crimes, suppressed Klan activity and enforced civil rights provisions for individuals. Hundreds of Klansmen were arrested and prosecuted and the movement went into decline.

Towards the end of the nineteenth century, however, racial tension began once again to build in the southern states. There was a series of lynchings of black men and laws were passed in the South preventing blacks from voting. The result was a migration from the South to the northern states. Known as the Great Migration, it paved the way for the second wave of Ku Klux Klan activity.

The southern blacks had moved to the great cities of the North, creating resentment amongst their white inhabitants. There was also a great deal of antipathy to the notion of black men who had enlisted in the Army when the United States had entered the First World War being armed. Astonishingly, some black soldiers, having returned from fighting in Europe were lynched, still wearing the uniform of their country. In 1915, William J. Simmons reformed the Ku Klux Klan. He was a preacher whose views had been greatly influenced by the three novels that made up Thomas Dickson Jr's *The Ku Klux Klan* trilogy and DW Griffith's 1905 film *Birth of a Nation*, that was based on the second book of the trilogy, *The Clansman*.

The second Klan was founded in Atlanta, but it was now opposed to Jews, Roman Catholics and immigrants as well as blacks and it harboured particular loathing for the National Association for the Advancement of Coloured People (NAACP).

This was the golden age of the Ku Klux Klan. Under the leadership of Hiram W. Evans, elected Imperial Grand Wizard in 1922, and with the burning cross as its symbol, membership rocketed. It is estimated that by the middle of the nineteen-twenties, about fifteen per cent of all American men – almost five million – were Klansmen. They were mostly lower to middle class men, worried about their jobs that they felt were under threat from the wave of immigrants arriving from the South and from Europe. Between 1918 and 1927, four hundred and sixteen African-Americans were killed in race attacks. White southerners were still trying to prevent black people from voting. In Ocoee,

Florida, after two black people had dared to cast their votes, the local black community was attacked. Six African-Americans died as well as two of their white assailants.

Later in the decade, however, the tide turned once more. In Alabama in 1927, a group of Klan vigilantes instigated a campaign of terror that attacked blacks as well as whites that they thought had broken the race rules, or at least the race rules as perceived by Klan members. The media began to come out against such activity, describing it as 'un-American'. The authorities responded by coming down hard upon the perpetrators. Lists of Klan membership were released and people, no longer able to hide their identities behind their masks, began to drift away. By 1930, membership numbers had plummeted until there were no more than 30,000 adherents.

In 1944, it disappeared altogether as an organization when it was presented by the American government with a tax bill for $685,000 that it was unable to pay. It had not gone completely, however. In Alabama in the late 1940s, the houses of successful African-Americans were victims of a bombing campaign by Klan members.

The Ku Klux Klan name was appropriated by many disparate groups in the 1950s as the movement for civil rights in the United States began to gain momentum. Civil rights activists became the new targets. Following the bombing of forty houses in Birmingham owned by black families in 1951 and 1952, the city was was given the nickname 'Bombingham'.

The outrages continued throughout the 1950s and 1960s. On Christmas Eve 1951, NAACP activists Harry and Harriet Moore died when their home was bombed; in 1957 Willie Edwards Jr was forced by Klansmen to jump 125 feet to his death from a bridge over the Alabama River; in 1963 NAACP activist Medgar Evers was shot dead on the driveway of his house by Klansmen; in 1963 the 16th Street Baptist Church in Birmingham was bombed killing four young black girls; in 1964, three civil rights workers were brutally murdered in Mississippi; that same year two black teenagers, Henry Hezekiah Dee and Charles Eddie Moore were also murdered in Mississippi.

Klan sympathizers and, indeed, members, continued to occupy positions of power across the South. Klansman Bull Connor was the Birmingham Police Commissioner which meant that the Klan was free to operate as it liked in his jurisdiction. Thus, when the Freedom Riders, a group of black civil rights activists who were testing out the newly legislated de-segregation of America's transport system, rode into town on their buses, Connor told the Klan they had fifteen minutes to attack the buses before his officers would intervene.

Eventually, however, civil rights legislation was introduced to protect voting rights, housing and a great deal more, bringing to an end the third phase of the Ku Klux Klan.

It began to re-group and modernize itself under the leadership of David Duke who founded the Louisiana-based Knights of the Ku Klux Klan in 1974. A holocaust-denier, notorious for wearing a Nazi uniform on campus while a student. He presented the modern Klansman as well-groomed, educated and professional and for the first time women were allowed to become members. He described the Klan as 'not anti-black', but 'pro-white' and 'pro-Christian'. He left in 1980 to form the National Association for the Advancement of White people.

The Klan has remained active in the decades since. In 1979, Klansmen and members of the American Nazi Party shot dead five civil rights demonstrators in Greensboro, North Carolina; in 1980, three Klansmen shot dead four elderly black women in Chattanooga, Tennessee.

In 1981, Michael Donald was lynched in Alabama and two local Klan members were charged with the murder, one of whom, Henry Hays, was sentenced to death. Michael Donald's mother, Beulah Mae, resolved to use the case of her son's murder to bring an end to the Ku Klux Klan in Alabama.

She filed suit against the United Klans of America which was the largest and most violent Ku Klux Klan organization at the time. The all-white jury found the Klan to have been responsible for her son's murder and ordered it to pay her seven million dollars. As a result, it was forced to hand over all its assets, including its national headquarters in Tuscaloosa. When Henry Hays was executed in 1997 for the murder of Michael Donald, it was the first time since 1913 that a white man had been executed in that state for a crime against a black man.

There are now reckoned to be around 5,000–8,000 Ku Klux Klan members in the United States, spread across 179 chapters. These days they take issue with illegal immigration, urban crime and same-sex marriage, as well as, of course African-Americans. A number of their chapters are now engaged in alliances with other white supremacist groups like the Neo-Nazis who share a similar brand of hate.

PART TWO

VOODOO CURSES AND HEXES

DEATH BY VOODOO

It is an astonishing phenomenon, found all around the world. The suggestion to someone that he or she is going to die by someone to whom have been ascribed the powers of magic or sorcery, will often result in the death of the person who has been cursed. Terrified and often abandoned by his family and friends, the victim's strength simply ebbs away until the body can no longer survive. In other words, he or she literally dies of fear.

Is death in such circumstances the result of physiological changes in the body brought on by terror? Or is it indeed the result of a supernatural power that enters the body by way of a pointed bone or a drink or even just a whispered curse. Do witch doctors and voodoo practitioners really have such extraordinary powers?

Stories of 'voodoo death' emanate from all round the world, from South America, Africa, Australia, New Zealand and the islands of the Pacific as well as amongst the people of Haiti, famous, of course for its voodoo practitioners.

The phenomenon was first noticed in South

America by the Spanish explorer and naturalist, Soares de Souza, around 1587. He observed death by fright amongst the Tupi-nambas Indians when men would die after being condemned by a medicine man.

In Africa, similar instances were recorded. A.G. Leonard in his book *The Lower Niger and its Tribes* records:

> *I have seen more than one hardened old Haussa soldier dying steadily and by inches because he believed himself to be bewitched; no nourishment or medicines that were given to him had the slightest effect either to check the mischief or to improve his condition in any way, and nothing was able to divert him from a fate which he considered inevitable. In the same way, and under very similar conditions, I have seen Kru-men and others die in spite of every effort that was made to save them, simply because they had made up their minds, not (as we thought at the time) to die, but that being in the clutch of malignant demons they were bound to die.*

Another story has been told of a young man in the Congo in 1682 who had spent the night at a friend's house. The friend had prepared a wild hen for breakfast the following morning. Unfortunately, the eating of wild hen by the young was strictly forbidden but the host lied to the young man it was not a wild one. They ate and the young man went on his way, hale and hearty. Several years later, he returned and was asked if he would like to eat a wild hen. The young man told his host that he had been instructed by a medicine man not to eat wild hen. His host laughed and explained that he had eaten one last time and no harm had come to him. The young man was horrified, immediately fell ill and within twenty-four hours, was dead.

In another case of death by suggestion, a Maori woman in New Zealand had eaten some fruit but was informed that she had taken it from a place that was taboo, that was sacred to the memory of a dead chief. She was dead by the middle of the following day.

A story from Australia tells of a group of aborigines, non-converts to Christianity, including a famous witch doctor by the name of Nebo, who were camped outside a mission at Mona Mona in North Queensland. One of the senior workers at the mission was a native named Rob who had been converted to Christianity. The mission's medical practitioner, Dr Lambert, arrived one day to discover that Rob was very ill. The doctor examined him but could find absolutely nothing wrong with him. Rob was in a great deal of distress, however, and was obviously seriously ill.

The missionary explained to the doctor that Nebo had been seen by Rob pointing a bone at him – a means of placing a curse on someone – and as a result was convinced that he would die. Dr Lambert immediately went out to Nebo and threatened him with the cessation of the food that he had been getting from the mission if he did not lift the curse. The witch doctor agreed to go and see Rob.

He leaned over the sick man's bed and explained to him that it had all been a misunderstanding; he had merely been joking and had not pointed the bone at him. Dr Lambert later described the relief that was felt by Rob as instant. By the evening, he was back working in the mission as if nothing had happened.

Dr Herbert Basedow, in his book *The Australian Aboriginal*, describes the true horror engendered in a person when he realizes that he has had the bone pointed at him:

> *The man who discovers that he is being boned by any enemy is, indeed, a pitiable sight. He stands aghast, with his eyes staring at the treacherous pointer, and*

*with his hands lifted as though to ward off the lethal
medium, which he imagines is pouring into his body.
His cheeks blanch and his eyes become glassy and the
expression of his face becomes horribly distorted...
He attempts to shriek but usually the sound chokes in
his throat, and all that one might see is froth at his
mouth. His body begins to tremble and the muscles
twist involuntarily. He sways backwards and falls to
the ground, and after a short time appears to be in a
swoon; but soon after he writhes as if in mortal agony,
and, covering his face with his hands, begins to moan.
After a while he becomes very composed and crawls
to his wurley. From this time onwards he sickens and
frets, refusing to eat and keeping aloof from the daily
affairs of the tribe. Unless help is forthcoming in the
shape of a counter-charm administered by the hands
of the Nan-garri, or medicine-man, his death is only a
matter of a comparatively short time. If the coming of
the medicine-man is opportune he might be saved.*

To save the man, the Nangarri, or witch doctor,
approaches the grief-stricken and terrified relatives,
holding a small item that could be a bone, a stick,
a pebble or a talon, that he claims to have taken
from the victim who has been cursed and which, he
claims, is the cause of his problems. Now that it is

removed, the curse is lifted and the afflicted person has nothing to fear. At that moment, the victim immediately begins to feel better.

Walter Cannon, the anthropologist who related these stories, investigated the question of how a state of fear can kill someone. He arrived at a physiological reason.

Fear, he explained is one of our most deep-seated emotions. Its effects are felt in the nervous system and in the endocrine apparatus, the sympathetic-adrenal system. He postulated that voodoo death may, in fact, result from a state of shock due to a persistent outpouring of adrenalin and a depletion of the adrenal corticosteroid hormones. This could cause a dramatic reduction in blood pressure that will result in death. Victims are indeed frightened to death, he concluded.

Death is not the only horrific outcome of a voodoo curse, however. As has been attested to by films and literature, the undead feature in this brand of sorcery, in the form of the zombie.

A zombie is an undead monster or a person in an entranced state who is controlled by a *bokor* or a wizard. They occurred initially in West African voodoo but migrated to Haitian Vodou and New Orleans Voodoo. They became well-known through

George Romero's 1968 horror film *The Night of the Living Dead* and have appeared in every form of entertainment media. They are usually hungry for human flesh, especially the brains and are often the result of a pandemic of some kind that causes the dead to come to life.

In West African Vodou, a bokor, or sorcerer can bring a dead person back to life and the zombie, having no will of his or her own, will remain under the control of the bokor.

'Zombi' is also the name of the Voodoo snake, Iwa Damballah Wedo which is of Niger-Congo origin and means 'god'. In the West African tradition there is also the zombie astral – a part of the soul of a human being that is captured by a *bokor* and used to make him more powerful. It is traditionally kept in a bottle which the *bokor* sells to people as a talisman that will bring success in business or good health. A zombie, however is merely a temporary spiritual being. After a time, God will take the soul back. However, another, more straightforward method of getting a zombie to return to its grave is to feed it salt.

The place most associated with the practice of Voodoo, is, of course, Haiti. There are countless cases of the living dead being observed there. In

1937, the American folklorist and anthropologist, Zora Neale Hurston, was in a Haitian village when a woman turned up who was said to have died and been buried in 1907 when she was twenty-nine years old.

Like Walter Cannon, Hurston wondered about the reason why Voodoo seemed so compelling and credible. '… if science ever gets to the bottom of Voodoo in Haiti and Africa, it will be found that some important medical secrets, still unknown to medical science, give it its power, rather than gestures of ceremony.' Like him, she thought there might be a good explanation for its miraculous power.

Another scientist, the ethno-botanist, Wade Davis, writing many years later, presented a pharmacological cause for zombiism. He claimed that a person could be turned into a zombie by the mixing of two special powders in a person's bloodstream and that they were usually introduced via a wound.

The first coup de poudre, includes Tetrodotoxin, a powerful and potentially fatal Neurotoxin that is found in the flesh of the puffer fish. The second powder, he claimed, consisted of dissociative drugs such as datura which is often used as a hallucinogen. Mixed together, these substances will induce a death-like state in which the victim will be totally under the control of the bokor or sorcerer.

These powders were often fired by way of a blow-dart into the body of a victim that rendered him immobile within minutes. The breath slows as does the heart and the victim seems to all intents and purposes to be dead. He is fully aware of what is going on around him, but can make no sign whatsoever.

In Haiti, the heat means that people are buried very quickly after death and as long as the bokor can dig his victim up within eight hours of burial, he will not be asphyxiated in the ground. An ancient voodoo ritual is then performed over the zombie's body, in which the bokor takes possession of the soul, replacing it with the *loa*, or spirit that he or she controls. The trapped soul of the victim is then put in a bottle or clay jar which is wrapped in a fragment of the victim's clothing, an item of jewellery or another personal possession and then hidden in a place known only to the *bokor*.

A concoction known as the 'zombie's cucumber' is used to revive the victim. The being is a shell of its living self, with no speech and no memory and it will often be used for farm labour or construction work. In one well-known case from 1918, a voodoo priest named Ti Joseph ran a gang of zombified labourers for the American Sugar Corporation.

In Haiti, this practice has been legislated for and is tantamount to attempted murder in the eyes of the law. The Haitian Penal Code's Article 249 states:

It shall also be qualified as attempted murder the employment which may be made against any person of substances which, without causing actual death, produce a lethargic coma more or less prolonged. If, after the person had been buried, the act shall be considered murder no matter what result follows.

The most famous recent example of zombiism arose from the cruel rule of the hated dictator, Papa Doc Duvalier, who ruled Haiti from 1957 until 1971. He had a private army of enforcers that was rumoured to consist of zombies – the notorious Tonton Macoutes. They were believed to be in a constant state of trance and unquestioningly followed every order he gave them.

He attempted to instill fear in his people, modelling himself on Baron Samedi, one of the *loa* – spirits – of Haitian voodoo. Like Samedi, Duvallier took to wearing a top hat, black tuxedo and dark glasses. He even adopted the strong nasal tone of the *loa* when talking. Duvallier was a devout voodooist, like a great many people in Haiti and he led a voodoo church that boasted a large congregation. He claimed that he was immortal and that he would rule Haiti forever, promising that he would rise from the dead and return to rule again. He died of a heart attack but he never did return and just to make sure a guard was put on his tomb.

THE LaLAURIE SLAVE MURDERS

Was it true? Or did embellishment through the years by countless authors, journalists and gossips turn it into the story we know today – a story of horror and cruelty that, if it is, indeed, true, is surely one of the worst examples of man's inhumanity to man in American history.

Delphine Macarty was born around 1775, one of the five children of Barthelmy Louis Macarty. Barthelmy's father – also known as Barthelmy – had brought his family to New Orleans from Ireland in 1730. Her mother – Marie Jeanne Lovable, also know as the widow Lecomte, and Barthelmy became prominent members of the white Creole community of the city and Delphine's cousin, Augustin de Macarty served as mayor between 1815 and 1820.

However, one other story suggests that Delphine's parents were actually killed during the slave uprising in that late nineteenth century in Port au Prince. This loss of her parents might go some way towards explaining her attitude to slaves, although nothing could justify what would ensue.

Delphine would marry three times, the first in 1800. Her first husband, Don Ramon de Lopez y Angullo was a high-ranking officer in the service of Spain who by 1804 was consul general for Spain in Louisiana. That year, the couple left on a trip to Spain but in Havana, on their way to Madrid, Don Ramon died, leaving Delphine a widow for the first time. She continued on the journey, giving birth to a daughter – Marie Borgia Delphine Lopez y Angulla de la Candelaria, nicknamed 'Borquita' – at sea. After a short stay in Spain, she returned to New Orleans with her daughter.

In 1808, she married again. Her new husband, Jean Blanque, was a prominent banker, merchant, lawyer and legislator. He purchased a house for his new family at 409 Royal Street, the house becoming known as Villa Blanque. Together, he and Delphine had four children – Marie Louise Pauline, Louise Marie Laure, Marie Louise Jeanne, and Jeanne Pierre Paulin Blanque.

She was widowed for a second time when Blanque died in 1816, and it took her nine years to find her third husband. Dr Leonard Louis Nicolas LaLaurie was a good deal younger than her but they married on 25 June 1825.

In 1831, Delphine purchased a property at 1140

Royal Street which she managed in her own name. By 1832, she had built a three-storey mansion on the land, with attached slave quarters. With her husband she moved into the house that would become one of the most notorious buildings in the United States.

In America at that time, it was usual for well-off, prominent families to retain the services of a number of slaves. And the LaLauries were no different. The house had a slave quarters and they maintained a number of servants there. It would be Delphine LaLaurie's treatment of these slaves that would bring disgrace to her house and to her name.

There had been suspicions that she did not treat her slaves well at the Royal Street mansion. They were observed by New Orleans residents to be 'singularly haggard and wretched' but it was noted that Delphine LaLaurie was polite to blacks generally, and some said she did care for their wellbeing. However, it was reported that she chained her cook to the kitchen stove and that her daughters were beaten when they tried to give food to the slaves. In her favour, it must be added that she did, in fact, free two of her own slaves – a Jean Louis in 1819 and a Devince in 1832. But the rumours became so strong that a local lawyer was sent to her house to remind her of the laws that applied to the welfare of slaves. He claimed later to have found no real evidence of mistreatment.

There was a story after that visit, however, that gave support to her mistreatment. A young slave woman was seen falling to her death from the roof of the mansion, apparently trying to evade a whipping by her mistress. This time, the authorities instigated a full investigation and it found against Delphine LaLaurie. She was declared guilty of illegal cruelty and forced to forfeit nine of her slaves. She and her husband immediately bought the nine slaves back, however, using one of their relatives as a phony buyer and soon they were back in the Royal Street slave quarters.

Things began to seriously unravel for the LaLaurie family on 10 April 1834 when a fire broke out in the slave quarters at the mansion. Passersby ran onto the grounds to offer help but when they requested the keys Delphine refused to hand them over. The helpers instead broke down the doors and found seven slaves, horrifically mutilated. The true story of the horror that had been unfolding behind the mansion's gates was finally exposed.

Several of them were suspended by the neck with their limbs – as the local newspaper, *The*

New Orleans Bee, put it: 'apparently stretched and torn from one extremity to the other'. Others were naked and chained to the wall, their eyes gouged out. Some had had their fingernails pulled out by the roots while others had been skinned on parts of their body, the exposed flesh poisoned and festering. There were stories of men with their tongues sewn together, people with their intestines pulled out and knotted around their waists. It was reported that a man had a hole in his skull and that a stick had been poked in to stir his brains around. A victim had her arms amputated and her skin peeled off in a circular pattern, making her look as one report described it 'like a human caterpillar'. Still another woman who sat in a cage, had had her limbs broken and then re-set at odd angles so that she 'resembled a human crab'. Some had had animal excrement stuffed in their mouths which had then been sewn shut, leaving them to starve to death. A small boy had had the skin of his face peeled back, revealing the muscles, veins and bloody flesh beneath it. A girl wore a suit made from the skin of several dead slaves.

One man who entered the quarters spoke of seeing a woman slave wearing an iron dog collar and an old woman who had a serious wound to the head and was unable to walk. Most showed signs of having been whipped on the buttocks. Most horrific of all, however, was an elderly man whose penis had been cut into five equal strands. Each of these was attached to a hook and the body was hoisted to the ceiling with two candles placed in his empty eye sockets, making a dreadful chandelier.

Cups and saucers, encrusted with a dried flaky red substance and bottles showing the same signs, suggested that blood had been drunk.

When told about the condition of her slaves, Delphine LaLaurie is reported to have responded angrily, shouting that 'some people would do better to stay home than to come to others' houses to dictate laws and meddle with other people's business.'

News of this gruesome discovery spread quickly through New Orleans and people were at first disgusted and then angry. A mob gathered and attacked the mansion, according to the newspaper 'destroying and demolishing everything upon which they could lay their hands.' The police were called and by the time they succeeded in dispersing the angry crowd, the Royal Street mansion had been seriously damaged, with 'scarcely anything [remaining] but the walls'.

The slaves who had been found were removed from their incarceration and taken to the local police station where they were available for viewing by a curious public. *The Bee* reported that by 12 April, four thousand people had come to view the suffering that had been endured by the slaves.

Two of the slaves died following their rescue but it was also reported that bodies were found buried in the grounds of the mansion, including the remains of a child.

Another story later emerged of a young thief who, having broken into the mansion, discovered a bucket on the floor containing human genitalia and next to it the body of a man. It seemed that the man had been force-fed the body parts until he choked to death.

Yet another story has LaLaurie killing a local activist Adam Wescount, reportedly gouging out his eyes and leaving his body to be eaten by birds.

It is claimed that Delphine LaLaurie fled New Orleans after the ransacking of her property, taking a coach to the waterfront from where she was conveyed by schooner to Mobile, Alabama and then on to Paris. One report suggests that she later died in a boar-hunting accident in France.

There is one final twist to the story. It is said that when the house was being renovated at the end of the 1960s, no fewer than seventy-five human skeletons were discovered beneath the floorboards of the third storey.

The house of horrors had given up its final gruesome secret.

MERCY BROWN – THE VAMPIRE OF RHODE ISLAND

Vampires are everywhere in the 21st century. From *Buffy the Vampire Slayer* to the phenomenally successful *Twilight*, our films, books and television programmes demonstrate our fascination with these otherworldly creatures.

It all began in nineteenth century New England in the United States where around twelve cases of vampirism were reported. Unlike the vampires of the twentieth and twenty-first century, these were not the kind who wore cloaks and had fangs, Instead, as is often the case with such things, they were an explanation for evil, a means of physically embodying something that was attacking a community.

It has often been said that such creatures as werewolves were invented in the popular imagination in medieval times as a way to explain brutal serial killings. An unknown evil that was attacking people within one area could then be described and given a physical presence. So it probably was with the vampires of New England, and in particular those of Rhode Island towards the end of the century.

The evil that was creating panic amongst the population at that time was the illness of consumption, now known as tuberculosis At the time it was wiping out entire families and one in four deaths was caused by it. The people of the time, without the cure for the illness that we now have, found something else to blame it on – vampires. Usually, the first one in the family to die was thought to be the vampire who had returned from the grave to suck out the life force of the other family members. Often there were reports from those left behind of a force crushing their chests, suffocating them. This was put down to their recently dead brother, sister, father or mother.

Amongst the symptoms of consumption were the gradual loss of strength and skin tone. The victim becomes pale and the loss of appetite results in him or her literally wasting away. It was probably this look of the consumptive – pale and thin – that provided us with the modern image of the vampire. This was coupled with the fact that during the later stages of consumption, the sufferer would often wake up with blood on his or her face, neck, nightclothes and bedding. Suspected of being a vampire, a corpse had to be disinterred immediately for examination and destruction. Growth of the hair and nails and the presence of blood signalled that the dead person was a vampire. The heart and vital organs would be burned to prevent the curse from spreading to other members of the family in question.

In Rhode Island at the end of the nineteenth century there were several cases where vampirism was suspected. In 1796, Stephen Staples wrote to Cumberland Town Council, requesting permission to carry out what he described as 'an experiment'. He wanted to dig up a daughter who had recently passed away in order to save the life of another who was ailing. There is no record of what the 'experiment' was, but it was undoubtedly to do with vampirism.

In 1799, well-to-do Exeter farmer, Stuckley 'Snuffy' Tillinghast, had a dream in which half of his orchard died. Shortly after his daughter Sarah died, his other children became ill and began to complain that Sarah was returning at night to press on their chests, making it difficult to breathe. Six of his fourteen children died before they decided to dig up Sarah's body. She was found to have fresh blood in her heart and in her veins and was, therefore, to their minds, a vampire. They burned her heart but it is recorded that this did not prevent a seventh child from dying.

A similar story was told in Foster in 1827 where Nancy, the nineteen-year-old daughter of Captain Levi Young was exhumed and burned, the fumes being inhaled by other family members, although this did not prevent another eight children from dying. In Peacedale, William G. Rose had the remains of his late daughter Ruth Ellen disinterred in 1874 and in West Greenwich in 1889, the same happened to nineteen-year-old Nelly L. Vaughn. It is rumoured that nothing will grow on her grave.

The most famous of all the Rhode Island vampires, however, was Mercy Brown who died aged nineteen during the bitterly cold winter of 1892. She was the third in her family to die, her mother Mary being the first to succumb on 8 December 1883 at the age of thirty-six. Seven months later, on 6 June 1884, her twenty-year-old sister Mary Olive followed her to the grave.

Mary's twenty-four-year-old brother Edwin was next to become ill and in order to try to cure him, he was sent to live in the arid climate of Colorado. Late in 1891, however, he returned to Exeter with the disease continuing to ravage his body. He had, in effect, come home to die.

Mercy's battle with consumption was considerably shorter than her brother's. Consumption could sometimes take years to kill the sufferer but it could also end a life within a short period. She had what was known as the 'galloping' variety of the illness and her struggle for survival ended after only a few months on 18 January 1892. In that freezing cold winter, however, the ground was frozen solid and it proved impossible to dig a grave. She was interred, therefore, in a crypt in the Chestnut Hill Cemetery behind the local Baptist Church.

Following her funeral, Edwin's condition deteriorated and his father, George Brown, became increasingly frantic, faced with the loss of Edwin and with two surviving and as yet unafflicted daughters to consider. He must have believed that his family was labouring under some kind of curse and, speaking to neighbours and friends, it is likely that this feeling was heartily endorsed. Soon, they were talking about what it could possibly be and they arrived at the conclusion that his family was under vampire attack from beyond the grave. The neighbours began to insist that he do something. But which of the already dead was the perpetrator? Was it his wife or Mary Olive, who were the first to die, after all? Or was it Mercy? George Brown decided that he would remove Mercy from her crypt and investigate whether she was responsible for the terrible scourge with which his family had been afflicted.

On 17 March 1892, George and some friends, accompanied by a doctor from the town of Metcalf, named Wickford, went to the cemetery to exhume the corpses of the three Brown women.

The two Marys were in an advanced state of decomposition, not unexpected given that they had been dead for ten years. When Mercy was examined, however, they noticed that she had moved within her coffin, one report suggesting that she had turned over and, remarkably, this might actually have been true. Before embalming became common practice, bodies could move during decomposition. They were even known to sit up or jerk.

Most disconcerting for them was the fact that her body seemed to be quite fresh, a realisation reinforced when the doctor cut out her heart and discovered that there was blood in it. Even this can be explained, however, because apparently blood can, in certain circumstances, coagulate and then become liquid again.

The doctor drained the fluid from her organs and her heart was burned on a nearby stone wall. Her liver and her lungs may also have been burned. Some of the ashes were mixed with water and given to Edwin to drink. It failed to bring an improvement to his condition, however, and he died just under two months later, on 2 May.

It is unknown whether the remaining Brown girls succumbed to the illness or whether they survived and the inhabitants of Exeter believed they had defeated the vampire curse. George certainly remained unaffected by it it, dying at the age of eighty in 1922.

Mercy Brown was the last of the Rhode Island vampires and following her exhumation, no one was ever dug up again as a suspected vampire, because it was discovered that tuberculosis was actually spread by bacteria and not by an undead family member thirsty for blood.

THE PENNSYLVANIA DUTCH HEX MURDER

Pow-wow is a system of folk religion and magic practised by Dutch settlers in the state of Pennsylvania in the United States, a unique combination of Christian theology and shamanistic belief. In Europe, of course, practitioners of shamanism were called witches and were persecuted for centuries. The art came to Pennsylvania with Dutch settlers but has now been outlawed for several generations.

The name 'Pow-wow' is derived from the book *Pow-wows*, or the *Long Lost Friend*, written by John George Hohman. It is a collection of spells, incantations and remedies for both human beings and animals. Published in German in 1820, an English version appeared in 1846 and became very influential. It assures its owner that:

> *Whoever carries this book with him, is safe from all his enemies, visible or invisible; and whoever has this book with him cannot die without the holy corpse of Jesus Christ, nor drowned in any water, nor burn up in any fire, nor can any unjust sentence be passed upon him. So help me.*

Of course, as in all such arts, there were people who misused Pow-wow, accepting payment for casting spells on others. These 'hexenmeisters' became deeply feared by the people of Pennsylvania and it is reported that even the police were afraid of their mysterious powers.

It was into such a world that John Blymire was born in 1895 in York County, Pennsylvania. His family were steeped in the Pow-wow tradition, both his father and grandfather being hexenmeisters. He would inherit their healing abilities.

At the age of five, Blymire fell ill, diagnosed as suffering from opnema, a wasting away of the body. It was immediately suspected that the illness had been caused by someone casting a spell on the boy, but it is more likely to have been the result of a poor diet and malnutrition. This was a common problem amongst children at the time.

When the illness proved too serious even for his father and grandfather to cure him, he was taken to powerful Pow-wow healer and distant relative, Nelson Rehmeyer. Rehmeyer succeeded in healing the boy.

Blymire was himself practising Pow-wow within a couple of years and at the age of nine he carried out his first successful cure. He was not the most powerful of hexenmeisters, but people sought him out. Otherwise, however, he was a quiet and introverted child who had no friends.

Aged thirteen, he left school to take up employment in a cigar factory in York, supplementing what he earned at the factory with earnings from his work as a healer. He kept himself very much to himself but an incident one day brought him to the attention of his workmates. At the end of their shift, Blymire and his colleagues were leaving the factory to make their way home. Suddenly, someone screamed that a mad dog was coming along the street towards them. Sure enough, a large collie, its mouth en-circled by foam, was approaching them. Everyone panicked, scrambling to get back inside the factory. But Blymire suddenly emerged from the terrified crowd, placing himself between it and the rabid dog. He concentrated and uttered an incantation before making the sign of the cross over the dog's head. It immediately stopped foaming at the mouth and seemed to calm down. Blymire walked off, the dog trotting tamely along at his heels. It was impressive.

Not long after, however, he fell ill again with the opnema from which he had suffered as a child. He was certain that another hexenmeister had cursed him, perhaps someone jealous of his powers. He decided to leave his job and put all his efforts into discovering who was behind the hex that he was sure had been placed on him. Meanwhile, he worked at odd jobs and earned a living from his skills as a hexenmeister.

At this time, he was living in boarding houses and it was at one of these that he met Lily, the woman who became his wife. It seemed that everything was getting better. His health improved and it looked as if the hex had been removed or had lost its power. He found a steady job and grew his business as a Pow-wow.

Before too long, things started to go wrong, however. His and Lily's first child died just a few weeks after being born and the same fate befell their second. Once again, his health began to fail and, to make matters worse, he lost his job.

Blymire sought the help of his fellow witches to find out who was placing spells on him. One of these, Andrew C. Lenhart was a very powerful Pow-wow, much feared in the region, even by police officers and local politicians. He told Blymire that the hex had been conjured up by someone very close to him and Blymire became irrationally convinced that it was his wife Lily. Life at home became unbearable and Lily became terrified of her husband. Eventually, her father hired a lawyer who engaged a psychiatrist to examine Blymire. He was found to be suffering from psychoneurosis and was committed to a state mental hospital. He did not remain there for long, however, merely walking out the door. It was too late, however. By this time, Lily had divorced him.

It was 1928 and Blymire had returned to work at his old job in the cigar factory in York and it was there that he made the acquaintance of fourteen-year-old John Curry, a boy whose life had already been blighted by abuse. Curry believed that his dreadful existence was the result of a hex.

Another man who believed he was hexed was farmer Milton J. Hess. He and his wife had taken great care to obey all the strictures provided to them by Pow-wows and they seemed to work for a while. Their farm flourished, crops were plentiful, chickens laid and cows provided good milk. His wife ran a successful stall at the farmer's market.

For no apparent reason, in 1926 things began to go wrong. Crops failed, chickens were stolen or failed to lay and cows stopped producing milk. Hess became ill and his wife became depressed at the way things were going, withdrawing into herself and not communicating with the other members of her family. Hess had to find work as a truck driver to keep the wolf from the door.

In June 1928, Blymire met Hess at the Widow Detwiler's boarding house. The two men became friends, often discussing hexes and Blymire's work as a Pow-wow. Around this time, he was consulting with a woman named Nellie Noll, popularly known as the 'Witch of Marietta' or the 'River Witch', still trying to find out who was placing curses on him. She told him that the person responsible was the 'Witch of Rehmeyer Hollow', Nelson Rehmeyer, the man who had cured Blymire when he was a boy all those years ago.

Blymire visited Hess at his farm where he saw for himself how bad things were for the farmer and his family. He returned to Nellie Noll and was told that Rehmeyer was also responsible for hexing the Hess family. She added that he was also behind the problems of young John Curry.

When he asked her what he could do to put an end to these curses, Nellie Noll instructed him to try to get his hands on Rehmeyer's copy of Hohman's *Pow-wows*, or the *Long Lost Friend* and burn it. If that proved impossible, she suggested that he obtain a lock of his hair and bury it in the ground at a depth of between six and eight feet.

Blymire, Hess and Curry met to formulate a plan to deal with Rehmeyer. Also present were Hess's brothers Clayton and Wilbert. Clayton who had a car, offered to drive them there.

On the day, Wilbert dropped out but the others set off for Rehmeyer's house. When they arrived, however, he was not at home. They walked to his ex-wife's house where they were told he was probably at his girlfriend's. They decided to return to the house and wait but by the time they got back there, a light was burning in the windows. They knocked on the door and Rehmeyer opened it and genially invited them into his parlour.

They chatted about the time when Rehmeyer had cured Blymire of his opnema and in further conversation Blymire established that Rehmeyer did indeed possess a copy of the book that he needed to find. He tried to use his powers to will Rehmeyer to hand it over, but he was not powerful enough to control the other man's mind. They could, of course, have used force but Blymire decided against this because the other man was large and could prove very difficult to overpower.

They stayed the night at the house and in the morning Rehmeyer got up and made breakfast for them before they left. On the night of Wednesday 27

November, Blymire, Curry and Wilbert Hess returned to Rehmeyer Hollow with a length of rope they had cut up into a number of shorter lengths. There was a full moon and it was the night before Thanksgiving.

They demanded the book but when he refused to hand it over they attacked him, Blymire looping a length of rope around the old witch's neck. As Rehmeyer struggled to free himself, Curry grabbed a piece of wood and struck Rehmeyer on the head with it. Rehmeyer fell to the ground where they viciously kicked him in the head and the face. Before long, the Witch of Rehmeyer Hollow was dead.

They ransacked the house and found a little money but then decided to try to get rid of any evidence by setting fire to the building. The fire failed to take, however, and next morning a neighbour discovered Rehmeyer's body.

Blymire, Curry and Wilbert Hess were arrested shortly after and charged with murder.

At their trial which began on 9 January 1929, the judge banned any mention of hexes and witchcraft. This left their motive as simple robbery. In one of the quickest trials in Pennsylvania judicial history, all three were found guilty, Blymire and Curry of murder in the first degree, Wilbert Hess of murder in the second degree.

Blymire and Curry were sentenced to life imprisonment and Wilbert was sentenced to ten to twenty years. In 1934, Curry and Hess were paroled. Curry became an artist and died in 1962 but Blymire remained in prison until 1953 when he returned to York where he led a quiet life and worked as a janitor.

THE LONELY HEARTS KILLERS

'I'm no average killer!' Raymond Fernandez had told the officers who arrested him. 'I have a way with women, a power over them,' he continued.

Indeed, this thin, well-dressed, slightly bald, thirty-five-year-old believed that he was the possessor of an uncanny power over women that was gained by the use of Voodoo. Sent to prison shortly after the Second World War, he shared a cell with a Haitian man who taught him some of the mysteries of the ancient West African religion, Vodun.

Released from prison, he began to seduce lonely women over great distances by sending them envelopes containing magical Voodoo powder or by obtaining a lock of his victim's hair. They were women who subscribed to lonely hearts clubs who were desperate for love and companionship. Fernandez was willing to provide that, but only until he had emptied their bank accounts, at which point he vanished into thin air. The women, often embarrassed and humiliated, rarely reported their experience to the police and Fernandez calmly moved on to his next lonely woman.

He had been born in Hawaii in 1914, to parents of Spanish descent but when he was three the family had moved to Bridgeport, Connecticut. Always a sickly child, he was a disappointment to his father and in order to make something of himself, decided in 1932, when he was eighteen years old, to go and work on his uncle's farm near the village of Orgiva in southern Spain. It was a good decision. After two years, and by now a handsome, well-built young man, he fell in love with and married a local woman, Encarnacion Robles.

At the outbreak of the Second World War, Spain declared its neutrality, but Fernandez served in its merchant navy. He then began to work for the British government as a spy and although little is known of his activities during this time, the Defence Security Office in Gibraltar described him as 'entirely loyal to the Allied cause' and added that he 'carried out his duties which were sometimes difficult and dangerous, extremely well.'

The war over, Fernandez decided to return to the United States where he hoped to find work before sending for his wife and their two children. He found passage on a freighter bound for Curacao in the Dutch West Indies but it was to be a fateful journey. One day, as he was coming up onto deck, a steel hatch came crashing down on his head, seriously injuring him. On arrival in port, he was rushed to hospital where he remained from December 1945 until his release in March 1946.

The accident had changed him, however. When he left hospital, he was moody, distant and irascible, a far cry from the sociable, courteous young man who had boarded ship in Spain.

He took another ship from Curacao to Mobile in Alabama but during the journey stole clothing and other items from the ship's storeroom. They were clearly identified as belonging to the ship and he was arrested as he tried to pass through customs. He was sent to prison for a year and it was during that time that he learned about Vodun.

He believed himself to be an *oungan*, or priest, who got his magical powers from *loa* – spirits. He read everything about the religion of Vodun that he could find, including material about human sacrifice and torture, although these were not practiced in Vodun.

When he was released from prison, he moved in with his sister in Brooklyn but his family worried about him. Since the accident, he had lost much of his hair and his horrific scar was visible on top of his head. He suffered from debilitating headaches and often locked himself away in his room for days. He also began writing in response to lonely hearts letters.

One such was from a woman, Jane Thompson, who had recently split up with her husband. After she and Raymond had finally met, he persuaded her to buy tickets to Spain for both of them. In October 1947 they embarked on a cruise liner bound for Spain, travelling as husband and wife.

In Spain, he took Jane to see his wife and children and, strange though it was, the three seemed to hit it off, being seen dining out in the nearby town. On the night of 7 November, however, Fernandez was seen running from their hotel room. Next morning, Jane Thompson was found dead. The Spanish police removed her body and buried it in great haste without even troubling to have an autopsy. Fernandez got out of town as fast as he could, catching the next ship bound for America. Arriving in New York City, he made straight for Jane Thompson's apartment and using a forged will, took possession of it, conveniently ignoring the fact that Jane's elderly mother still lived there.

His correspondence with lonely hearts club women continued and one of the women he wrote to was Martha Seabrook Beck, a large lady who worked as a nurse at a children's hospital in Pensacola, Florida.

Born in Milton, Florida, in 1919, Martha had always been large due to a glandular condition. At school, she had been bullied and humiliated because of her size and at home, she later claimed, she was a victim of sexual abuse at the hands of her brother. Her teenage years were spent in a well of loneliness and depression.

In 1942, she enrolled in a nursing school and did well, graduating at the age of twenty-two at the top of her class. Her size, however, made it difficult for her to find work as a nurse and for a while she worked in a funeral home preparing bodies for funerals. Moving to California, she worked as a nurse at a US Army hospital. She dated soldiers that she met in the town's bars and inevitably fell pregnant. When she told the baby's father, however, he was horrified and tried to kill himself. She fled back to Florida.

Back home, she made a great pretence of having been married but that her husband had been killed in action. In spring, 1944, she gave birth to a baby girl. When she became pregnant again later that year, the baby's father married her but it was short-lived and six months later the marriage was over. She found the job at the children's hospital and, desperately lonely, placed an advertisement in *Mother Dinene's Family Club for Lonely Hearts*. It was that advertisement that Raymond Fernandez saw.

He wrote to her and as usual asked for a lock of her hair and performed the Voodoo ritual that would, he believed, make him irresistible to her. They finally met on 28 December when he stepped off a train in Pensacola, surprised to find a seriously overweight woman awaiting him – she had failed to mention her size in the advert.

Soon the two were sharing a bed and when he told her that he would come back for her or that he would send money to enable her and her children to come and live with him in New York, she was overjoyed, taking it as a proposal of marriage. When he realized that she was telling people she was getting married again, he wrote to her explaining that she had misunderstood him. Martha responded by threatening suicide and he capitulated, writing back to invite her to come and visit him in New York.

She arrived in January 1948, but he wanted nothing to do with her children. He told her to abandon them outside a Salvation Army shelter and she obliged. She would not see them again until two years later, after she had been sentenced to die in the electric chair.

Soon, he was explaining to her how he made his money and the two decided to become a partnership. From that point on, America's widows, spinsters and divorcees were no longer safe.

Their first victim was Esther Henne with whom Fernandez had been corresponding for some time. They travelled together to Pennsylvania, Martha posing as his sister-in-law and within a month Fernandez and Esther Henne were man and wife.

Back in New York, Fernandez tried to persuade his new wife to sign over her insurance policies and pension to him. But Henne had somehow heard about the mysterious death of Jane Thompson and fled back to Pennsylvania. Their next victim would not be so lucky.

He married Myrtle Young in Arkansas in 1948 but soon tired of this wife. He drugged her and bundled her on a bus back to Arkansas to get rid of her. She was in a coma by the time the bus reached its destination and she died in hospital the following day.

Janet Fay was a wealthy sixty-six-year-old widow who lived in Albany, New York. He married her and in January 1949, they moved into an apartment on Long Island with Martha pretending to be Fernandez's sister. On the first night, however, Martha was consumed with jealousy when she saw

Raymond in bed with his latest wife. She claimed later to have suffered a blackout during which she bludgeoned Janet. As his latest conquest lay bleeding on the floor, Fernandez strangled her with a scarf.

They tidied up the mess, shoved Janet's body into a closet and went to bed. Next day, they crammed the corpse into a trunk that they left with his sister before burying it in the cellar of a house they were renting.

To maintain the charade that all was well, however, Fernandez posted typed letters to Janet's family. They became suspicious, realizing that Janet had never typed or owned a typewriter in her life. They alerted the police.

Martha and Fernandez were long gone, however. They travelled to Grand Rapids in Michigan where they moved in with forty-one-year-old widow, Delphine Downing and her two-year-old daughter, Rainelle. Delphine was unaware that the new man in her life was bald and when she walked in on him without his toupee in the bathroom one morning, she was furious, accusing him of deceiving her. Martha persuaded her to take some sleeping pills to calm herself down and Fernandez went to get the gun that had belonged to Delphine's husband. As Delphine drifted off to sleep, he placed the barrel of the gun, wrapped in a towel to muffle the noise, against her temple and pulled the trigger. Delphine's young daughter Rainelle watched all this happen and, of course, she presented the next problem.

Rainelle was crying hysterically as Fernandez ransacked the house looking for valuables. It was driving him to distraction and also raising the possibility that someone would arrive enquiring about what was happening. Unable to take it any more, he ordered Martha to kill the girl. She refused at first, but then filled the bath with water and drowned Rainelle. They buried mother and daughter next to each other in the basement of the house.

Instead of getting out of town as fast as they could, Martha and Fernandez bizarrely chose next to go to the movies. Returning afterwards to the house, they began to pack but as they did so there was a knock at the door. They opened it to find the police who had been called by suspicious neighbours.

Their trial was the sensation of the boiling hot summer of 1949. Reporters described in great detail the relationship between Martha Beck and Raymond Fernandez. She was nicknamed 'Big Martha', the taunts of her miserable childhood coming back to haunt her.

On 18 August, the jury returned a guilty verdict and

they were each sentenced to die in the electric chair at new York's Sing Sing prison on 10 October.

On the day, Raymond was the first to be executed. Although relations between him and Martha had alternated in the press between love and hate in the previous two months, at the last minute she had sent him a note telling him that she loved him. He exclaimed on receiving it, 'Now I am ready to die. Tonight I will die like a man.'

His last words were, 'I want to shout it out! I love Martha! What do the public know about love?' But as he approached the chair, the courage her love had given him deserted him and he had to be dragged, struggling to his death.

It was Martha's turn a few minutes later. She wedged her huge, grotesquely overweight body into the chair, mouthed the word, 'So long,' and was dead by 11.42 pm.

THE MURDER OF EMMETT TILL

Mississippi, in the 1950s, was the poorest state in the United States and the Delta counties were the poorest part of Mississippi. In Tallahatchie County, the average income in 1949 was $690 and for black families it was just $462. These poor people were sharecroppers, living on land owned by whites. They did not vote and had few legal rights.

Mamie Carthan was born in the tiny Delta town of Webb, Mississippi but when she was two, her family moved north to Argo, Illinois, like thousands of other black families, to escape poverty and the racial injustices being meted out on a daily basis to blacks in the south.

Mamie married Louis Till but the couple separated in 1942, leaving her to bring up their only child with the help of her mother. Emmett had been born in 1941 and was known to friends and family as 'Bobo' or 'Bo'. As a child, he suffered from polio but he grew to become a large young man, five feet six and a hundred and sixty pounds by the time he was twelve. His childhood illness had left him with a stutter but he was a lively, witty youth.

In the summer of 1955, Mamie decided to send Bo for a holiday with some relatives who still lived in Mississippi. Her cousin Moses 'Preacher' Wright lived in a town called Money in Leflore County. A sharecropper, who scraped a living harvesting cotton on his twenty-five acres, he lived with his wife and three sons in a six-room wooden shack.

Mamie knew it would be difficult for her son to adapt to life in Mississippi. He would find that things were very different to the big city. Before he left on the train, she schooled him in how to behave and how to speak. She instructed him to say 'yes, sir' and 'no, ma'am' and warned him to watch what he said.

It must have been quite an experience for the boy, arriving in the Delta. It is a vast area with few major towns and many communities that are no more than a couple of houses and a petrol station. Race relations would have been strange to him. There was segregation everywhere and the idea of sex between blacks and whites was abhorred to the extent that there were even laws against it. Sexual intercourse with a member of another race was punishable by a fine of $500 and ten years' imprisonment.

But Mississippi was not alone in its antipathy to blacks. South Carolina Governor ben 'Pitchfork'

Tillman once said in a disgraceful speech, that sex between races was 'the one crime that warrants lynching; and Governor as I am, I would lead a mob to lynch the Negro who ravishes a white woman.' Meanwhile, Mississippi Governor James K. Varddman once said, 'If it is necessary, every Negro in the state will be lynched; it will be done to maintain white supremacy.' And, indeed, lynchings did frequently happen in Leflore and Tallahatchie Counties. The reasons were astonishing – inflammatory language, loitering, demanding respect, testifying against a white man and trying to exercise the right to vote.

It was, without doubt, an alien world to a teenager from Chicago.

Emmett quickly made friends in Money and on 24 August, he and some of them drove to a local grocery store to buy sodas and some bubble gum.

Bryant's Grocery sat on Money's only intersection. It was run by twenty-four-year-old Roy Bryant and his pretty twenty-one-year-old wife Carolyn, who were both white and who lived in a room behind the store. Carolyn was a good-looking woman and her long, black hair and striking eyes had won her several beauty contests. She and Roy had married when she was seventeen and they had two children.

But the grocery business did not bring in enough money and Roy had to do some trucking on the side to make ends meet.

Being from the big city, Emmett Till was a lot more worldly than boys of his age with whom he was hanging out in Leflore County. He bragged to them about his escapades with girls in Chicago and in his wallet he carried a picture of a white girl that he claimed was his girlfriend. The other boys were impressed and encouraged him to go into the store and strike up a conversation with Carolyn Bryant who was on her own behind the counter. That week Roy was driving a truck to Texas and was not due to return for a few days.

Emmett entered the store and there are several different versions of what actually happened. One suggests that he put his arms around the woman's waist and said such things as 'I've got something for you, baby.' Other reports suggested that he did not actually touch her but did make some crude remarks. At the later trial, Carolyn testified that he said 'What's the matter baby, can't you take it? You needn't be afraid of me!'

Carolyn was sufficiently upset by what he said that she went into the back room and returned with a pistol. Then, just as he was leaving the store,

Emmett is reported to have whistled at her and shouted out 'Bye Baby!'

By then, however, realizing the seriousness of what was taking place, his friends had hustled him away from the store.

Soon word was spreading around town about what had happened. Inevitably, it got to Roy Bryant when he returned and he resolved to do something about it. He spoke with one of his brothers, World War Two veteran JW Milam and in the early hours of 28 August, the two of them drove to Preacher Wright's house and banged on the door. When Preacher opened the door, he was confronted by a pistol and the two men asking for Emmett.

The boy was wakened and told to get dressed. They told Moses that if he was not the right boy they would bring him back. Moses waited, but no one came back and it was the last time Emmett Till's family saw him alive. Moses reported the abduction to the local sheriff the following morning and Deputy Sheriff John Ed Cochran picked up Bryant and Milam later that day. They admitted that they had indeed taken the boy but claimed to have let him go unharmed a little later.

The sheriff launched a search, assisted by hundreds of local people but there was no sign of

Emmett. The press became interested and soon the story was featuring in the national media.

Three days later, on 31 August, a white boy fishing in the Tallahatchie River near a place called Pecan Point, saw a body in the water. He ran home to tell his parents and soon the police arrived to remove the corpse from the water. It was, of course, Emmett Till. He had been brutally beaten to the extent that one of his eyes was hanging out of its socket. A large fan, weighing almost eighty pounds, had been tied to his neck with a length of barbed wire and there was a bullet hole just above his right ear.

Emmett's body was put into a sealed coffin and transported, at her request, back to his mother Mamie in Chicago, this despite the wish of the Tallahatchie sheriff that he be buried immediately. The coffin arrived in Chicago on 2 September and Mamie fainted when she saw her son's body, so horrific was the damage that had been done to it.

She asked that the coffin be left open at Roberts Temple Church so that the violence that had been done to Emmett's face was there for the 250,000 people who filed past his coffin to see. It was an unforgettable sight; many fainted and all wept.

On 6 September, as they laid Emmett Till to rest, J. W. Milam and Roy Bryant were indicted for his murder. The trial began on a hot and humid 19 September 1955 with the national media out in force. When black Congressman, Charles C. Diggs Jr. turned up, there was outrage in Mississippi. They found it difficult to believe that a black man could be a Congressman. There were no black jurors, however, which was astonishing, given that sixty-five per cent of the population of Tallahatchie County were black.

The jury retired to deliberate on 23 September, and one hour and seven minutes later, it returned an astonishing verdict of not guilty.

There was national outrage with the verdict being denounced in newspapers across the United States as well as across the rest of the world. Meanwhile, the feelings in Mississippi were summed up by its own *Jackson Daily News* – 'Practically all the evidence against the defendants was circumstantial evidence; it is best for all concerned that the Bryant-Milam case be forgotten as quickly as possible. It has received far more publicity than it should have been given.' Realizing that the rule of double jeopardy protected them from further prosecution, J. W. Milam and Roy Bryant sold their story to *Look* magazine, and in the article they admitted the murder. It was published on 24 January 1956.

They told how they drove for seventy-five miles that night along country roads before going to Milam's woodshed and beating Emmett, inflicting terrible injuries on him. Till bravely, but stubbornly, refused to cry out, however, antagonizing the two hate-filled men even more. 'I never hurt a nigger in my life,' said Milam. 'I like niggers. In their place. I know how to work 'em. But I just decided it was time a few people were put on notice.'

They got back into the truck and stopped at a nearby factory where, amongst the rubbish, they found the heavy electric fan. They then drove back out into the Delta, stopping eventually at the river where they made the boy strip off all of his clothes.

Milam asked him if he still maintained that he had had a white woman and Emmett answered that he had. Milam raised his gun and shot Emmett above his right ear at point blank range. They then tied the fan to him using the barbed wire and tossed his body in the river.

When the article was published, there was national outrage but nothing could be done and the story faded into memory.

After the trial, Moses Wright had to uproot his family and leave Leflore County. He had testified against a white man and that meant that he was no longer safe. Roy Bryant returned to his store but he discovered that his black customers refused to shop with him. He was forced to close and move his family to Texas where he died of cancer in 1990.

No one was ever convicted of any charges relating to the murder of Emmett Till.

THE ZODIAC KILLER

The Jack the Ripper case in which five prostitutes were murdered by an unknown assailant in Whitechapel in London in 1888, is undoubtedly the greatest murder mystery of all time. The second-greatest, however, has to be the case of the Zodiac Killer, a serial killer who stalked Northern California in the late 1960s and early 1970s. In a series of letters to San Francisco newspapers, the Zodiac taunted police officers investigating the case and provided complex cryptograms or ciphers, three of which have never been solved. Although a number of suspects have been touted, there has never been conclusive evidence against any of them.

The first murders that were attributed to the Zodiac Killer occurred on 20 December 1968 at Lake Herman Road just outside the city of Benicia in the San Francisco Bay Area.

At around ten past eleven that night, sixteen-year-old Betty Lou Jensen and David Faraday, enjoying their first date together, were parked near the gates of a pumping station just east of Lake Herman, a well-known hang-out for young courting couples.

They had told Betty's parents that they were going to a Christmas concert but instead had driven to this isolated location. As they sat there a car drew up beside them and a man got out carrying either a .22 calibre rifle or a handgun that took .22 ammunition. He had started out behind the car, blasting out the right rear window before shooting out the left rear tyre. As he came round to the front, the terrified teenagers scrambled out of the vehicle through the passenger door.

Betty Lou started to run towards the road but was gunned down by five bullets in the back about thirty feet from the vehicle.

Faraday, on the other hand, was killed at close range with a single bullet to the head. Ten shots had been fired in total before the shooter left the scene.

Despite the best efforts of investigators from half a dozen law enforcement agencies and the offer of a substantial reward, the killer was never found. It was a murder that was seemingly motiveless, had been witnessed by no one and, therefore, had no suspects.

Just under seven months later, shortly after midnight on Saturday 4 July 1969, twenty-two-year-old Darlene Ferrin and 19 year-old Michael Mageau were parked in the Blue Rock Springs Park in Vallejo, just four miles from where Betty Lou Jensen and David Faraday had been murdered. While they sat there with the car lights out and the radio playing, a car drove into the car park and parked beside them. It then almost immediately reversed and drove off, but returned about ten minutes later, parking behind them.

The driver got out carrying a flashlight and walked up to the couple's car. He pointed the flashlight into the car and Mageau, thinking that it must be a police officer, began to reach for his driving licence. Suddenly, however, the sound of gunfire shattered the silence and Mageau realized that the man had also been carrying a gun, later discovered to be a Luger 9mm.

The first bullets struck Mageau, wounding him in the face and body and travelling right through him and hitting Darlene. He shot five times before turning and walking away from the vehicle. Hearing Mageau moaning, however, he returned and shot each of them twice more.

Darlene Ferrin was pronounced dead at the hospital but, astonishingly, Mageau survived, despite receiving multiple gunshot wounds to his chest, neck and face.

The following day, a man phoned the Vallejo

Police Department to claim that he had carried out the attack. He also claimed responsibility for the shooting of Betty Lou Jensen and David Faraday.

On 1 August, the first of the letters arrived. Three, in total, were sent to the *Vallejo Times-Herald*, the *San Francisco Chronicle* and the *San Francisco Examiner*. They claimed responsibility for the two shooting incidents and each included one third of a 408-symbol cryptogram. He claimed that in this cipher lay the secret of his identity. He insisted that they be printed on each paper's front page or he would carry out more killings, possibly up to a dozen over the weekend. When the cryptogram was deciphered, it read as follows, with spelling errors:

I LIKE KILLING PEOPLE BECAUSE IT IS SO MUCH FUN IT IS MORE FUN THAN KILLING WILD GAME IN THE FORREST BECAUSE MAN IS THE MOST DANGEROUE ANIMAL OF ALL TO KILL SOMETHING GIVES ME THE MOST THRILLING EXPERENCE IT IS EVEN BETTER THAN GETTING YOUR ROCKS OFF WITH A GIRL THE BEST PART IS THAE WHEN I DIE I WILL BE REBORN IN PARADICE AND ALL THE I HAVE KILLED WILL BECOME MY SLAVES I WILL NOT GIVE YOU MY NAME BECAUSE YOU WILL TRY TO SLOI DOWN

OR STOP MY COLLECTING OF SLAVES FOR MY
AFTERLIFE EBEORIETEMETHHPITI

The meaning of the last eighteen letters has never
been deciphered and the murders that are threatened
in the letter did not occur.

On 7 August, the letter writer called himself
the Zodiac for the first time. He wrote to the *San
Francisco Examiner* using the greeting, 'Dear Editor,
This is the Zodiac speaking'. Vallejo Police Chief,
Jack E. Stiltz had said that he was unsure whether
the first letters had been written by the killer and he
had requested that he write again, providing more
facts by which they could confirm that he was the
killer. This letter was a response to that appeal. The
letter did, indeed, contain details of the killings of
which the public were unaware.

On 27 September, he struck again and this attack
would demonstrate the oddness of the Zodiac Killer
case.

Lake Berryessa is the largest lake in Napa County,
California and is popular with local people. College
students, Bryan Hartnell and Cecilia Shephard were
enjoying a picnic there that Saturday, at Twin Oak
Ridge, a peninsula on the lake's western shore,
when they were approached by a man, between five

feet eight and six feet tall, with dark hair and dark, disheveled clothing. Hartnell described him as in his thirties and 'fairly unremarkable.'

As he approached the couple, he suddenly ducked behind some trees and they were surprised to see him re-emerge wearing a curious four-cornered black hood with a bib that dropped almost to his waist. Embroidered on it was the crossed-circle design that had appeared as part of the cryptogram the Zodiac had sent the newspapers. On his belt, he wore a long knife in a wooden sheath. In his hand was a large semi-automatic pistol. He told the surprised couple that he was an escaped convict from Deer Lodge, Montana and that he needed money and their car to escape to Mexico. He produced pre-cut lengths of plastic clothes line and instructed Shephard to tie Hartnell up. He then tied her up.

He told them he was going to have to stab them but Hartnell begged to be stabbed first as he could not bear to see his girlfriend in pain. 'I'll do just that,' the killer callously replied.

Hartnell was stabbed six times and Shephard, who died of her wounds two days later, received ten stab wounds. He left them for dead and using a black magic marker, drew his crossed-circle logo on the couple's car along with 'Vallejo 12-20-68 7-4-

69 Sept 27-69-6:30 by knife.' Those were the dates of his other attacks.

At 7.40 pm, he called the Napa County Sheriff's office from a phone box to report the incident and to claim responsibility.

On 11 October, a cab driven by Paul Stine was hailed by a man at the intersection of Mason and Geary Streets in San Francisco. He asked to be taken to Presidio Heights. During the journey, the passenger shot Stine in the temple with a 9mm pistol and stole his wallet and car keys. He also cut off a piece of the driver's bloodstained shirt. Three teenage witnesses saw the man wiping down the car to make sure he had left no fingerprints before walking away.

Unfortunately, the call that went out to police officers in the vicinity described the killer as black and officers in one patrol car consequently thought nothing of it when they drove past a man walking out of the area. They had driven past the Zodiac Killer.

At least there was a description. He was thirty-five to forty-five years old, medium to heavy build, medium complexion with light coloured hair that was possibly going grey at the back.

Another Zodiac missive arrived at the *San*

Francisco Chronicle on 14 October. This time he was threatening even worse crimes:

> *This is the Zodiac speaking. I am the murderer of the taxi driver over by Washington St + Maple St last night, to prove this here is a blood stained piece of his shirt. I am the same man who did in the people in the north bay area ... School children make nice targets, I think I shall wipe out a school bus some morning. Just shoot out the frunt tire + then pick off the kiddies as they come bouncing out.*

Enclosed with the letter was a piece of the shirt he had cut off the cabbie.

Officers were worried. The fact that he had broken his usual pattern to murder a lone male in downtown San Francisco implied that anything was possible, even the mowing down of schoolchildren. Bus drivers in the Bay area were issued with instructions about what to do if they were fired upon.

The Zodiac was now national news which brought with it its own problems, tip-offs flooding in from every part of America.

The letters kept coming. One arrived on 8 November, containing a 340-letter cryptogram that has never been deciphered. He sent one to the well-known lawyer Melvin Belli asking him to help him. In the envelope was another swatch of the taxi driver Paul Stine's shirt.

On the night of 22 March 1970, a man indicated that something was wrong to a pregnant woman driving with her ten-month-old daughter on Highway 132 near Modesto. Katherine Johns pulled off the road and the man fixed one of her wheels which he said he had noticed was wobbling. When she pulled away, however, the wheel he had purportedly fixed fell off. The man returned, offering to drive her to a gas station for help. She climbed in his car and they drove off but when he seemed reluctant to stop at the gas stations they were passing, she became concerned. For ninety minutes they drove.

He suddenly told her that he was going to kill her and then throw the baby out after her, but at an intersection she leapt out of the car with her baby and ran into a field where she hid. The man sat in his car for a while before closing the car door and driving off.

When she arrived at a police station to report the incident, she instantly recognized the man as being the same as the composite sketch on a poster of the man who had killed Paul Stine. Astonishingly, the desk sergeant at the police station was terrified that the Zodiac killer was going to turn up and kill all of them. He made the frightened woman and her baby wait in a nearby restaurant.

When her car was found, it was burned out. The man had returned to it and torched it.

He threatened to attack schoolchildren again in a letter of 20 April and again on 28 April. Other letters spoke of how he wanted the people of San Francisco to wear badges with his logo, the crossed circle, on them. He used odd references to Gilbert and Sullivan's *The Mikado* in one letter and in another discussed the tortures his 'slaves' – his victims – would undergo at his hands in the afterlife. On 27 October, he wrote 'Peek-a-boo, you are doomed'.

An 31 October letter suggested that the Zodiac had killed before the murders of David Faraday and Betty Lou Jenson. He directed police to the 30 October 1966 killing of eighteen-year-old Riverside City College student Cheri Jo Bates and they did, indeed, believe there was a strong possibility that he had been involved.

Then it stopped. There was no communication for three years but he re-surfaced in 1974 with a letter that referred to the film *The Exorcist* that had recently come out – 'the best satirical comedy that I have ever seen.'

Several more followed and then the last communication ever received from the Zodiac Killer arrived on 8 July1974, postmarked San Rafael. It was an attack on the conservative *San Francisco Chronicle* columnist, Count Marco Spinelli

Since then there has been no further communication and the cases involving the Zodiac Killer remain unsolved.

CHARLES MANSON

PROSECUTOR VINCENT BUGLIOSI: What is a creepy-crawling mission?

LINDA KASABIAN: A creepy-crawling mission is where you creepy-crawl into people's houses and you take things which actually belong to you in the beginning, because it actually belongs to everybody. I remember one specific instance where the girls made Charlie a long, black cape, and one of the girls was fitting it to him, and he sort of said, 'Now when I go creepy-crawling, people won't see me because they will think I am a bush or a tree.'

It was 28 July 1970, and the trial of Charles Manson and his group of followers, known as the Family, had many months still to go before verdicts were reached. Linda Kasabian, a Family member, had turned state's witness and was describing the escapades that Manson led and encouraged, deliberate terrorization of the Hollywood film community through eerie activities and eventually the vicious killing of nine people.

Manson's life was a car crash from the outset. Born in Cincinnati in 1934 to sixteen-year-old prostitute and alcoholic Ada Kathleen Maddox, all he ever knew about his father was that his name was Scott and he was a colonel in the armed forces.

When Charlie was just five years old, his mother was sent to prison for five years for an armed robbery committed with her brother. Charlie was sent to a quiet town in West Virginia where he was looked after by an aunt and uncle. When his mother was paroled in 1942, he went back to her and a life that involved living in cheap motel rooms and a series of men who entered and exited his mother's life.

When he was thirteen years old, Kathleen tried to have him placed in a foster home but no such home being available, he was sent instead to Gibault School for Boys in Terre Haute, Indiana. He hated it and after ten months he walked out and returned home to his mother. She did not want him around, however, and Charlie was left to fend for himself, aged just fourteen.

Needing cash to rent a room, he robbed a grocery store, but further robberies resulted in him being arrested and being sent to an Indianapolis juvenile centre. Following his escape the day after arriving, he was sent to Boys Town. He was there a mere four days before making a break for it with another inmate. They tried to make for the home of the other boy's uncle, committing two armed robberies en route. During the second, however, they were caught and Manson soon found himself at the Indiana Boys School. It was a brutal environment and Manson was abused sexually and physically. He escaped in 1951 with two other boys but they were apprehended in Utah and having committed numerous robberies and a stolen car across the state line, he was sent to the National Training School for Boys in Washington DC.

He was seventeen, illiterate and dangerously anti-social.

He was next sent to a minimum-security facility but just before a parole hearing, he put a razor to another inmate's throat and sodomized him. They sent him to the Federal Reformatory at Chillicothe. There, he seems to have learned his lesson at last. He became a model inmate and was released on parole in 1954.

In January, 1955, he married but, with his first child on the way, was arrested again, for car theft and, again having driven it across the state line, faced another federal charge. He was sent to Terminal Island prison in San Pedro, California. Meanwhile, his son, Charles Manson, Jr was born – but his marriage was over.

He was released on parole in 1958, but a year later was given a ten-year suspended sentence for trying to cash a forged US Treasury cheque. Shortly after, he was arrested for transporting a woman across a state line for the purpose of prostitution and his ten year sentence was invoked. He was sent to the United States Penitentiary at McNeil Island.

By March 1967, when he walked through the prison gates having been given an early release, he had been locked up for more than half his life. He regarded prison as his home and actually requested that he be allowed to stay, a request that was turned down.

He travelled to San Francisco which, at that point in time, was the centre of the cultural universe. The 'Summer of Love' was just beginning and young people from all over the world rushed there to be part of it.

Manson had learned to play guitar in prison and earned money by busking while living in the San Francisco hippie stronghold, Haight-Ashbury. He had soon moved in with Mary Brunner, a librarian at Berkeley University. He then began to gather a group of mostly young women who looked upon him as a guru. Soon, there were eighteen women living in Mary Brunner's house and by the autumn, the group were living in Topanga Canyon.

One day, a couple of the girls were picked up while hitchhiking by Beach Boy Dennis Wilson, who took them back to his house. They stayed and the rest of the Family moved in. It was an expensive few months for Wilson who also fell under Manson's spell, even paying for studio time for him to record the songs he had been writing. He promised to introduce him to influential people in the music business, one of whom was the producer Terry Melcher, son of the movie star, Doris Day. It was a promise he would live to regret.

The Family became a pain in the neck for Wilson but he finally managed to get them out of his mansion. They moved to Spahn's Movie Ranch before moving to a couple of ranches near Death Valley.

It was now late 1968 and The Beatles had just released their *White Album*. Manson was a fanatical Beatles fan and in his twisted mind he believed they were speaking directly to him through these songs. He assimilated them into his perverted philosophy in which he claimed that America's blacks would rise up and start to slaughter white people. The

White Album, he claimed, supported his prediction. He appropriated a song title from the album as the name for his vision of chaos – 'Helter Skelter'. The family, he added, would be safe while the uprising was taking place. They would hide in a 'bottomless pit', a secret city beneath Death Valley.

In order to get his philosophy out there, he decided to write an album of songs containing coded messages instructing people to initiate the carnage and invited Terry Melcher out to hear them. The Family made huge preparations and when Melcher failed to show up, Manson was furious and swore revenge. It would be a double-edged sword. He would take revenge on Melcher and he would show the blacks what needed to be done. His target was 10050 Cielo Drive where he believed Melcher lived.

When he investigated, however, he found out that Melcher had moved out and since February 1969, the house had been leased by Polish film director Roman Polanski and his beautiful, pregnant actress wife, Sharon Tate.

Manson was undeterred and Helter Skelter was unleashed.

The killing began on 25 July 1969 when Family associate Bobby Beausoleil, Mary Brunner and Susan Atkins visited musician Gary Hinman on Manson's orders to persuade him to give Manson money that he had inherited. When Hinman refused, he was stabbed to death by Beausoleil and the women used his blood to smear the message, 'political piggy' on his wall. Beausoleil was arrested driving Hinman's car on 6 August.

Two days later, family members Charles 'Tex' Watson, Patricia Krenwinkel, Linda Kasabian and Susan Atkins were dispatched to the Polanski house with orders from Manson to 'totally destroy everyone in it as gruesome as you can.'

The first to die was eighteen-year-old Stephen Parent who had been visiting the property's caretaker. He was killed as he drove out of the property.

Inside the house, were thirty-three-year-old Wojciech Fryowski, a friend of Polanski, thirty-three-year-old celebrity hair stylist Jay Sebring, twenty-five-year-old coffee heiress Abigail Folger and twenty-six-year-old Sharon Tate.

Fryowski woke to Watson hissing at him, 'I'm the devil, and I'm here to do the devil's work.'

They were all gathered together in the living room and Tate and Sebring were tied together by the neck, the other end of the rope being thrown over a roof beam. Watson began to stab Folger repeatedly and Fryowski was bludgeoned on the head and then shot twice. Folger ran out to the pool area, bleeding profusely, but Krenwinkel and Watson pursued her and stabbed her again. Meanwhile, Sharon Tate pleaded for the life of her unborn child but Atkins and Watson between them stabbed her sixteen times.

Before they left, they left something 'witchy' as Manson had requested; they smeared the word 'Pig' on the front door with Sharon Tate's blood.

The following night, Krenwenkel, Watson and Leslie Van Houten broke into the Los Feliz, Los Angeles home of Leno LaBianca, a retired supermarket executive and his wife, Rosemary. They stabbed Leno with a bayonet and, after she had put up a desperate fight in the bedroom, they stabbed Rosemary forty-one times. Watson carved the word 'war' on Leno's chest and 'rise' and 'Death to Pigs' was smeared in blood on the walls of the house. 'Helter Skelter' was also smeared but was misspelt as 'Healther Skelter'.

Surprisingly, it took months for the Tate, Hinman and LaBianca murders to be linked. Police put the Tate killings down to a drug deal gone wrong and suggestions that 'a guy named Charlie' and a bunch of hippies might have been involved, were not investigated.

At the end of August, however, someone finally realized that the victim's blood had been used to write on the walls of Hinman's apartment as in the other two cases. Investigations inevitably led back to Charles Manson and the Family.

The desert ranches where Manson and his people were staying were raided in October and a dozen people, Manson included, were arrested. At around the same time, Susan Atkins confessed that she had been involved in the Hinman murder.

The trial was a circus at times, with Manson hamming it up and at one point shaving his hair off, a gesture that was copied by the girls. They even tried to twist their stories to spare him, but eventually, on 25 January 1971, Manson, Krenwinkel, and Atkins were found guilty of all seven charges of murder and Leslie Van Houten was found guilty of two counts of murder. Tex Watson was found guilty on all seven counts later in the year. They were sentenced to death, but their sentences were commuted to life after the US Supreme Court declared the death penalty unconstitutional in 1972.

Charles Manson, Leslie van Houten, Patricia Krenwinkel and Bobby Beausoleil are still incarcerated, more than forty years after their terrible crimes. Susan Atkins died in prison in 2009.

ERVIL LEBARON AND THE CHURCH OF THE LAMB OF GOD

Ervil LeBaron liked cars. They were one of his passions. He had others, of course, and one of those was 'blood Atonement', the controversial Mormon doctrine that says that in the case of murder, even the atonement of Jesus does not apply. Only the shedding of the blood of the one who has committed the sin of murder will make things right. For LeBaron, however, blood atonement meant killing anyone who, in his eyes, had done him, or his church, the Church of the Lamb of God, wrong and twenty-five to thirty people are thought to have lost their lives because of it.

Polygamy had divided the Church of Jesus Christ of the Latter Day Saints almost from its founding in 1823 by Joseph Smith after he had been visited, as he claimed, by an angel named Moroni who showed him gold plates on which were inscribed ancient scriptures. Although as time went on, Smith publicly rejected polygamy, he is believed to have privately taken thirty-three wives. Outlawed in 1862 by the United States government, the Mormon Church ceased advocating it in 1890.

It was a decision, however, that dismayed many, leading them to split from the main church and establish their own communities where polygamy was not frowned upon. In 1924, one Mormon, Alma Dayer LeBaron, claimed that the voice of God had told him to travel to a remote part of northern Mexico with his two wives and eight children in order to live the life he had chosen. There, he established a settlement – Colonia LeBaron – and a year later, his ninth child was born, a son he named Ervil. Ervil would later be responsible for the murders of around twenty people and even long after his death, his followers would continue his evil work

Before Alma died in 1951, his son Joel assumed the leadership of the community, founding the Church of the First-Born of the Fulnes (sic) of Time, assisted by his handsome, six foot four brother, Ervil. The colony grew and before long a nursery, primary school and community kitchen and laundry were opened. The people of the settlement became known as 'Firstborners'.

The two men, however, were polar opposites. While Joel was a quiet man of religion, his brother was brash, wore flashy clothes and drove fast cars.

He rarely did any of the physical labour that was required around the community, claiming that his role was as a spiritual leader – he studied scripture and prayed instead, he claimed. He was also a serial womanizer and the age and marital status of the women he pursued were irrelevant to him. He told them that God had instructed him to take them. Astonishingly, the other families at Colonia LeBaron were only too happy to hand over their adolescent daughters to him in marriage. He would, in fact, take thirteen wives and father more than fifty children, all more members for the church, of course. Two of those wives, however, would die for him and two more would kill for him.

As he reached the age of forty, Ervil was tired of being second-in-command. Matters came to a head over a beachfront settlement Joel had established at Los Molinos in Baja California, Mexico. Joel and Ervil disagreed on what should be done with this land, Joel seeing it as a communal farm, Ervil envisioning a tourist resort. Ervil flew wealthy potential investors down to look at the property. To Joel, however, this was just another of his brother's get-rich-quick schemes, of which he had seen many over the years, and this one, like the others, came to nothing.

In reality, the church had no money, although

to see Ervil driving around in his gold Impala –
nicknamed the 'Golden Calf' by Firstborners – it was
not immediately obvious. When quizzed about it,
he said he needed it to impress potential converts.

Meanwhile, he was beginning to adopt some odd
and frightening views. He came up with a series
of decrees based on the Ten Commandments that
he called the Civil Law, appointing himself chief
enforcer. And just as in Moses' time, breaching the
Ten Commandments was punishable by death, he
believed the same should apply to the Civil Law.
He explained to the terrified congregation that he
would apply ancient means of execution such as
stoning, disembowelment and beheading.

It was only the beginning. Blood atonement
had arrived. In 1972, Ervil demanded a share of
the leadership of Colonia LeBaron but his brother
rejected his request. Additionally, he told him, he was
removing him from his position in the church. With
the colony divided by this split, Ervil moved away
to found his own church, the Church of the Lamb
of God. From San Diego, in southern California, he
railed against his brother. Eventually, on 20 August
1972, some of Ervil's men shot Joel dead.

As a warrant was issued for his arrest, Ervil was
horrified to learn that instead of turning to him, as

he had anticipated, the members of his late brother's church appointed his younger brother Verlan as leader.

In December 1972, he gave himself up at a police station in Ensenada. He was sentenced to twelve years in prison, but, remarkably, was free after just a day behind bars when the Mexican Supreme Court quashed his conviction.

There was paranoia now on both sides. Ervil – now known as 'Lord Annointed', 'One Might' or 'Prophet of God' by his followers, was armed at all times and feared that Joel's people might try to avenge their leader's death. Verlan, on the other hand, was terrified that he might be next. He fled to Nicaragua.

With Verlan gone, Erlan believed that the money the Firstborners had been paying to the church down at Colonia LeBaron should now be paid to him. He quoted the Civil Law at them, making it clear that if they failed to pay, they would die.

When they ignored him, he took terrible action, sending his men to Colonia LeBaron where they firebombed houses and shot Firstborners as they rushed to put out the fires. At the end of that horrific night, two were dead and thirteen injured. Ervil was by now completely off the rails, behaving like an emperor, deciding on his followers' marriages and using women and girls as payment to those of his men who had done him a good turn or served him well. The church moved to Utah where leaders of other polygamous sects were astonished to find him demanding a tenth of their income. Naturally, they showed him the door.

It was around this time, however, that the killing started in earnest. He heard that a Firstborner back in Mexico, Noemi Zarate, was threatening to inform on him to the police and sent one of his many wives, Vonda White, to silence her. Vonda shot Noemi dead while she was driving with her in the foothills of the San Pedro Mountains.

Bob Simons was a Mormon who lived on a ranch near Grantsville, Utah. Desirous of Simons' ranch, Ervil had him shot in a remote location on 2 April 1975.

Vietnam veteran, Dean Vest, was next. At six foot eight, Vest was a man mountain who had acted as the church's military mind until his wife left him and he decided to leave. Leaving the church was, of course, a breach of one of Ervil's major Civil Law rules and blood atonement was the punishment. Five foot three Vonda White once again acted as the weapon of the Lord Annointed. As Vest crouched over her broken washing machine, trying to repair it, she shot him dead with a Colt .38 revolver.

It was 1975 and Ervil had turned fifty. That did not stop him marrying sixteen-year-old Rena Chynoweth. He had already been molesting her for four years, anyway. He ordered her to kill his former friend, Rulon Allred who was withholding money from him. She was arrested and tried for the murder, but was acquitted for lack of evidence. Meanwhile, Vonda had been given life for the murder of Dean Vest.

Terrified followers were beginning to leave the church and things were beginning to unravel. Finally, on 1 June 1979, Ervil was arrested south of Mexico City.

He was sentenced to life imprisonment but, just a year into his sentence, was found dead of a heart attack in his cell on 16 August 1981. Strangely, just a few hours later on the same day, Verlan LeBaron was killed in a car crash in Mexico.

Ervil had used his year in prison well, writing the 500-page book, *Book of the New Covenants*, that included a commandment to kill disobedient church members whose names were on a list compiled by him. Twenty copies were printed and distributed.

The elimination of the people on the list began. In June 1983, his twenty-year-old son Isaac who had testified against him, committed suicide in highly suspicious circumstances. A few months later, his wife Lorna was strangled. His oldest son, thirty-three-year-old Arturo, who had assumed leadership of the church on his father's demise, was shot dead by a rival 'prophet' in December of that year.

Unfortunately, the next in line to run matters, Ervil's son, Heber, was almost as insane as his father. He launched a campaign of revenge on Firstborners who had betrayed his father. Four died between 1984 and 1988. Then, on one dreadful day, 27 June 1988, another four former followers died, three of them almost simultaneously at 4 pm. Duane Chynoweth and his eight-year-old daughter were shot and killed while out shopping and Eddie Marston, who was a stepson of Ervil was also shot dead. Meanwhile, that same day, Mark Chynoweth was shot to death in his office in Houston, Texas.

Seven were arrested for the '4 o'clock murders' and five were convicted of murder. Heber was sent to prison for life while Aaron LeBaron, another of Ervil's sons, received a forty-five-year sentence. The last suspect, Joseph LeBaron was arrested in May 2010.

Many of Ervil LeBaron's family members and former disciples remain in hiding to this day in fear of his blood atonement being visited upon them.

SON OF SAM

The man known as the '.44 Caliber Killer' was hogging the headlines. He had launched his deadly campaign, seemingly aimed at random couples seated in cars in the early hours of the morning in various boroughs of New York, on 29 July 1976 and by 17 April 1977. Five were dead and a number had been seriously wounded.

However, following the latest shootings, which had ended the young lives of Alexander Esau and Valentina Suriani, a letter was discovered lying on the street. It was addressed to New York Police Department Captain Joseph Borelli, one of the key members of the Omega task force, headed by Deputy Inspector Timothy Dowd, that had been created to find the killer. Borelli's name had appeared frequently in articles about the killings and the killer now had a message for him. It read, complete with spelling mistakes:

Dear Captain Joseph Borrelli,
I am deeply hurt by your calling me a wemon hater. I am not. But I am a monster. I am the 'Son of Sam.' I am

a little brat. When father Sam gets drunk he gets mean. He beats his family. Sometimes he ties me up to the back of the house. Other times he locks me in the garage. Sam loves to drink blood. 'Go out and kill,' commands father Sam. 'Behind our house some rest. Mostly young – raped and slaughtered – their blood drained – just bones now. Papa Sam keeps me locked in the attic too. I can't get out but I look out the attic window and watch the world go by. I feel like an outsider. I am on a different wavelength then everybody else – programmed too kill. However, to stop me you must kill me. Attention all police: Shoot me first – shoot to kill or else keep out of my way or you will die! Papa Sam is old now. He needs some blood to preserve his youth. He has had too many heart attacks. 'Ugh, me hoot, it hurts, sonny boy.' I miss my pretty princess most of all. She's resting in our ladies house. But I'll see her soon. I am the 'Monster' – 'Beelzebub' – the chubby behemouth. I love to hunt. Prowling the streets looking for fair game – tasty meat. The wemon of Queens are prettyist of all. It must be the water they drink. I live for the hunt – my life. Blood for papa. Mr Borrelli, sir, I don't want to kill anymore. No sur, no more but I must, 'honour thy father.' I want to make love to the world. I love people. I don't belong on earth. Return me to yahoos. To the people of Queens, I love you. And I want to wish all of you a happy Easter. May God bless you in this life and in the next.

A week earlier, retired city worker, Sam Carr, who lived in the New York borough of Yonkers with his wife and children, had received a bizarre letter. It concerned his dog, a black Labrador named Harvey. The writer was complaining about the dog's barking. Then, two days after the 17 April murders, another, more threatening letter arrived, bearing the same handwriting. It read:

I have asked you kindly to stop that dog from howling all day long, yet he continues to do so. I pleaded with you. I told you how this is destroying my family. We have no peace, no rest. Now I know what kind of a person you are and what kind of a family you are. You are cruel and inconsiderate. You have no love for any other human beings. Your selfish, Mr Carr. My life is destroyed now. I have nothing to lose anymore. I can see that there shall be no peace in my life, or my families life until I end yours.

Carr immediately called the police but there was nothing they could do. Ten days later, Sam Carr heard a gunshot from his backyard. He ran out to find his dog lying on the ground bleeding and caught sight of a man wearing jeans and a yellow shirt running away. The letter to Borelli had not been given to the newspapers and no one thought to link the letter to Sam Carr with Son of Sam.

The killer known as the '.44 Caliber Killer' who would evolve into the much more frightening Son of Sam struck for the first time at just after one in the morning of 29 July 1976. Eighteen-year-old brunette Donna Lauria and her nineteen-year-old friend, Jody Valenti, were shot as they chatted in Jody's car outside the entrance to the apartment building in which Lauria lived in the Bronx. A man suddenly appeared at the passenger window of the car, pulled out a Charter Arms .44 and pumped five bullets into the interior of the vehicle. Hit in the neck, Donna was killed instantly. Jody was hit in the thigh, but pressed on the car's horn, frightening their assailant away, but only after he had continued to click the empty chambers of the gun for a few seconds.

It seemed entirely motiveless and police began to think it must have been a case of mistaken identity. The alternative was that it had been a lone psycho. That was not exactly reassuring because if that was the case, there was every possibility he would strike again. He did – again and again.

Twenty-year-old Carl Denaro and his college friend Rosemary Keenan were the next couple to sense a shadow by the passenger window. Sitting talking in Rosemary's Volkswagen Beetle after spending the evening with friends at a bar in Queens, celebrating Carl's enlistment in the US Air Force, they sat horrifies as the window of the car exploded and bullets whizzed past them. Carl received a serious head wound but Rosemary had the presence of mind to slam her foot on the accelerator and speed away from their assailant. Carl later had a metal plate inserted in his skull, but at least both survived.

Just over a month later, sixteen-year-old Donna DeMasi and her friend eighteen-year-old, Joanne Lomino, were saying goodnight outside Joanne's house after spending the evening at the movies. Suddenly, out of the darkness, a man appeared and in a strange high-pitched voice began to ask them for directions. 'Can you tell me how to get...' he began. But he never finished his sentence. Instead, he pulled out a revolver and shot the girls before running away. Although both victims survived, Joanne was rendered paraplegic by her wounds.

Two months later, on 30 January, Christine Freund was fatally wounded as she sat talking to her fiancé, John Diel in his car in Queens.

The police launched Operation Omega to catch the killer and it was now exhaustively investigating the backgrounds of all the victims, but they could find no connection, apart from the fact that they had all been shot by a man with a .44 gun. It did, indeed, appear that the attacks were random.

Following the fatal shooting of Virginia Voskecherian as she walked home from college on 8 March, police did at last get a description of their perpetrator. After he shot her, he ran past a man who was just walking round the corner of the street at that moment. 'Hi, mister!' he said cheerfully as he ran past.

He was a white male, twenty-five to thirty-six years old, six feet tall, of medium build and with dark hair. The bullet that killed Voskecherian was confirmed as being from the same one used in the first attack the previous year.

After the 17 April murders and the letter to Captain Borelli, another letter turned up. It was sent to the famous *New York Daily News* reporter, Jimmy Breslin. The murderer wrote:

Hello from the cracks in the sidewalks of NYC and from the ants that dwell in these cracks and feed in the

dried blood of the dead that has settled into the cracks.
Hello from the gutters of NYC, which is filled with dog
manure, vomit, stale wine, urine, and blood. Hello from
the sewers of NYC which swallow up these delicacies
when they are washed away by the sweeper trucks.
Don't think because you haven't heard [from me]
for a while that I went to sleep. No, rather, I am still
here. Like a spirit roaming the night. Thirsty, hungry,
seldom stopping to rest; anxious to please Sam. Sam's
a thirsty lad. He won't let me stop killing until he gets
his fill of blood. Tell me, Jim, what will you have for
July 29? You can forget about me if you like because I
don't care for publicity. However, you must not forget
Donna Lauria and you cannot let the people forget her
either. She was a very sweet girl. Not knowing what
the future holds, I shall say farewell and I will see
you at the next job? Or should I say you will see my
handiwork at the next job? Remember Ms. Lauria.
Thank you. In their blood and from the gutter – 'Sam's
creation' .44.

From that day on, the '.44 Caliber Killer' was known as 'Son of Sam'.

Four more people would be shot by Sam. On 26 June, in Queens, Salvatore Lupo and Judith Placido were wounded in their car and on Sunday

31 July, just over a year since the murder of Donna Lauria, 'Son of Sam' claimed his last victims. Stacy Moskowitz was shot and died later in hospital while her boyfriend Bobby Violante was hit twice in the face but survived. This time, however, Sam had been seen.

As he returned to his Ford Galaxie after the shooting, a woman walking her dog saw him tear a parking ticket from his car and throw it to the ground in anger. She also thought that she saw a gun. She called the police and reported the incident. They traced the ticket and the vehicle to which it had been issued.

David Berkowitz was arrested on 10 August 1977 outside his apartment building. New Yorkers could at last breathe a sigh of relief.

Berkowitz had a troubled childhood. Adopted at birth, he grew into a problem teenager – a loner, a petty thief, a pyromaniac and a bully. His adoptive mother having died, his father abandoned him and he failed to make a viable career for himself in the army. His step-sister, however, had given him an interest in the occult that would emerge during his questioning by investigators.

He claimed that others were involved in the

murders and that the dog he had shot was actually possessed by an ancient demon that ordered him to kill. He wrote to a newspaper that, 'There are other Sons out there, God help the world.' He has said that there are two dozen members of the satanic cult with which he was involved in New York and that it had links with others across the United States.

Nothing has ever been proved and Berkowitz, currently serving his life sentence at Sullivan Correctional Facility in Fallsburg, New York, will say no more for fear, he claims, of what might happen to his family.

He, too, fears the 'twenty-two disciples of hell he mentioned in his letter to Jimmy Breslin.

SHOKO ASAHARA

It was a simple but deadly plan. Aum members would carry *sarin* – the most deadly nerve toxin in the world – onto trains in bags. Five men had been chosen – Kenichi Hirose, Yasuo Hayashi, Masato Yokoyama, Toru Toyoda and Dr Ikuo Hayashi – and each was equipped with antidote pills so that they would survive the attacks.

On the morning of 20 March 1995, each was dropped at a different station where they boarded Metro trains passing through Kasumigaseki and Nagatacho stations, where the Japanese government was based. This was to be an attack on the very heart of the nation.

On the Chiyoda Line, just before 8 am, Ikuo Hayashi punctured one of his bags of *sarin* as the train approached the Shin-Ochanomizu station, the stop for the central business district in Chiyoda. He left the train which carried on for four stations. The bag was disposed of by station attendants at Kasumigaseki station, two of whom died. Two hundred and thirty-one people were injured in this attack.

On the Marunouchi Line, Knichi Hirose dropped his packets to the floor as the train approached Ochanomizu station and punctured them with the tip of an umbrella. He left the train which carried on for fourteen stops to Nakano-sakaue station where two seriously affected people were carried from the carriage in which the *sarin* had been dropped. One of them later died. Three hundred and fifty-eight were seriously injured.

On the Ikebukuru Line, Masato Yokoyama, wearing a wig and fake spectacles, failed to puncture his packages properly. However, they remained on the train even after it had been searched by station attendants. No one died, but more than two hundred people were poisoned.

Toru Toyoda punctured his packages on arriving at Ebisu station on the Hibiya Line. One person died and five hundred and thirty-two were injured.

Meanwhile, on the Naka-Meguro Line Yasuo Hayashi punctured the three packets he was carrying at Akihabara station and left the train. By the next stop, passengers were beginning to feel the effects and someone kicked the packages out onto the station platform. There were four fatalities in the station as a result. Some remained on the train, however, and after another couple of stops, passengers were becoming very ill. This attack was responsible for eight deaths and two hundred and seventy-five seriously ill people.

The attacks had killed a total of thirteen people and severely injured fifty while almost a thousand others suffered from temporary problems with their sight. Altogether, around 5,500 people were treated in hospitals and many were permanently injured. When it was revealed that sarin gas had been the agent used, Japan went into panic, especially the people living and working in Tokyo.

The authorities suspected one body of being behind the attack – Aum Shinrikyo, the religious organization run by Shoko Asahara.

Asahara had been born Chizuo Matsumoto in 1955. While still a child, he had gone blind in his left eye and was teased and bullied at school as a result. Eventually, his parents sent him to a school for the blind, but as the only partially sighted pupil in a class of blind children, it was his turn to become a bully.

He had boasted that one day he would be prime minister of Japan, but this plan had to be abandoned when he failed to gain entry to Tokyo University. Instead, he settled down, marrying and having the first of his six children. He launched the Matsumoto

Acupuncture Clinic, with money provided by his wife's parents. A range of dubious but expensive herbal remedies followed.

By this time, he was spending a great deal of time in meditation and was exploring spirituality and fortune-telling. He was soon boasting of being able to see the auras that surrounded evil people.

He decided to found his own religion, registering a company – Aum Incorporated – that he ran from his rented one-bedroom flat in the Shibuya district of Tokyo. A yoga and meditation club to begin with, he opened yoga schools across the country, establishing a reputation as a caring and charismatic leader.

Inside, however, Matsumoto was a mess. He began to believe that Armageddon was at hand and that he had been chosen to survive it and become the leader of a race of people with the purest of spirits. He announced this to his small group of followers, grew his hair and his beard and began to dress in long, flowing robes. He also legally changed his name to Shoko Asahara.

He travelled extensively, recruiting new followers. He met the Dalai Lama while on a visit to Daramasala in India and received his blessing for Aum Shinrikyo, or Aum Supreme Truth, as he was calling his religion. He wrote a book, delivered lectures and began describing himself as a 'venerable master'. He claimed to have healing powers and for a fee of more than £200, he would lay his hands on sick people.

He asked followers for donations and millions of yen flowed into the organization's coffers. Meanwhile, he began to devise a philosophy for his religion, incorporating elements of Christianity, Buddhism and Hinduism and even the sixteenth century French seer, Nostradamus. He predicted the end of the world would occur in 2003, giving an added impetus to those thinking of making a donation.

He devised other, bizarre ways of raising cash, allowing followers to drink his blood in return for a payment of almost £5,000 and a couple of pints of his bathwater could be purchased for £500.

By 1988 Aum Shinrikyo had grown. There were 1,500 followers in Japan and Asahara had opened an office in New York, hoping to find adherents in the United States. Now extremely wealthy, he decided to use some of his money to purchase land at the foot of Mount Fuji on which he planned to construct a temple and a headquarters for his religion. It was very basic, no more than prefabricated huts, but that did not deter hundreds of followers from coming to hear him talk, at a cost of around £1,500 a week. Many gave up their jobs, their friends and family to devote their lives to him. He called them his monks or nuns. They donated everything they owned to Aum Shinrikyo – houses, cars, savings and valuables. He also took possession of their credit cards, making sure, of course, that he also had their pin numbers.

Children ran away from home to join him, but like other followers they endured a tough regime. Aum Shinrikyo adherents were regularly deprived of sleep and fed only meagre rations. Breaching the strict rules within the compound resulted in swift and harsh punishment – offenders were starved and locked in tiny rooms in which they were subjected to recordings of lectures by Asahara played for days on end.

Needless to say, there were many complaints. Many people saw it as a cult, an anti-social organization that was exerting a bad influence on Japanese youth. Even a victory in the courts that meant that Aum Shinrikyo could call itself a religion – enjoying the tax concessions that brought – did not endear it to the older generation or the authorities who were becoming increasingly suspicious of Asahara's activities.

Within the organization itself, however, there was a growing sense of disillusionment. Many felt that the change to their lives that the leader had promised had failed to materialize. One man expressing a desire to leave was told that he must be mentally ill. Asahara described his condition as 'heat within the head', and ordered that he be immersed repeatedly in freezing water. He died of hypothermia. Another who wanted to leave had his neck broken by one of Asahara's henchmen. Asahara was not prosecuted for these crimes but was becoming increasingly paranoid.

Tsutsumi Sakamoto was a lawyer engaged by some parents whose children had run away from home to join the sect. On 3 November 1989, he, his wife and their small child were murdered by members of Aum Shinrikyo on the orders of Shoko Asahara. He described what they had done as 'holy work', declaring that the baby, although an innocent victim, would be re-born in a higher world.

Arrogantly, Asahara called a press conference to allay the inevitable suspicions that his organization was behind the disappearance of the Sakamoto family who at that point were still believed to be victims of a kidnapping. He denied involvement.

In the laboratories at the compound, Asahara's scientists were working in his Supreme Science

Institute on various projects designed to create agents of mass destruction. His chief scientists, Hideo Murai and Seiichi Endo succeeded in creating Clostridium botulinum, one of the most powerful toxins known to man. Asahara was eager to try it out on the people of Tokyo and devised a plan in which a truck would spray the toxin close to the Japanese parliament in the centre of the capital. He intended to disable the centre of government and seize power for himself. But, when the toxin was exposed to oxygen, it neutralized and was ineffective.

In order to understand more about chemical weapons, he travelled to Moscow and, while there, even discussed obtaining nuclear weapons. Meanwhile, Aum was changing, becoming increasingly militarized, adherents undergoing military training and being drilled.

Aum's wealth was estimated to be around a billion dollars and as his followers starved and scraped by on very little, Asahara was enjoying the benefits of such wealth, owning a fleet of very expensive cars that included a Rolls Royce, a number of Mercedes as well as a couple of luxury yachts.

He targetted the marriage of Japanese Crown prince Naruhito on 9 June 1993, fitting a truck with a means of spraying the toxin created by his scientists onto the streets of Tokyo. Not a single casualty was reported, however. Once again, they went back to the drawing board.

Later that year, they sprayed anthrax from the top of a building in Tokyo onto the streets below and although people reported upset stomachs and pets became ill, there were no serious injuries.

Sarin gas was the next toxin to be tried. After testing it on a herd of sheep on a remote farm in Australia owned by Asahara, they decided to strike at a group of judges who had found against Aum the previous year. Two trucks were dispatched to the dormitory in which the judges lodged but when the device that was supposed to mix the gas, malfunctioned, a cloud of deadly hydrogen chloride gas was released into the air. The wind blew it away from the dormitory and into a group of houses. Seven people were killed and one hundred and fifty were taken to hospital.

It was time, the increasingly unstable Asahara decided, to launch a major attack using sarin gas. Plans were made for the attacks on the Tokyo subway.

Following the attacks, the authorities planned a huge raid on the Aum Shinrikyo facility. Word got out, however, and Asahara was able to flee in his Rolls Royce while his followers frenziedly began to destroy the evidence that would implicate the religion.

On 22 March, more than one thousand police officers raided the Mount Fuji headquarters, finding tons of dangerous chemicals and arresting around a hundred members of the sect. They uncovered a torture chamber in the basement and prison cells, many of which were still occupied by adherents who had contravened one of Asahara's rules. In a safe a million dollars was found.

On the run, Asahara produced a booklet that predicted, amongst other things, a huge disaster that would take place on 15 April 1995. The government declared a state of emergency but the day passed without incident.

Cyanide devices began to be discovered in Tokyo's subway system, left by cult members who were still on the loose. The city remained terrified.

On 23 April, as he emerged from a car at Aum's Tokyo headquarters, Aum scientist Hideo Murai was stabbed to death by a man enraged by what the cult had perpetrated in the subway.

In the six weeks following the initial raid, 150 members had been arrested but Asahara remained free until 16 May when he was discovered hiding behind a wall in an Aum building that had already been searched by police on a number of occasions. He was meditating when discovered.

Following what was described as Japan's 'trial of the century' Asahara was sentenced to death, a sentence upheld by the Japanese Supreme Court in 2006. He is now in prison awaiting execution.

ROCH 'MOSES' THÉRIAULT

Jim Jones, David Koresh and Roch 'Moses' Thériault; they were all the same. They got religion, became heavily involved up with one religious movement, devoting all their time to it and then came to the conclusion that they were bigger than the movement, deciding they should be at the head of their own movement, leading their weak, submissive and often vulnerable followers to salvation. Their powerful mixture of charisma, manipulativeness and authority meant that their insane dogma was swallowed hook, line and sinker by their disciples and they could lead them anywhere. Eventually it all ended in megalomania, a belief that the leader was the new messiah and that when Armageddon arrived – and he will usually have prophesied it – they would be the 'Chosen People'. Sadly, it all ended in debauchery, corruption and death.

Born in Saguenay Valley in Quebec, Roch Thériault had a pretty normal childhood, although he would later claim that his father was abusive. His family was devoutly Catholic and, as often happens, their close relationship with the Catholic Church alienated Roch from it. Throughout his life he had an intense dislike of Catholicism.

By the age of twenty, he was married to a woman named Francine Grenier and with her he had two sons, Roch Jr and François.

In his twenties, Thériault began to change. He became irrationally obsessed with medicine following an operation for ulcers and also began to drink heavily and have affairs. His wife soon tired of his philandering and walked out but Thériault had soon moved in with another woman named Gisele.

The most important change in him, however, was that he became interested once again in religion, attending services held by the Seventh Day Adventist Church. The Seventh Day Adventists were distinguished by their observance of Saturday as the Sabbath and by their emphasis on the imminent second coming of Jesus Christ. From its ranks would come David Koresh who would lead his splinter group, the Branch Davidians, to death in the siege at the Mount Carmel Centre in Waco, Texas in 1993.

Like Koresh later, Thériault had extreme views which made his fellow Adventists distinctly uncomfortable. He was obsessed with the Apocalypse and adopted an Old Testament approach to life in which males were superior and women were mere chattels, there only to serve the needs of men. Nonetheless, there were a number of people who were attracted to his charismatic personality. They were twenty-one-year-old Solange Boilard, nineteen-year-old Chantal Labrie, twenty-year-old Francine Laflamme, twenty-year-old Nicole Ruel, twenty-year-old Josée Pelletier, Jacques Fiset who was in his mid-twenties, twenty-four-year-old Claude Ouellette, twenty-four-year-old Jacques Giguère, his twenty-three-year-old wife Maryse and their six-month-old daughter. They all fell under the spell of this man who seemed so different to the rest and appeared to offer them more hope than they could find in the church.

His apotheosis to something approaching divinity in their eyes began in 1977 while they were on an Adventist retreat at Lake Rousseau in Ontario. Thériault hiked into the woods to meditate and on his return informed them that he had had a vision from God who had told him that the rocky outcrop on which he was kneeling was now a holy place.

He moved his group of followers to Sainte-Marie about 65 kilometres from Quebec City where they opened the Healthy Living Clinic a shop selling alternative medicines, organic food and holistic literature. He insisted on them all wearing a uniform, an ankle-length tunic, green for the women and beige for the men. His robe was brown.

As he began to attract more followers, Gisele noticed that the women of the group had begun to compete for his attention. Fearing she might lose him to one of them, she persuaded him to marry her. On 8 January 1978 their wedding took place at an Adventist church in Montreal.

Meanwhile, the Adventists were becoming increasingly concerned about Thériault's group. They were particularly worried about the girls and approached many of their parents, including Gisele's, trying to get them to persuade their daughters to leave him. His hold over them was too great, however. Even when the police turned up, they were unable to persuade them to leave him. In fact, they would not even speak to the officers.

In March 1978, Geraldine Gagné Auclair arrived at the Healthy Living Clinic. She had been undergoing treatment for leukaemia at a hospital in Quebec City but her husband had met Thériault who had persuaded him to let him visit his wife in hospital. Thériault argued loudly with her doctors over her treatment, especially about the quantity of drugs she was being prescribed. He convinced her husband to check her out of the hospital and bring her to his clinic. His treatment for Geraldine was grape juice and organic food and, needless to say, the very sick woman did not last long. 'You know, when God wants people,' Thériault told her husband and his followers, 'he takes them. It was Geraldine's time.'

It was all too much for the Seventh Day Adventists and in March 1978, they expelled Thériault from the church. Not that it bothered him. Soon, even though he had no authority to perform marriages, he was performing them for his followers. They had not actually expressed a desire to marry each other; he just decided they should. The sermon delivered by him after the ceremony harped on his old theme – the woman's subservience to her husband.

Gisele who was now pregnant was beginning to feel rejected as he bathed in the adulation of his followers and did not have much time for her. She delivered an ultimatum to him. Either he finished with the commune or she would leave him. His response was to punch her in the face and restrict her to her room for two days.

But things were not going well with the clinic. They owed large sums of money and the Seventh Day Adventists who had been supplying them with health food and literature stopped supplying. They simply climbed into their vehicles and left it all behind.

For a while they wandered, but by July 1978 they were in the wilderness of the Gaspé Peninsula in Quebec. Here Thériault shared with the group his vision for the future. He prophesied that on 17 February 1979, the world would end with a great storm. They, God's chosen, would be saved but only if they had already established themselves in the Appalachian foothills.

They travelled to southeastern Canada where they set out on foot and hiked for a couple of days until they came to an isolated hill beside a small body of water known as Lac Sec. They stopped and made their home there, erecting tents and beginning the construction of a large communal cabin. It was hard work, clearing the land, digging a well and surviving on limited rations. He provided a new uniform, though – dark blue wraparound smocks.

Not that Thériault did much work. He was always too ill and, in fact, claimed to be suffering from cancer. But some found it too hard and left.

The cabin was finished in September when, to celebrate, Thériault decided to re-name them all with names from the Bible. He assumed the name Moses. Shortly after, he annulled all the marriages in the commune, apart from his own. He then started to marry all the women himself. The strict Adventist diet was next to go. He started to drink again after being sober for two years and he prostituted one of the women to a local grocer in exchange for meat, milk and cheese for himself.

His sermons became even stranger, rambling on drunkenly for hours. Anyone who fell asleep during one was struck on the head with a heavy club. His regime became even harsher. On one occasion, when one woman ate two more pancakes than her allocation Thériault punched her, breaking two of her ribs. In another punishment, people who had transgressed were made to stand naked in the snow for hours on end.

Maryse Grenier was a reluctant member of the group and had always been a problem. When she talked about leaving the commune, Thériault ordered her husband Jacques Giguère to punish her by chopping off one of her toes. Jacques understandably hesitated and Thériault snarled at him, 'What are you, a faggot? Don't you have any balls? If you want to be a man, you have to learn how to teach your woman a lesson.' Further hesitation led Thériault to threaten that he would do it himself, only he would chop off all her toes. Reluctantly, Jacques picked up the axe and did as he was told.

The day he had predicted for the end of the world

came and went without incident but Thériault shrugged it off, complaining that he could not be expected to understand the timing that God had tried to explain to him. It made no difference. No one left.

In late 1980, the mentally unstable Guy Veer joined the group. He was given the responsibility of looking after the 'outsider' children, those of whom Thériault was not the father. However, when two-year-old Samuel Ouellette would not stop crying one night, Veer lost his temper, punching the child a number of times and killing him. Six months later, a drunk Thériault decided that Veer should be castrated for his crime. Thériault performed the procedure but a short while later, when Veer escaped and told local people about Samuel's death, Thériault was arrested and sentenced to two years' imprisonment.

Released in February 1984, he took his followers to a place near Lindsay in Ontario where they began to build a new cabin. Now calling himself 'Rock', he announced to his relieved followers that he was no longer drinking and that there would be no more violence. It did not last long, however. Soon, he was drinking again and the violence resumed

Worried about the children in the camp, the

authorities raided it removing them to foster homes. They were lucky. Occasionally, Thériault would hold two children over a fire and laugh while their mothers pleaded for their child to be saved. There was sexual abuse too.

In autumn 1988, when Solange Boilard fell ill, Thériault convinced her that there was a problem with her liver. He persuaded her that she needed an operation and he would, of course, perform it. After giving her an enema and then putting a tube down her throat and ordering everyone to suck and blow on it, he made an incision on her right side. He tore out a strip of tissue and told her she would be alright. It soon became obvious that she was far from alright when blood began to pour from her mouth. She died shortly after.

Thériault was beside himself and is reported to have tried to kill himself a number of times, but when he did not die, he announced it to be God's will. He ordered Solange's body to be exhumed and poured vinegar on her to keep the worms at bay. A few days later he ordered her to be dug up again. This time he told Jacques Giguère to drill a hole in her head into which he masturbated, convinced that his seed would revive her.

Things began to unravel even further. On 26

July 1989, he stuck a knife into Gabrielle Lavalle's hand, fixing it to a table. He walked away, but on his return, saw that her arm had turned blue and began sawing it off. He then took a meat cleaver to it and amputated it. She did not make a sound but a few days later escaped and went to a hospital where her feeble story about how she had lost her arm was not believed. The truth came out and shortly after Thériault was arrested and charged with first degree murder. In 1993, he was found guilty and sentenced to life imprisonment.

Since being in prison, he has had had two more children following conjugal visits by two of his women followers.

JEFF LUNDGREN AND THE KIRTLAND KILLINGS

He brought the little girls out to the barn one at a time on the innocent pretext of seeing a horse. When each of them came in, she was grabbed and bound with duct tape. Then Jeff Lundgren stepped forward and pumped bullets into their tiny bodies and with his associates, buried them beside their mother and father who had already been dispatched. Lime was poured over the bodies and soil was poured into their graves. The men went about the work quietly and seemingly unconcerned. It might even be said they showed a callous disregard for what had just happened – the murders of four people. Emotion was unnecessary, however, because as Jeff Lundrgren told them, it had to be done. It was, after all, 'God's will'.

Jeffrey Don Lundgren came into the world on 3 May 1950, in Independence, Missouri, the son of Don and Lois Lundgren. The Lundgren family were devout members of the Reorganized Church of the Latter Day Saints, a group that had broken away from the main Mormon church in 1860.

Within the walls of the Lundgren home, life was harsh and tightly disciplined. Don was not afraid to dish out severe punishments for even the smallest infraction and Lois was a distant woman who was not a lot better than her husband. Lundgren would later claim that his treatment as a child amounted to physical abuse that led to him being the way he was, but it has never been confirmed that this was actually the case.

As a child, Jeff was unpopular with classmates, viewed as an arrogant loner. He was also cruel. A neighbour recalls him nailing a rabbit to a piece of wood and viciously beating it to death. He would certainly confirm the notion that children who are cruel to animals invariably grow up to be violent adults. After high school, Jeff enrolled at Central Missouri State University where he majored in electronics. In his sophomore year, his life centred on an RLDS sorority house where he met fellow students Keith Johnson and Alice Keehler who would become his wife.

Alice's life was not much different from her future husband's. She, too, had been a victim of violence as a child, from a father who suffered from multiple sclerosis and was unable to work. He took his frustrations out on his family.

Like Jeff Lundgren, she had also been a loner, preferring to spend her time at the local church than with her schoolfriends. They were made for each other and shortly after meeting had become inseparable.

In 1969, now married and with Alice pregnant, the couple dropped out of college much to the disappointment of Don and Lois Lundgren. Jeff enlisted in the United States Navy and in December 1970 his son Damon Paul was born. He remained in the Navy for four years and a few weeks before his honourable discharge, Alice gave birth to their second son, Jason.

After his discharge from the Navy, they lived in San Diego where they became active in the local RLDS church. They moved back to Independence but Jeff's irascible and irresponsible nature made it difficult for him to hold down a job for any period of time. He took it out on Alice and the children, of whom there were now three. On one occasion, he pushed his wife down a flight of stairs, rupturing her spleen. Nonetheless, their fourth child, Caleb was born in September 1980. It was suspected by some of their friends, however, that she had the baby in a last-ditch effort to keep the failing marriage together.

By 1981, Jeff was beginning to question the way the RLDS church was going. The ordination of women priests appalled him and when they asked him to join its lay priesthood, he said no. Instead, he formed his own Mormon splinter group.

He had developed a charismatic style that appealed to people and they flocked to his meetings. People also began to make donations that enabled him and his family to live.

Soon, however, he announced that God was telling him to move. The place that had been chosen for him was Kirtland, Ohio. Once there, he told them, the Lord would imbue him with his true power.

A number of his followers travelled to Ohio with him, moving into his house and living communally. He and Alice found jobs as tour guides at the RLDS's temple in Kirtland. In return for their work, they received free board and lodging and $125 a week. The church later estimated that he had stolen around $25,000 from them during his time working for them

Lundgren's state of mind was becoming even more questionable. He started to present himself to his followers as a prophet, a new Joseph Smith, the founder of the Church of the Latter Day Saints. He prophesied the date on which Jesus Christ was going to return to earth – 3 May 1988 which also happened to be his thirty-eighth birthday. He devised a plan for his followers to seize the temple in Kirtland that day, killing anyone who got in their way. The nature of the group changed. Once, they had read the Bible and debated the scriptures; now they wore uniforms, marched and stockpiled weapons.

Several months before the fateful day, Lundgren suddenly announced that he had had a vision. He had been told that if they wanted to see God, they should sacrifice one of the families in the group who had been causing him some trouble. The Avery family had followed Lundgren to Ohio, but Dennis Avery had kept for himself some of the money he had received when he had sold his house in Independence. This had deeply irritated Lundgren.

The Averys had purchased a farm in Ohio. On 10 April, shortly before they were due to move in, Lundgren ordered two of his men to dig a pit in a barn on the farm. It had to be big enough to hold five bodies, he ominously told them.

A week later, he and his people helped the Averys to move their belongings into the farm and then they all sat down to dinner at a nearby motel. Back at the farm, Dennis Avery was asked to come out to the barn under some innocent pretext. Once there, Lundgren tried to render him unconscious with a stun gun but it failed to work. They grabbed him and as he pleaded for mercy, bound him with duct tape and threw him into the pit that had been dug a week earlier. The sound of a chainsaw drowned out the sound of two bullets being fired into Dennis Avery's back.

They enticed Dennis's wife Cheryl out to the barn. As the duct tape was wound around her, she put up a mighty struggle but once again the sound of a chainsaw drowned out the noise of the three bullets that were pumped into her body. Fifteen-year-old Trina Avery was next and then they brought in the girls.

The following day they headed for West Virginia where Lundgren said he had to await a sign from God that would lead him to the 'golden sword' that had been spoken about in the Book of Mormon. Meanwhile, he was full of himself following the Averys' murder, delighting in the power he had over these people. They were terrified of him and not without reason. He boasted about the murders, going over every detail again and again.

At Davis, in the remote Canaan Valley, sixty miles southwest of Wheeling, they constructed a military-style compound, digging foxholes and ensuring that guards were posted on a regular basis. They adopted a shoot-to-kill policy and they even had an anti-aircraft sub-machine gun that could shoot down any helicopters that the authorities sent to spy on them.

Lundgren's teachings became more extreme as the summer progressed. Married men were ordered to hand over their wives to him so that he could 'cleanse' them with his seed and it was patently obvious to them that anyone who objected would suffer a similar fate to the one suffered by the Averys. There was a great deal of unease within the group, however, and for the first time, members began to doubt their leader.

They moved to Missouri and then he decided to break the group up over the winter and get back together again the following summer. Each man was told to get a job and save his earnings, ready to hand it over when they re-grouped.

By this time, it was becoming obvious to Jeff that he was beginning to lose control. There were members of the group who would not be returning and what was to stop them going to the police and telling them about the Avery killings? He took his family and a follower named Danny Kraft to Southern

California where they stashed their weapons cache in a storage locker. They went into hiding.

Lundgren's old university friend Keith Johnson was the first to crack. The guilt of what he had been part of proved too much and he organized a meeting with agents of the FBI. They were incredulous but when officers from the Kirtland Police Department checked the barn, they realized that Johnson was telling the truth.

News of the find flushed out other members of the cult. In the hope of receiving leniency from the courts, they began to tell their stories. Arrest warrants were issued for the Lundgrens and ten other members of the group. Soon, Jeff and Alice Lundgren were arrested at a Santa Fe motel, just six miles from the Mexican border.

It took the jury just one day to reach a verdict in the case against Alice Lundgren. Found guilty of all five murder charges, she was sentenced to twenty years for each, to run consecutively. She went to prison for a hundred years.

Jeff Lundgren's trial began on 23 August 1990. It took two hours to find him guilty of five first degree murders and he was sentenced to death for each one. On 26 October 2006, Jeffrey Don Lundgren was executed by lethal injection at the Southern

Ohio Correctional Facility in Lucasville. His last words were: 'I want to profess my love for God, my family, my children and my beloved Kathryn,' – he had divorced Alice and married Keith Johnson's wife Kathryn while in prison – 'I am because you are.'

PART THREE

KIDNAPPING AND SEXUAL SLAVERY

COUNTESS ERZSÉBET BÁTHORY

Her aunt was rumoured to be a witch, she had an uncle who was an alchemist and a devil-worshipper and her brother was a paedophile. Her nurse was said to be a practitioner of black magic and was reputed to have been involved in the sacrifice of children. Countess Erzsébet Báthory, however, outdid them all. She was one of the most prolific women killers there has ever been.

She was born in either 1560 or 1561, into the powerful Báthory family and grew up on an estate in Transylvania in Hungary. Her family included counts, princes, bishops and cardinals and she was a cousin of the prime minister, György Thurso. Her uncle Stephen had been King of Poland.

As a child, it is thought that she suffered from epilepsy and there is evidence of mental instability in the family, her cousin Prince Stephen, famous for attempting to unite Europe against the invading Ottoman Turks, displaying the extraordinary and callous savagery of a psychopath.

She was promiscuous from an early age, falling pregnant to a peasant at the age of fourteen. A year later, however, she married the powerful Count Ferencz Nádasdy whose family, like hers, was known for its ruthless cruelty. There were 4,500 guests at the wedding which took place in the palace of Varanno.

In those troubled times, her husband was constantly at war, leaving his young wife to indulge whatever wicked pastimes she could come up with but when he was home, he demonstrated a catalogue of unsavoury habits, including the savage beating of young servant girls. He also took pleasure in leaving them staked out in the countryside with honey smeared all over their naked bodies, victims of insects or other creatures. He also liked to pour water over their naked bodies in winter, leaving them to freeze to death. When he was feeling particularly amorous, he would bring back a black magic spell for his wife from his travels.

Witchcraft began to play a big part in her life and she was rumoured to carry around with her a parchment that had been fashioned from a caul, the membrane that surrounds a baby's face and head in the womb and sometimes covers it when it is born. In medieval times, it was imbued with all kinds of magical powers and a caul on a newborn baby was a sign of good luck or an indication that the child was destined for greatness. On the caul was inscribed an incantation that would protect Erzsébet from evil.

After her marriage, she had moved into her husband's castle, Castle Csejthe, now a ruin in modern-day western Slovakia. He had given it to her as a wedding present along with the Csejthe country house and seventeen neighbouring villages and it was there that her reign of terror began.

She had learned from her husband the art of beating someone until they were within an inch of their lives and she used this skill relentlessly. She would write to him while he was on his campaigns, detailing her latest incidents of cruelty. She missed him, of course, but that did not prevent her from taking countless lovers in his absence and their gender was irrelevant to her. She surrounded herself with an entourage of people who were adept in the black arts of sorcery and alchemy and she had even learned about drinking blood from one man who visited the castle. She was also reputed to bathe in blood.

Her husband died in 1604 after an illness lasting three years and the countess was a widow at the age of forty-four. She spent some time in Vienna but returned to her estates where she would live for the remainder of her life.

Many young girls had been disappearing from neighbouring villages. It was reported that a carriage, drawn by powerful black stallions, would drive through the villages collecting young girls who believed they were being taken to the castle to work as servants but would never be seen again.

Even the daughters of noble families were not safe. She offered to teach them social graces but like the other girls, they disappeared beyond the gates of the castle and were never seen again.

Everyone had been afraid to speak out against her and, eventually, she began to think she was invincible, she could do whatever she wanted.

Between 1602 and 1604, following wild rumours, a Lutheran minister, István Magyar, began to complain publicly and at the court in Vienna about the atrocities that were reported to be occurring at Castle Csejthe. The authorities, however, were slow to respond and it was not until 1610 that King Matthias ordered György Thurzo, his prime minister and Erzsébet's cousin, to investigate. It was not a small undertaking as the Báthory family was extremely wealthy and powerful.

Thurso's party travelled to the castle to carry out its investigation. It was hoped that although she was a practitioner of the black arts who had no qualms about harming others, she would open the gates of the castle to them on seeing the colours of her cousin. On the night they arrived, they were informed that she was holding one of her late-night gatherings. These events were known to be wild and during them screams were often heard from within the massive castle walls.

However, on 30 December 1610, as they approached, they noticed that the windows of the castle were in darkness. They were surprised to find that there was no guard at the gates and were able to ride in unchallenged. They entered a great hall and were horrified to find the body of a partly-clothed young girl lying on the floor. She was unnaturally pale as if the blood had been drained from her body. Another girl lay nearby, close to death and also looking as if her blood had been drained from her body. Another woman was found chained to a post. She had been whipped and again she she was very pale.

In the dungeons they discovered cells crammed with women and children, screaming and wailing. Everywhere there was the stench of decomposition.

The castle displayed signs of a drunken orgy having taken place and implements of torture were scattered around. However, there was not a trace of the Countess. She had fled when she heard that an investigation was being launched that night.

A plan had been concocted before the party had set out for Castle Csejthe between her family and the government for her to be spirited away to a convent. It was believed that a trial and execution would constitute too much of a scandal and a noble family would be disgraced. Moreover, the king owed her a large sum of money which placed him in an embarrassing position.

Nonetheless, a trial was held, although she failed to attend any of its session. It began on 2 January 1611 and there were twenty-one judges, headed by Judge Theodosius de Szulo of the Royal Supreme Court.

Many of the witnesses who testified had actually been victims of her extraordinary cruelty or were members of the families of girls who had gone missing. Her accomplices also testified and it was their testimony that was most damning. Each of them was asked the same eleven questions.

Ficzko, a dwarf who worked for Erzsébet, testified that he was uncertain how many women he helped to kill, but believed that thirty-seven girls had been murdered, an estimate that was thought by many to be very conservative. He described how if the girls did not come willingly, they were beaten unconscious and carried to the castle. He described the types of torture that were practiced, explaining how they tied the hands and arms very tightly with Viennese cord, and then beat them until the whole body was black as charcoal and their skin was rent and torn. One girl, he said, suffered more than two hundred blows before dying.

Dorko, another accomplice and procurer, used shears to cut the girls' fingers off and then slit their veins with scissors.

A nurse, Ilona Joo, admittted that she had taken part in the murder of around fifty girls. She described pushing red-hot pokers into victims' mouths or up their noses and how on one occasion her mistress the Countess had stuck her fingers into the mouth of one girl and pulled so hard the sides split open. The judges learned that victims were forced to indulge in deviant sexual practices and one was even made to strip flesh off her own arm.

Countess Erzsébet Báthory and her servants were convicted of eighty murders, although King Mathias wrote in a letter that there may have been as many as 300 and one estimate puts the number at 650.

Her accomplices were tortured and executed – their fingers were pulled off and they were buried alive, burned at the stake or beheaded but the Countess was imprisoned for life, proclaiming her innocence throughout. King Mathias had demanded that she be executed, but her connections proved too powerful.

Instead, she was put under house arrest in her own castle, locked up in a small suite of rooms whose walls and windows had been bricked up. Meanwhile, she persisted in her claims that she was innocent of all charges, blaming the girls' deaths on a whole range of illnesses from disease to blood poisoning.

On 21 August 1614, three years after she had been incarcerated, she was found dead. Initially, she was buried in the church at Csejthe, but the villagers were so disgusted at having her body in their churchyard that she had to be reinterred at the Báthory family crypt at Ecsed.

COLLEEN STAN

Cameron Hooker's favourite movie was 1975's *Story of O,* which tells how an independent young woman is taken by her lover to a château in Roissy in France where she voluntarily becomes a slave. Branded with the initials of her master, she is subjected to sexual sado-masochistic rituals. Hooker, with the compliance of his submissive wife Janice decided that he was going to make his fantasy real. He went out looking for a woman who would become his sex slave. On Thursday, 19 May 1977, as he drove with his wife and baby through the town of Red Bluff, he found her standing at the side of the road, hitchhiking. His dream was about to become chilling reality.

Twenty-year-old Colleen Stan had left her hometown of Eugene, Oregon, to hitchhike across the state line to wish a friend happy birthday in the northern Californian town of Westwood. It was a journey of four hundred miles and, not having the cash to take a bus, she decided to hitch. It had gone well and by the afternoon, she was only fifty miles from her destination.

A couple of cars had already stopped, but she was

careful and being dubious about them, she let them travel on. When the blue Dodge Colt pulled up, however, with a clean-cut man, woman and baby inside, she figured it was safe.

Their names were Janice and Cameron Hooker and they seemed nice, chatting away to her as they headed down the Interstate, although she became uneasy when she realized that the man was constantly observing her in the rear-view mirror. She reassured herself, however, that as his wife and child were in the car, nothing untoward was likely to happen.

Cameron asked her if it would be alright to make a slight detour. They wanted to see some spectacular ice caves that were nearby. She told him that was fine and a few miles further on, they pulled off onto a dirt road which they drove along for a while before he stopped the car. He suddenly pulled out a knife and held it to her throat. He then told her to do as she was told, tied her hands and ankles and blindfolded and gagged her.

He then produced a bizarre contraption – a large, metal-hinged plywood box that he placed over her head putting her into total darkness and rendering her barely able to breathe. He covered her with a sleeping bag and she felt the car drive off again.

When they stopped, he took off the box and pushed her out of the car and into a house. She was led down some stairs into a basement. He ordered her to stand on a chest freezer and with a leather strap tied her hands above her head to pipes in the ceiling. She was still blindfolded.

He kicked away the freezer from beneath her, leaving her hanging by the wrists from the ceiling. She kicked and screamed but he threatened to cut her vocal chords if she continued, hinting that he had done it before. He then slowly undressed her and began whipping her back and front till it stung.

He left and returned with his wife and to Colleen's disgust they started to have sex on the floor below her. After they had finished, he took her down and locked her in a sitting position in a large wooden box. She was unable to move and he placed the head box back on, making it difficult once more for her to breathe. When she began to scream, Hooker returned and tied a strap tightly around her chest that silenced her but made it even more difficult to breathe. She remained like that for the remainder of that terrifying night.

Little did she know that this long night was just the beginning of seven years of captivity.

The Hookers had met in 1973 when loner

Cameron met epileptic fifteen-year-old Janice. They were a good fit – she was malleable, which suited him, and she was happy to find a man. He was obsessed with violent pornography and she was so eager to please him that she would go along with anything he wanted to do. By 1975, they were married.

Soon, however, he was eager to expand his fantasies and he did a deal with his wife. If he allowed Janice to have the baby she so badly desired, she would allow him to find a sex slave. He launched his search.

The day after she had been kidnapped, he starved Colleen all day before finally feeding her with potatoes and water. He hung her up again and then he put the head box back on. Next day was much the same, but she was beginning to learn that if she did not do as she was told, she would be punished – hung and whipped.

Naturally, her family in Eugene became worried and she was reported missing. When no leads emerged, the case faded away, however. Her family were convinced she had been murdered or kidnapped by a religious cult but nothing came to light.

Colleen spent her days chained, blindfolded, hung naked and whipped by Hooker. At other times, he would push her head under water until she blacked out. Meanwhile, however, he was working on a new idea, a box shaped a little like a coffin. He put her sleeping bag in it, put earplugs in her ears and chained her up inside. She would be left in the box until he wanted her.

Meantime, he continued to whip her and beat her and to add a little more spice, he burned her body with a heat lamp. He would also electrocute her and sometimes choke her.

After a few months, he decided that as well as satisfy his base instincts with her, he could also get her to work. He constructed a wooden cell under the stairs of his house and in there she had enough room to shell nuts or do macramé. She was delighted with even this small improvement in her conditions and she began to look forward to her time under the stairs.

After about eight months, Hooker introduced a new twist. He presented her with a contract that bound her to him as a slave. He told her that she would have the slave name 'K' and forced her to sign, adding that he had paid $1,500 to register with a body called the Slave Company. They watched over all such arrangements and had probably bugged the house, he told her. More sinisterly, he informed her that they knew who her family was and should she disobey or try to escape they would be in grave danger. Janice was also his slave, he told her.

Incredibly, the gullible woman believed it all.

Now known in the house as K, Colleen was allowed to do household chores but when Hooker shouted out 'Attention!' she had to immediately stop what she was doing, take off her clothes, stand on tiptoe and reach up until her hands touched the top of the doorframe. She wore a slave collar and even had a slave registration card that he made for her.

Despite all his abuse over the months, he had never raped her. Finally, many months after she had been kidnapped, she was brought into the Hookers' marital bed, but Janice decided she did not like what was going on and left the room, Hooker finally had intercourse with her. This would become a regular occurrence.

He introduced another of his boxes after the family moved into a trailer that was short of space. It was a ventilated wooden box that fitted under his and his wife's water bed. It would become Colleen's home for twenty-three hours a day. She heard them making love above her and even listened as Janice gave birth to their second child on the bed.

As the years passed, he started to allow her to

work outside in the yard where neighbours who saw her believed her to be a live-in babysitter. She was even allowed to go jogging. He would always be sure to let her know, however, that the Company was watching her every move and she always returned.

She even went out drinking with Janice one night. They met some men and went home with them. Hooker agreed afterwards to let Janice continue having an affair with one of them.

Eventually, Janice wanted her husband to set Colleen free. She was becoming jealous of the attention he was lavishing on the younger woman but he was not ready for that yet. Instead, he had Colleen say goodbye to all the neighbours as if she was going away and confined her to the box under the bed again.

Astonishingly, three and a half years after she was kidnapped, she was permitted to visit her family. He dropped her off at the house, pretending to be her boyfriend and picked her up again twenty-four hours later. Ever fearful of the Company, she told them nothing about her captivity and they did not press her, fearful that if they asked too many questions, they would lose her forever. She returned to Red Bluff with her kidnapper.

Cameron's fantasy was growing. He was talking about having as many as five slaves and tried to build a dungeon to house them in the yard. It flooded, however, and the idea had to be shelved for the moment.

But Janice was changing. She had started going to church and was riddled with guilt about Colleen. Eventually, she blurted out to Colleen that the Company did not exist and that the contract was not worth the paper it was printed on. Colleen immediately quit the job at a motel that Cameron had found for her, stayed one more night in the trailer and the following day called Cameron at work to tell him she knew everything and was going home. He cried down the phone line.

In another twist to this bizarre story, Colleen did not tell her parents or even inform the police about what she had endured for the past seven years. It was only when Janice finally walked out on Cameron three months later that the truth came out. She told her pastor who, with her permission called the police.

Janice also told detectives that her husband had kidnapped, tortured and killed a missing girl, Marie Spannake, before he kidnapped Colleen Stan. Although her body was never found and no charges could, therefore, be brought in that case, for the kidnapping and sexual assaults on Collen, he was sentenced to a total of 104 years in prison.

JIM JONES AND THE PEOPLE'S TEMPLE

Today, nothing remains of Jonestown apart from a rusting oil tank turned on its side. The settlement where several hundred people lived their lives has vanished into the earth of the jungle in which it stood, the buildings mostly destroyed by fire in the 1980s and the jungle and weeds have swallowed up any other evidence of the settlement's existence. There is silence where once there was noise, and peace where once there was horror. In this jungle clearing in Guyana, on 18 November 1978, 913 members of the People's Temple ended their lives by drinking poison. It was a dreadful end to an extraordinary story.

Born part-Cherokee in Crete, Indiana in 1931, the young Jim Jones found it difficult to make friends and received little love from his parents. He used religion, therefore, as his way into society and by 1947, aged just sixteen, he was preaching on street corners to whoever would stop and listen. After graduation from Richmond High School, he became a full-time preacher, delivering an unusual message of racial integration but when his views proved to be unpopular with the leaders of the church to which he was affiliated, he resolved to create his own church. Amongst other things, he sold monkeys as pets door-to-door to raise funds and by 1956 had established the Wings of Deliverance Church, soon to be re-named the People's Temple and located in Indianapolis.

His message of integration stretched beyond colour to include the poor and disadvantaged.

Jones's church became a beacon for the unemployed, for drug addicts and for ex-convicts. He practised what he preached. He and his wife, Marceline had a son, but they also adopted a black child and a Korean child.

His church was not a free ride for its members. He demanded devotion, dedication and sacrifice, attracting new members by using stunts such as healing. He claimed to be able to heal cancers, make the blind see and the lame walk. He also told his followers that he was a seer, that he could foretell the future and, to their surprise and delight, he often conjured up revelations about individual members. They were unaware, however, that he regularly sent Temple members out the night before one of these fortune-telling sessions to go through the dustbins of the people involved. Nonetheless, it did not prevent him from calling himself the reincarnation of Jesus Christ, a claim believed by many of the simple, naïve and fairly desperate people he attracted.

As a member, there were financial commitments. Initially on joining, donations were purely voluntary, but the longer someone was a member, the greater the financial burden placed on him or her. Eventually a follower was expected to pool his or her income with the other members. In return they were given room and board and a weekly allowance of two dollars. They lived communally at the People's Temple, Jones telling them it was the only place where they would be protected from earthly temptations and the evils of modern life.

Increasingly, he stirred up paranoia amongst his congregation. He told them that the outside world was suspicious of them and would work against them to bring an end to their community. Anyone who dissented even a little from Jones's views became a hated figure and those who left were detested. Doubts were not permitted and everyone was encouraged to report any instance. Children reported their parents and parents their children.

In the midst of this febrile atmosphere, Jones

claims to have had a vision of a nuclear attack, the Midwest being the target. He decided to move the People's Temple to a safer place but first scouted out some locations. Leaving the church in the hands of his assistants, he spent two years travelling, visiting Hawaii and Brazil, teaching English in order to support himself. On the way back from Brazil, he visited Guyana on the northern coast of South America where he was particularly impressed by the socialist policies of the government.

Back in Indianapolis, he read a magazine article that said that Mendocino County, California would be safe in the event of a nuclear attack. He moved his congregation there and found part-time teaching work while his wife Marceline was employed as a social worker at Mendocino State Hospital.

His marriage was in trouble by this time, however. Marceline was tired of her husband's extra-marital affairs and his increasing drug use. He used a variety of drugs to control his mood swings. Amongst these were the sedative Quaaludes that his son Stephen used in a failed suicide attempt.

The church was also in trouble, numbers having slumped to just sixty-eight. In an effort to revive it and to obtain valuable tax exemptions, Jones affiliated the People's Temple with the Disciples of Christ, a church that boasted 1.5 million members. His new partners paid little attention to Jones, however, and he continued to baptize new members of the People's Temple 'in the holy name of socialism'. To his mind, socialism, or his form of communalism, was the manifestation of God and only through this could anyone achieve true freedom, justice and equality. It worked and by 1973, his congregation had grown to more than two thousand.

In 1974, he returned to Guyana, having obtained permission from the Guyanese government to begin the construction of a commune on three hundred acres of land about a hundred and forty kilometres from the capital Georgetown. He named it Jonestown.

Back in California, he began to prepare his followers for the move to Guyana.

They believed it would be a paradise on earth, but, of course, it was far from that. They had to work six days a week, from seven in the morning until six at night in temperatures that often reached a hundred degrees Fahrenheit. Meals consisted of little more than rice and beans, while Jones dined on eggs, meat, fruit, salads and soft drinks that he kept in his own private refrigerator.

Discipline was rigorous and punishment harsh.

Recalcitrant members were imprisoned in a six foot by three foot plywood box and problem children were forced to spend the night at the bottom of a well, sometimes hanging upside down. Anyone who tried to flee from the encampment was restrained and incapacitated by drugs. Armed guards patrolled constantly.

Meanwhile Jones was claiming the welfare payments of his followers which amounted to around $65,000 a month and his wealth by this time was estimated to be in the region of $26 million.

In November 1978, a group of United States officials visited Jonestown to investigate complaints made by concerned relatives about Jonestown. The group was led by Congressman Leo Ryan, and included his legal advisor, Jackie Speier, now herself a member of Congress; Neville Annibourne, representing Guyana's Ministry of Information; Richard Dwyer, Deputy Chief of Mission of the US Embassy to Guyana at Georgetown (believed by some to have been a CIA officer); reporters Tim Reiterman (*San Francisco Examiner*) and Don Harris (NBC); Greg Robinson; Steve Sung; Bob Flick; Charles Krause; Ron Javers; Bob Brown; and relatives' representatives Anthony Katsaris, Jim Cobb and Carolyn Houston Boyd. The party arrived on 14 November, but Jones refused to allow them access to Jonestown.

On the morning of Friday, 17 November, they flew to Port Kaituma airstrip, ten kilometers from the camp, regardless of whether Jones was willing to see them or not. Initially, only Ryan and three others were allowed in, but the remainder were finally allowed in after sunset.

Jones and his followers put on a show for them, staging a reception and a concert for their visitors. They were shown round by carefully selected members and everyone they met seemed cheerful and happy.

Two members initiated an escape attempt that night, however. Vernon Gosney slipped a note to Don Harris, mistaking him for Congressman Ryan. It read: 'Dear Congressman, Vernon Gosney and Monica Bagby. Please help us get out of Jonestown.'

Ryan and his people were allowed to remain in Jonestown that night while everyone else spent the night at the airport. The following morning, when Jones awoke, the NBC crew handed him Vernon Gosney's note, Jones was furious. Then another two families – the Parks and the Bogues – stepped forward and said they also wanted to leave with

Ryan's group. Christopher O'Neal and Harold Cordell joined their ranks.

Jones grudgingly gave them permission to leave and provided them with some money and their passports. He seemed to become reconciled to the idea and told them they could come back any time they wanted to. Later, when Jones heard that another two families – the Matthews and the Wilsons had left the camp that morning, he was very upset. Others lined up to leave and negotiations began that went on all afternoon.

Ryan decided to let a small group leave at around three in the afternoon from the airstrip while he would remain behind with other members of his party while another plane was chartered. Suddenly, however, just after the first group had left, Temple member Don Sly attacked Ryan with a knife. The Congressman was unhurt but it was decided that it would be best if he left. His party, accompanied by around sixteen Temple members left for the airstrip at around 4.30 pm.

They were using two planes – a six-passenger Cessna and a slightly larger Twin Otter and at around 5.20 the Cessna started its preparations for take-off. At the far end of the runway, however, Temple member Larry Layton, who was actually a Jones loyalist, pulled out a gun inside the plane and started shooting, wounding Monica Bagby and Vernon Gosney. Dale Parks disarmed him.

Meanwhile, Congressman Ryan and his party were boarding the Twin Otter but as they did so, a tractor approached the landing strip with a trailer attached. The members of Jones's armed guard who were on board opened fire when they got to within thirty feet of the plane, running round it, guns blazing. Cameraman Bob Brown's camera captured the attack, even though as it rolled, he was shot dead.

Congressman Ryan and newsmen Brown, Robinson and Harris as well as People's Temple defector Patricia Parks were also killed.

A Guyanese plane would come to evacuate the dead and wounded the following morning.

Meanwhile, back at Jonestown, Jim Jones called a meeting before which his assistants had filled a metal vat with Valium, chloryl hydrate and possibly cyanide. Jones announced, 'One of the people on that plane, is gonna shoot the pilot, I know that. I didn't plan it but I know it's going to happen. They're gonna shoot that pilot and down comes the plane into the jungle and we had better not have any of our children left when it's over, because they'll parachute in here on us …' He added, 'They'll torture our children, they'll torture some of our people here, they'll torture our seniors. We cannot have this.' He explained that they were all going to drink the mixture and end it. 'All it is, is taking a drink to take ... to go to sleep. That's what death is, sleep.'

They had practiced it before. 'White Nights' he had called them. Tonight, however, was no practice.

The children were first to die, poison being squirted into their mouths with a syringe. They were led away and the adults followed amidst anguished screams and cries. When it was done, Jones and his closest supporters came together, gave a final cheer and shot each other dead with handguns.

Jim Jones was found slumped in a deck-chair, with a bullet wound to the head. Around him lay the bodies of 913 members of his People's Temple.

Paradise on earth had just become Hell on earth.

ROBERT BERDELLA

There are some killers who take murder to a whole new level. Even for hardened policemen as well as hardened true crime writers, it must be said, their crimes are difficult to take in. Men such as Dennis Neilsen, John Wayne Gacy and Jeffrey Dahmer are some of the names that spring to mind, names that send a shudder of disgust down the spine. To that list could be added Robert Berdella, the Kansas City Butcher.

Bob Berdella was born in Ohio in 1949 and had a relatively uneventful childhood. At school, he excelled particularly in art. When his father died when Bob was sixteen, however, he seemed to change and became a loner. He also realized around that time that he was gay.

His talent for art led him in 1967 to study at the Kansas City Art Institute. His ambitions to find a career teaching art came to nothing, however. Instead, he found a job as a chef but in his spare time, he was dealing drugs and he was arrested a couple of times for the possession of LSD and marijuana. No charges were pressed on either occasion.

In 1969, he bought a house at 4315 Charlotte and opened a novelty shop – Bob's Bizarre Bazaar – selling a wide variety of items as well as catering for people with an interest in the occult.

His first victim was his friend, Jerry Howell whom he murdered in 1984. Berdella and he had engaged in a sexual relationship for several months but Howell owed Berdella money after he had helped him with some legal fees. Berdella was not impressed.

On the evening of 4 July, Berdella took Howell home with him. In the house, he laced his drinks with tranquilizers and before long Howell passed out. Berdella then repeatedly raped him, further assaulting him with a carrot and a cucumber. Before going to work, he bound Howell and on returning that evening picked up his assault where he had left off, injecting him with drugs to keep him quiet. He beat him with a metal pole and by around ten o'clock that evening Howell was dead.

He decided to cut the body up to make for easier disposal but before doing so, he realized that he would have to drain it of blood. He hung it up by the feet, draining the blood from him and taking a lot of photographs in the process. He then cut it down and with kitchen knives and a chainsaw cut it up into pieces small enough to be disposed of easily. These pieces he put into plastic bags which he left outside on the street along with bags filled with Howell's clothes and the implements with which he had dismembered him, to be collected, by the garbage men at the end of the weekend. A few weeks later, he sat down and wrote about the incident.

On 10 April 1985, another friend, Robert Sheldon, became Berdella's second victim. He went about it in exactly the same way as with Howell but this time, he injected his victim in the left eye with drain cleaning fluid in an attempt to blind him and render him less able to escape. Eventually, however, Berdella became worried that Sheldon would be spotted by another of his visitors. After four days of torture, he pulled a plastic bag over his head and asphyxiated him. This time, after putting the body parts out with the trash, he put the head in the freezer before eventually burying it in his garden.

Two months later, he killed a young man named Mark Wallace, spicing up the torture with some electric shock treatment.

He killed Walter Ferris in September after Ferris had asked if he could stay at his house for a while and nine months later it was the turn of Todd

Stoops who was injected and brutally tortured.

He was viciously raped and Berdella also injected Drano into his eyes and voice box. Stoops finally died on 1 July and Berdella kept his dismembered body in his basement for a week before disposing of it.

His final murder victim was a male prostitute named Larry Pearson whom Berdella met in spring 1987. He kept Pearson around as a sex slave for about six weeks but when he started to fight back, Berdella drugged him and killed him. He kept his skull in a cupboard.

He was finally caught during Easter weekend, 1988. On the Saturday morning, someone phoned the police to tell them that there was a naked man in the neighbourhood. The police who went to investigate were astonished to find that not only was the report true but that the man was actually wearing a dog collar round his neck.

When they finally got to him, he was in a bad way. He was hardly able to talk and his eyes were puffy and red. He had scars and wounds on his wrists and mouth. A traffic warden who was on the scene told the officers that he had seen the man leap from the first-floor window of a house across the street. The address of the house was 4315 Charlotte Street.

The officers covered the naked man with a blanket

and he then told them a grim story.

His name, he told them, was Chris Bryson and he was twenty-two years old. Three days earlier, at around midnight on 29 March, he had been invited back to his house by a man driving a brown Toyota. The man, who introduced himself as Bob, drove him to the house on Charlotte Street and they went in.

It was messy. There was junk everywhere and the place smelled of dogs. Bob excused the mess by saying that he had been an art student and liked to collect stuff. He suggested that they went upstairs, to get away from the dogs and Bryson went first. Arriving at the top floor, Bryson was just turning to his new friend when he felt a sharp blow on the back of his head. He stumbled forward, stunned, but then turned to try to defend himself against any further blows. Just at that moment, however, he felt a stinging sensation in his neck. The other man had managed to inject him with something. Everything went dark.

When he awoke, he discovered that he was lying on a bed, his arms and legs tied to the bedposts. He was naked. He fell unconscious again and while he was under, Bob slipped the dog collar around his neck and took photos of him. He also sat down and began recording the incident in scribbled notes in a notebook.

When he awoke, he was subjected to a battery of sexual assaults before Bob drugged him again. The next time he awoke, he tried to make a noise, pleading for mercy, through the gag that had been stuffed in his mouth. It only irritated his captor who began jabbing him in the eye with his finger before rubbing a cotton bud covered in some unknown fluid in his eyes. It was agony for Bryson and he could do nothing to stop it.

Berdella started beating Bryson's hands with an iron pole and then attached an electrical device to his testicles. He sent a pulse of electricity through the device, making Bryson utter anguished, muffled screams. Bob now had a Polaroid camera and was taking photographs as Bryson writhed in agony.

When he next awoke, he had a fever. Bob came back and told him that he was his sex toy and he was going to keep him there for the rest of his life. If he misbehaved, he would re-introduce the tortures that he had already experienced. Chillingly, he added, 'You could end up in the trash, like the others.'

Bryson decided that the only way to survive was to cooperate. Meanwhile, he would await the slightest opportunity to escape.

He had found that opportunity one day when Bob tied his hands in front of him, rather than to the bedposts. As soon as Bob left the house that morning, Bryson had managed to burn his rope restraints with matches that he found and jumped out the window.

Officers wondered if this case was no more than a lover's tiff but on entering the house, they saw almost immediately that Bryson was telling the truth. Inside they found a couple of skulls and another was buried in the garden. There were human vertebrae in a bag in a cupboard and photographs of the victims and scribblings in notebooks described every horrific detail of these dreadful kidnappings.

Berdella was arrested and offered to make a full confession in exchange for not receiving the death penalty. The prosecution accepted it and he went to prison for life, denying that he had fed human flesh and bones to his dogs and that he had been involved in devil worship, this despite several articles of occult significance being found in his house.

Robert Berdella died in prison of a heart attack in October 1992 after he had written to a minister complaining that prison officers were not giving him his heart medication.

No one investigated these claims and his family was not informed of his passing.

GARY HEIDNIK

An industrial food mixer stood on a kitchen work-top. Blood was drying around its edges and slivers of unidentified material clung to its sides. It had been used very recently. Nearby was an oven dish and lying inside it was a human rib. When an officer gingerly opened the fridge door, to his utter disgust he found a human arm.

Gary Heidnik's childhood was as unhappy as the rest of his life. A disaster at school, he sought stability in the US Army, where he trained as a medic. He was discharged after fourteen months, however, when he was found to be suffering from schizoid personality disorder.

He kidnapped for the first time in 1978 when he signed the sister of a friend out of a mental hospital and locked her in the basement of his house at 3520 North Marshall Street, Philadelphia. He raped and sodomized her repeatedly before being arrested and convicted of a litany of charges – kidnapping, rape, unlawful restraint, false imprisonment, involuntary deviant sexual intercourse and interfering with the custody of a committed person. Initially sentenced to seven years in prison, his sentence was overturned on appeal and he was instead committed to a mental institution for three years. By 1983, he was back on the streets again.

A couple of years later, he married a girl called Betty whom he met through a matrimonial service. Needless to say, he treated her badly, beating and raping her and forcing her to join in sex sessions he had with other women. She walked out after just three months and reported him to the police. He was charged with assault, spousal rape and involuntary deviant sexual intercourse. When she failed to turn up for a preliminary hearing, however, the charges were dropped.

He did leave her something to remember him by. She gave birth to his son a few months later, a son he would never see, just like the four other children he said he had fathered by different women.

He did not need those children, however. He had resolved to kidnap ten women and keep them prisoner in his house, ready to do his bidding and bear his children. He launched the plan on 26 November 1986.

Josefina Rivera had a blazing row with her boyfriend and stormed out of the apartment she shared with him. The moment she stepped outside, she regretted her dramatic exit, however. It was teeming with rain. As she stood wondering where she was going to go to keep dry, a silver and white Cadillac pulled up beside her. Its driver, a bearded man, rolled down his window and asked her if she needed a lift. She hesitated but then decided that he looked okay and anyway, the warm and dry interior of the car was a far better prospect than standing in the rain.

They stopped at a diner and had coffee but she could not take her eyes off the expensive watch and jewellery he was wearing. When he invited her back to his place she said yes and they drove to his house, which, she was surprised to find, was a run-down building in a rough area. She was puzzled, however. He was clearly loaded because parked in front of the house was a 1971 Rolls Royce. Gary Heidnik did indeed have money. He had invested his Army disability cheque astutely and had more than half a million dollars in his bank account.

She noticed that to open the door he used an odd key. One half of the key appeared to have been cut off and the other half was left in the lock so that no one could gain entry without his half.

He started to give her a tour of the house but in one room he suddenly jumped her from behind and began to strangle her. Josefina struggled but she was no match for him. He produced a pair of handcuffs and cuffed her wrists together behind her back. He then pushed her ahead of him downstairs and into a damp basement room. He clamped manacles around her ankles and chained her to a large pipe that ran across the ceiling. He then pushed her down onto a filthy mattress that lay on the floor, lay down, placing his head on her lap and, astonishingly, fell asleep.

She had also eventually fallen asleep, but woke up later to find him gone. She looked around the room. There was a small window allowing a little light to enter. In the centre of the space a large, shallow hole had been dug in the concrete down into the earth below. When he returned a short while later, it was to this hole that he gave his attention, bringing a shovel to widen and deepen it. He reassured her that she would not be alone for long. He intended to kidnap other women who would keep her company. Then he raped her for the first of countless times.

Once he had gone again, she dragged her chains over to the window and began to shout for help. All she succeeded in doing was infuriating her captor who came running into the room with a large stick with which he proceeded to savagely beat her. He dragged her semi-conscious body over to the pit and suddenly she realized what it was intended for. It was a punishment pit. He tossed her down into it, bent her head down over her chest and covered it with a wooden panel that was weighted down to prevent her escape.

When she was eventually allowed out of the pit, she discovered that she was not alone. Sandy Lindsay was a friend of Heidnik that he had met at the Elwyn Institute, a local hospital for the mentally and physically disabled. He had fallen out with her after she fell pregnant with his child and had an abortion.

To put her family off the scent, he made Sandy write a letter to her mother in which she said that she had to get away for a while. He travelled to New York and posted it, leading them to believe that she was there.

The two women prayed that someone would find them, but the days, weeks and then months passed and still they remained in Heidnik's hellish basement, enduring repeated rape, hours in the pit and being chained by one arm to the pipe in the ceiling for hours at a time.

A police officer knocked on Heidnik's door one day, looking for Sandy Lindsay after her mother,

From June to September 1692, nineteen men and women, all convicted of witchcraft, were taken to Gallows Hill close to Salem Village, for hanging. This picture shows the execution of Bridget Bishop, who was the first woman to be executed as a result of the Salem Witch Trials. (Credit: Getty Images)

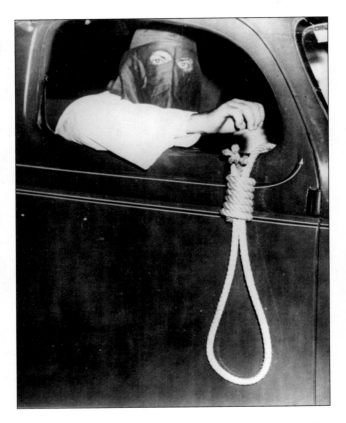

On 11 May 1939, seventy-five cars containing members of the Ku Klux Klan drove through the streets of Miami, Florida, to try and prevent black people from taking part in the election. This member of the organization made his point by carrying a noose. (Credit: Getty Images)

Members of the American white supremist movement, Ku Klux Klan, can be seen crawling out of a tunnel following one of their inclandestine meetings in November 1922. (Credit: Getty Images)

Raymond Fernandez used the home of his sister, Mrs Lena Cano, at 12-02 30th Drive, Astoria, Queens, to store the body of one of his victims, which he had locked inside a trunk. Fernandez and his common-law wife, Martha Beck, became known as 'The Lonely Hearts Killers' because they met each other and their victims through 'lonely hearts' advertisements in newspapers. (Credit: NY Daily News via Getty Images)

J. W. Milam stands trial for the murder of fourteen-year-old Emmett 'Bobo' Till in September 1955. Till was an African-American boy who was murdered in Mississippi after reportedly flirting with a white woman. (Credit: Time & Life Pictures/Getty Images)

Seventy-three-year-old Josef Fritzl went on trial in the Austrian town of Sankt Poelten on 15 March 2009. He was accused of imprisoning his daughter, Elizabeth, in the cellar of his house for almost a quarter of a century. During her incarceration, she was sexually abused by her father and bore seven children by him. (Credit: AFP/Getty Images)

A tiny door led to a sequence of underground rooms underneath Josef Fritzl's house. Bright decorations of red paint and white tiles, however, could not disguise the ramshackle state of the place his daughter had to call home for 24 years. (Credit: Getty Images)

Children from the Nigerian city of Eket protest after being branded as witches in February 2009. Several religious leaders were arrested on murder charges after they confessed to killing 110 children for being so-called witches. (Credit: AFP/Getty Images)

still suspicious about her daughter's disappearance, had told police that she had been hanging out with a man named Gary Heidnik. Heidnik did not open the door and the officer went away. The case vanished under a pile of other cases on someone's desk and was gradually forgotten.

In late December Heidnik kidnapped two more girls – twenty-one-year-old Lisa Thomas and twenty-three-year-old Deborah Dudley. Deborah was trouble from the outset, fighting and arguing with her captor. He doled out savage beatings to her as punishment.

In the middle of January, eighteen-year-old Jacqueline Askins arrived. There were now five girls chained up in Gary Heidnik's basement.

His treatment of them became even worse. If he had to leave them for any length of time, he would appoint one as leader. She was instructed to tell him of any misbehaviour in his absence and the miscreant would be beaten. If there had been nothing to report or the leader simply refused to tell him, he would beat them all.

He did not even feed them properly, eventually giving them tinned dog food to eat.

Inevitably, it took its toll on them and Sandy became ill and died. He dragged her body from the room and they were horrified to hear the sound of his power saw starting up. A short while later, one of Heidnik's dogs walked into the basement room with a long, meaty bone between its jaws. They knew where it had come from. What they did not know, however, was that he was using the food processor to grind up Sandy's flesh and mixing it with the dog food he was giving them to eat.

The house soon began to stink of rotting flesh, leading Heidnik's neighbours to call the police. However, when an officer arrived to investigate, Heidnik laughed it off, claiming to have overcooked a roast dinner. The officer apologized for disturbing him and left, glad to have a simple explanation that would not require any further investigation.

As if it could not become any more horrific, Heidnik, now paranoid that the girls were conspiring together against him, tried to make it impossible for them to communicate, trying to deafen them by gouging inside their ears with a screwdriver, their fearful screams stopped by gags stuffed into their mouths.

He also took care of Deborah's constant carping, taking her upstairs and showing her Sandy's head in a saucepan and other parts of her body that he was storing in the fridge. The message was obvious.

Soon, she was no longer a problem, however. He had started punishing the girls by electrocuting them with bare wires. One day, he ordered Josefina to fill the pit with water. He pushed the girls in and then touched Deborah with the bare wire. She was electrocuted and her body found its way into the freezer.

Josefina was now his favourite to the extent that she was allowed to sleep in his bed and spend time alone with him. Remarkably, she won his trust to such an extent that he also gave her permission to go home and visit her family, but only on the condition that when she returned, she brought with her another woman.

Naturally, she went straight to her boyfriend's flat and called the police. They initially refused to believe her, but as she showed them the wounds and scars on her body and the marks gouged into her skin by handcuffs and manacles, they began to come round.

Heidnik was picked up at a petrol station and charged with two counts of first-degree murder, five of rape, four of aggravated assault and one of involuntary deviate sexual intercourse. He was found guilty and displayed not a flicker of emotion as the death sentence was read out.

Gary Michael Heidnik, one of America's most dangerous and evil killers, was executed by lethal injection on 6 July 1999.

YAHWEH BEN YAHWEH

He was like a rock star, driving luxury cars and wearing satin tunics when he entered the church he had founded, a gold crown on his handsome head. he was idolized by his congregation and they called him 'King'. No wonder – his literature said that he could make the lame walk and the blind see. 'God wants you to be rich!' he would tell his excited audiences and they believed him.

It had not always been like that for him though. Born in 1935, the oldest of the fifteen children of a poor preacher in Kingfisher, Oklahoma, he started life as Hulon Mitchell. Leaving school, he enlisted in the US Air Force, also studying psychology at university. He married and had four children in four years but later divorced.

He threw himself into the growing Civil Rights movement on leaving the Air Force, working as an activist in Enid, Oklahoma, but, like many blacks, disappointed at the slow pace of change, he joined the Nation of Islam, a black Muslim organization that espoused separation rather than segregation for America's blacks.

Mitchell made the first of several name changes in his life, calling himself Mitchell X, in the style of one of the Nation of Islam leaders Malcolm X, the 'X' standing for his lost African name. By this time, he was living in Atlanta, studying the Koran and taking a Master's in economics. He was married again and spent his spare time selling the Nation's newspaper, *Muhammad Speaks*, on street corners. Once again, he changed his name, to Shah, meaning minister and he began preaching in a Nation church. Soon, however, he was being accused of molesting children and embezzling from the church. That particular incarnation of Hulon Mitchell disappeared.

He reappeared in Atlanta a short while later, however, using the name Father Michel and working with another preacher going by the name of Father Jone. He had to be careful, though, as the Black Muslims were still after him. Father Jone was shot dead in May 1969, but Mitchell did not let his partner's death faze him. He became even more outlandish. It was at this time that he entered his services to cries of 'King!'

He told his parishioners that God wanted them to be rich, but, of course, the only person who actually was getting rich was Father Michel. Before long, he left Atlanta and his family in his wake along with allegations of fraud and made for Orlando, Florida.

Brother Love was his next character, a street preacher who built up a small following and married for the third time. He established a new religion based on coded messages he claimed to have found in the Bible. It was based on the Black Hebrew movement and he claimed that Africans were the 'true Jews', descended from the Lost Tribes of Israel. White people had to be destroyed, he ranted in his new guise of Och Moshe Israel. He moved to Miami after, he claimed, a vision from God.

He had arrived now at his last incarnation. The Hebrew Yahweh ben Yahweh means 'God, son of God' and under that name, he urged people to join him, giving up friends and family and living together communally. Incomes and whatever money they had was pooled and children were schooled at home. Followers were also encouraged to assume biblical names such as Solomon and Gideon.

Doors were knocked on, leaflets distributed and inevitably the poor ghettos of the city provided rich pickings for the new religion.

In 1980, he bought a large warehouse in Liberty City, a suburb of Miami which was re-named the Yahweh Temple of Love. Mitchell and thirty of his followers moved in and established a café, a grocery store, a health centre and a bookshop in which the writings of the leader himself were the only books on offer.

'How many of you would die for Yahweh?' he would scream in the sermons he delivered at this time against a soundtrack of loud, aggressive rock music. 'Would you kill for Yahweh?' Around him would stand the Circle of Ten, ten young men armed with wooden staffs known as 'staffs of life' who guarded the temple and doled out punishment for the slightest breach of one of the leader's rules.

His behaviour was becoming increasingly erratic and his sexual activity was prodigious. At night he crept into the rooms of women followers. Age was of little importance to him and he is reported to have had sex with girls as young as ten years old.

He also had a bizarre approach to pregnancy and sex education. Midwifery classes featured instructions from him for the pregnant women to inspect each other's genitalia, while in male sex education classes he played pornographic videos of white women having sex with animals.

Dissent was sternly discouraged and harshly punished. One man, Ashton Green, who had left the Temple of Love, came back to visit some friends. The Circle of Ten were waiting for him. They shot him dead and then shot his wife and slit her throat. She did not die, however, and managing to get away, went to the police who, although unable to connect him to Ashton Green's murder, became very interested in the goings-on in the warehouse in Liberty City.

Another man, twenty-two-year-old Leonard Dupree was kicked to death by a crowd of around seventy Temple of Love people who believed he had been sent to assassinate their leader. The body was disposed of and they got away with it.

From the warehouse Mitchell launched a new business, a food distribution company that also brewed beer and made wine. He began to be lauded as a black role model by business commentators. Money was indeed flowing in, but his followers were seeing none of it. As he lived a life of increasing luxury and splendour, they lived in squalour in cramped conditions with no privacy.

His next initiative was to create what he called the Death Angels, a group of his followers with instructions to go out and murder white people. They were further ordered to return with a body part from their victim to prove they had actually done it.

One of the Death Angels, Robert Rozier, killed

a number of white men, mostly down-and-outs or drunks. Rozier was arrested for the 1986 murders of two men who had refused to move their families out of an apartment block purchased by the Temple of Love. He turned state's witness, providing information about the Temple of Love and agreeing to testify against Mitchell.

Mitchell was arrested along with fifteen of his disciples and charged with fourteen murders as well as extortion and racketeering.

In court, however, despite Rozier's chilling evidence on the murders he had committed on the instructions of Hulon Mitchell, the prosecution was unable to directly implicate Yahweh ben Yahweh in the killings. The judge described the case as 'the most violent case ever tried in a federal court: the indictment charges the sixteen defendants on trial with fourteen murders by means such as beheading, stabbing, occasionally by pistol shots, plus severing of body parts such as ears to prove the worthiness of the killer. They were also charged with arson of a slumbering neighborhood using Molotov cocktails. The perpetrators were ordered to wait outside the innocent victims' homes wearing ski masks and brandishing machetes to deter the victims from fleeing the flames.'

Mitchell was sentenced to eighteen years in prison but was released after ten. Under the terms of his parole, he was banned from having contact with the members of his former congregation which had now re-located to Canada, but when it was discovered that he was dying of prostate cancer the ban was relaxed and he was allowed to visit them.

Huron Mitchell, Mitchell X, Minister Shah, Father Michel, Brother Love and Yahweh ben Yahweh all died on 7 May 2007.

SISTER MARGARET ANN PAHL

It was like a scene from a cheap 1950s horror B-movie. Candle flames flickered on the walls of the chapel room in Toledo's Mercy Hospital. They surrounded the body of a seventy-one-year-old nun named Sister Margaret Ann Pahl who had been in the chapel that 5 April 1980, preparing it for the Easter services. She lay with her arms folded across her chest, the altar cloth draped over her body. The elderly nun had been strangled and stabbed thirty-one times in the neck and body through the altar cloth. Furthermore, and adding to the chilling strangeness of the murder, the wounds were in the shape of an upside-down cross an anti-Christ symbol, a sign of Satan. On her forehead was a smudge of blood suggesting that her killer had anointed her, humiliating her and her beliefs even in death. The way her body was posed suggested that this was perhaps no ordinary murder – people began to suspect that it might be a ritual killing.

It certainly looked like it, from the way the body was positioned. It had been placed deliberately and was intended to suggest that there was a deeper meaning to this killing.

Margaret Pahl was born into a devoutly Catholic family and she had cousins who were nuns. Therefore, it was not a great surprise when she announced as a teenager that she, too wanted to become a Sister of Mercy when she left school.

Not long after, she packed a few belongings and climbed into the family's Buick with her parents and her brothers and sisters and made the long trip to Our Lady of the Pines, a convent and retreat situated in the midst of sixty-three acres off Tiffin Street in Fremont.

Her sisters and parents wept as they waved goodbye to her. They were devastated to lose her, but, as her younger sister later said, 'She'd been called to be a nun. She just knew.'

At home, they found things laid out neatly in her room, each tagged with the name of the member of the family she wanted the item to go to.

Sister Margaret Ann was trained as a registered nurse, later becoming director of Mercy's school of nursing and then administrator at St. Charles Hospital in Oregon and Mercy Hospital in Tiffin.

By 1980, now seventy-one years old, she was having trouble with her hearing and was at last considering retirement. Nonetheless, she was still working, looking after the two chapels at Mercy

Hospital with a devotion second only to her devotion to her calling. Sister Margaret Ann was demanding; everything had to be done exactly as she wanted and exactly when she wanted. It became exasperating for those with whom she worked. A housekeeper told police that on Good Friday, 1980, Sister Margaret Ann was inconsolable because the chapel was not as perfect as she wanted it to be. She was even more upset when she was told that the priest had decided to shorten the normal Good Friday service. The housekeeper said that the elderly nun took her hand and cried, 'Why did they cheat God out of what was his?'

The following day, Sister Margaret Ann's alarm clock woke her up at 5 am in her upstairs living quarters at Mercy Hospital. She made her way downstairs and by 6.15, she was in the dining room where she picked up a tray that she stacked with cleaning cloths and incense from the storage cupboard to take to the chapel. She left the tray on a pew and went to the hospital cafeteria where she ate a breakfast of grapefruit, cereal and coffee and told a cafeteria worker she knew that she was going to St. Joseph's chapel.

She left the cafeteria at 6.45 am and returned to the chapel to prepare it for the busy Easter weekend that lay ahead. Shortly after 8 am, a young nun walking to the chapel, found what appeared to be a white linen altar cloth lying on the floor of the hallway leading to the chapel. She dropped it on a pew in the chapel, stopped momentarily at the organ and then went to the sacristy, a small room to the side of the altar to make a phone call.

When she opened the door and walked in, the scene in front of her made her momentarily freeze and then scream. On the polished marble floor of the sacristy lay the body of Sister Margaret Ann.

The coroner said that she had been strangled from behind by someone with large hands. There were a number of pieces of evidence, including the linen cloth that the young nun had picked up from the floor outside which seemed to have blood stains on it and a unique 'sword-like' letter opener with a medallion with the image of the US Capitol building on it, that was later retrieved from the quarters of a priest at the hospital, Father Gerry Robinson.

This priest was questioned closely about the murder. He had worked closely with the elderly nun and it was well known at Mercy Hospital that he did not see eye to eye with her. Her puncti-liousness irritated him and the two had had a strained relationship.

However, although he was the prime suspect in the eyes of investigators, they were unable to prove anything. The case remained unsolved for the next twenty-two years.

On a hot summer day in 2003, a forty-one-year-old woman went to the downtown headquarters of the Toledo Catholic Diocese for a meeting with the church review board. She was seeking reimbursement of $50,000 that she had spent on counselling as a result, she claimed of clerical sex abuse.

Questioned by the church officials on the board, she made a disturbing catalogue of accusations, claiming that she had been sexually abused not just by one, but by a whole group of priests from 1968 to 1975.

The assaults took place in the basement of St. Adelbert parish rectory on Warsaw Street and formed part of cult-like ceremonies. She described how children were molested at these events and were also ordered to look on while other children were similarly abused. The group of abusers called themselves the Sisters of Assumed Mary, or SAM and would chant Satanic verses, cut her with a knife as a sacrifice to Satan, drew an upside-down cross on her abdomen and forced her to drink the blood of sacrificed animals such as rabbits.

She detailed how the men dressed as nuns and performed their rituals while she lay on a table. If she made an attempt to get up she was restrained and forced back onto the table. They raped her repeatedly and forced her to perform sexual acts on them. The abuse became ever more horrific as the sessions continued and they started to torture her, holding lit matches to the soles of her feet and the corners of her eyes.

The woman's mother had a close relationship with several of the men and she also participated in the ceremonies which later took place in woods. She was a kind of high priestess of the group.

Several more women came forward to inform police that they had been similarly abused between the late nineteen-sixties and 1986, being forced to take part in cult-like ceremonies that involved altars and men dressed in robes.

Four clerics were named but one name stood out for police officers who had been around for a while – Father Gerry Robinson, now sixty-six years old and ministering to the sick and dying in nursing homes and hospitals. The woman told them that when she was fourteen years old, she had a sexual encounter with him in a room near the chapel of St. Vincent Mercy Medical Center, but that there had been none of the ritual associated with the other incidents.

Police re-opened the case of Sister Margaret Ann Pahl, studying the blood on the piece of cloth from 1980 and listening again to the tapes of the interviews with Father Robinson from back then.

A battery of forensic tests were carried out on the original evidence, including the letter opener and two forensic experts concluded that the small medallion with the image of the US Capitol building on the letter opener could be the source of the faint bloodstain on the altar cloth. DNA samples from the nun's body were also examined after her body had been exhumed for that purpose.

There was also a particularly revealing video of Robinson while he was being interviewed by police. Left alone in a room for a few minutes, he was filmed folding his hands and whispering in a barely audible voice the word 'sister'. He then prayed with his head bowed, uttering at one point the anguished words, 'Oh, my Jesus'.

On 23 April 2004, Father Gerry Robinson was arrested and charged with the murder of Sister Margaret Ann Pahl. He was released on bail of $200,000 which was raised on his behalf by a group of supporters. But the evidence against him was compelling and it took a jury just six hours to find him guilty of murder, only the second time in the United States that a priest has been convicted of murder.

On 11 May 2006, Gerry Robinson was sentenced to fifteen years to life in prison.

GERALD AND CHARLENE GALLEGO: THE 'LOVE SLAVE MURDERS'

Women found Gerald Gallego irresistible, a dangerous charmer who had married five times before he met Charlene Williams in a seedy poker bar in Sacramento in September 1977. But he was rotten to the core and he had come from a long line of people who were equally rotten. His ancestry was filled with murderers and child molesters.

He was born in 1946 while the father he never met was doing time in San Quentin. Eventually, in separate incidents, his father would kill two police officers in Mississippi and in 1955 became the first man to be executed in that state's brand new gas chamber. His mother was no innocent either, a prostitute who allowed Gerald to be used as a messenger for various pimps in the 1950s as she plied her trade on the streets of Sacramento's red light district.

He was first in trouble with the law at the age of six and by 1977, had been arrested at least twenty-three times. He had spent time in a variety of institutions that had all attempted to restore him to the straight and narrow – Fred C. Nelles School for Boys, the Preston School of Industry, the Deuel Vocational Institution, and the Vacaville Medical Facility. He had also spent time in various city and county jails.

Charlene Williams was born in 1956 into a rather different background. Her father Charles was an executive with a national supermarket chain. She was an only child and was brought up in the upmarket Sacramento suburb of Arden Park. At junior school, Charlene was a star pupil and displayed a talent for music, playing the violin to a high standard. By the time she got to high school, however, she had gone completely off the rails, alcohol, drugs and sex becoming her main interests. She only just graduated from high school but failed at college and dropped out. By the time she met Gerald Gallego, she had experienced two brief, failed marriages.

She liked Gerald from the start, describing him as 'a very nice clean-cut fellow,' and just a few days after they had met, he charmed her by sending her a dozen roses with a card attached that read, 'to a very sweet girl.' A few short weeks later and they had moved in together.

He immediately let her know how things were

going to be. She was going to be the bread-winner, supporting them both with her earnings as a clerk at a local supermarket. He started to control her, stipulating what she should wear and being very open about the flings he would occasionally enjoy with other women. She put up with it quite happily. She found him exciting and extremely sexy and would do anything to please him. When he described, therefore, his fantasies of having young sex slaves, she was happy to go along with it. In fact, it excited her.

On 11 September 1978, they parked their 1973 Dodge van – it had mountains airbrushed on the side panels – at the Country Club Shopping Plaza, just off Watt Avenue in Sacramento. Gerald explained to Charlene what she had to do. He told her to find two girls that she thought would be good sex slave material. She was then to lure them somehow back to the van. She demurred. She realized that this could all go very wrong and she could be arrested. But Gerald became irritated and told her to get on with it or there would be trouble.

Not long after, she found two girls that she thought looked suitable. Rhonda Scheffler, aged seventeen and sixteen-year-old Kippi Vaught were spending the afternoon shopping at the mall but when Charlene asked them if they'd like to get high, they leapt at the opportunity. They followed her out to the parking lot where she threw open the van's back doors. The two girls found themselves staring down the barrel of Gerald's .25 calibre handgun. The terrified girls were quickly bundled inside and their hands bound with tape. Gerald drove off, telling Charlene to watch them.

They drove east out of town on the I-80, making for the Sierra Nevada Mountains. When they arrived at Baxter, a little more than fifty miles away, they turned off the Interstate and drove into the foothills of the mountains. They stopped in the middle of nowhere and he ordered the girls out of the van at gunpoint. He walked off with them into the hills, taking a sleeping bag and leaving Charlene waiting at the van.

When he returned some hours later, he ordered Charlene to go and visit some friends in order to establish an alibi and told her to then take the van home and return in their Oldsmobile. When she returned later, the girls were bundled into the back seat of the Oldsmobile and he directed Charlene as she drove. Meanwhile, he talked to the girls as if he was about to free them. When he finally told Charlene to stop, however, and ordered the girls out of the vehicle, he took a tyre iron from the trunk and bludgeoned each of them on the head with it. As they lay bleeding on the ground, he shot them dead.

Gerald and Charlene, now married, decided the best policy would be to get away from California for a while until the heat died down. Incredibly, they were helped in this by Charles and Mercedes Williams, Charlene's parents, who, fearful of the loss of the family's good name, told Charlene to steal her cousin's birth certificate which gave Gerald an alias with which to obtain a driving licence and other official documents. He took the name of Robert Feil and Charles Williams got him a job driving trucks for a Houston supermarket.

Gerald hated the job, however, and by the following spring they were in Reno, Nevada where he worked as a driver for a meat distribution company and she found an office job. But Gerald had not given up on his sex slaves. He quit his job and began formulating another plan. The Washoe County Fair seemed as good a place as any to find them.

Brenda Judd, fourteen years old, and Sandra Colley, a year younger, were leaving the fairground to make their way home on 24 June 1974, when they were accosted by Charlene who asked them if they would distribute some leaflets for her for a few dollars. The girls immediately agreed and she told them the leaflets were in her van. Charlene and the two girls got into the van and Gerald, who had been following them, jumped in a moment later, gun in hand. He bound the girls and drove out to I-80, stopping at a hardware store to purchase a hammer and a shovel.

After a while, he asked Charlene to drive and got in the back where he began repeatedly raping the girls. They drove further into the Nevada hills before eventually stopping in a remote area known as Humboldt Sink.

For the next couple of hours, Gerald rested while he watched Charlene force the two girls to perform sexual acts on each other. When he was bored, he took his shovel from the van and dragged Sandra Colley from the van to a dried-up creek. He stepped behind and brought the shovel down on her head, a sound that Charlene would later describe to investigators as 'a loud splat like a flat rock hitting mud.' He then did the same to Brenda Judd before burying the two girls in a deep hole and placing a large rock over the grave.

The two girls were listed as runaways until Charlene confessed during the trial in 1982. Their bodies would not be found until 1999, twenty-five years after their murder.

They returned to Sacramento where Gerald had an affair with another woman but soon he was bored and experiencing his old urges again.

On 24 April 1980, they kidnapped two seventeen-year-olds, Stacey Ann Redican and Karen Twiggs with a promise of drugs in the back of their van. As before, Charlene drove while he raped them repeatedly. They drove to Limerick Canyon near Lovelock where Gerald battered the girls to death with a hammer that Charlene insisted on throwing out the window of the van on the drive back to Sacramento.

Shortly after, Gerald and Charlene re-married, but under his new name, Robert Feil. They went on holiday to Oregon but, ever on the alert for sex slaves, on 7 June, Gerald spotted pregnant twenty-one-year-old Linda Aguilar walking at the side of a highway. He stopped and asked the girl if she needed a lift. Tragically, she accepted his offer.

As before, Charlene took over the driving while Gerald climbed into the back to rape Linda. When they eventually stopped, he knocked her down with a rock and then strangled her. They found her body a month later but suspicion immediately fell on her boyfriend who had beaten her before.

Six weeks later, Gerald struck again. They had been drinking all day and wound up at the Sail Inn in West Sacramento. At closing time, however, instead of going home, they waited in the bar's car park. When Virginia Mochel, the waitress who had been serving them that evening, emerged, Gerald accosted her with his gun and ordered her into the van. This time, they drove home and while Charlene watched television, he remained in the van with Virginia, repeatedly raping her. His urges sated, he told Charlene to drive and while they drove, he strangled the girl. They dumped the body outside the town of Clarksburg.

The police investigation led to Gerald and Charlene because they had been at the inn that night, but when questioned they succeeded in putting them off the scent. The investigation gradually ran out of steam but it had been a close shave.

Gerald was becoming increasingly erratic in his behaviour and increasingly violent towards Charlene. It became so bad that she finally moved out, going back home to live with her parents. They met again for dinner on the night of 1 November and a drunk Gerald told Charlene he was intent on kidnapping more girls. After dinner, they cruised various shopping malls, looking for potential victims. In the early hours of the following morning, at a café at the Arfen Fair shopping centre, Gerald found what he was looking for, but Charlene was surprised to see that his targets were a man and a women.

In the car park, Gerald approached twenty-two-year-old Craig Miler and twenty-one-year-old Mary Sowers, gun in hand. They thought that if they did what they were told, this drunk would not harm them. So, they clambered into the van. Even when a college friend, passing by, leaned in the window and asked what they were doing, they merely nodded and said hello. Charlene, however, suddenly started shouting at their friend and sped away but not before the college friend had written down the number plate of the van.

Craig was shot three times in the head and dumped and Mary was raped in the bedroom of Gerald's apartment. He then drove her out into the country and shot her.

Next morning, police officers were waiting for them when Gerald drove Charlene home to her parents' house. They could not properly explain their movements the previous night but, although deeply suspicious, the detectives left.

The couple decided to go on the run, driving to

Reno, ditching their car and taking a bus to Salt Lake City.

Meanwhile, back in Sacramento, the evidence against them was piling up. Craig Miller's college friend identified Gerald as the man he had seen the previous night with his friends and Charles Williams told police that Robert Feil was really Gerald Gallego. Furthermore, bullets taken from Craig Miller's body matched some that Gerald had fired into the ceiling of a bar where he had worked.

Gerald and Charlene were by this time in Nebraska from where Carlene called her parents. They agreed to wire money to her, but they passed word to the FBI and agents were waiting for the couple when they walked into the Western Union office in Omaha.

In California, Charlene was sentenced to sixteen years and eight months in return for pleading guilty to the murder of Craig Miller and Mary Sowers and testifying against Gallego. In Nevada she struck a similar deal, admitting the murder of Karen Twiggs and Stacey Redcan, and received a similar sentence.

Gerald, arrogant as ever, defended himself but in both California and Nevada, he was sentenced to death, one of the few American criminals to earn the distinction of being sentenced to death in two different states.

Charlene was released from prison in 1997 and disappeared. In 2002, Gerald Gallego died of rectal cancer, aged fifty-six, at the Nevada prison system's regional medical centre.

ROBIN GECHT AND THE RIPPER CREW

It had been a few days now and the smell seemed to be getting worse. It was coming from somewhere behind the Moonlit Hotel in the Chicago suburb of Villa Park. Even though it was located in an area of down-at-heel shops, seedy bars and fast food outlets, the hotel manager thought it was a bit too much. On 1 June 1981, he ventured out into the rubbish-strewn field behind his establishment and came upon not the dead animal that he expected to find, but the remains of a young woman. She was the first victim of the gang of satanic killers who came to be known as the Ripper Crew.

Satanic worship had become popular in the 1980s, providing cheap thrills for bored youngsters and adults who should have known better. Robin Gecht was one such but he and his fellow Satanists took their pastime a little further than everyone else. In 1981 and 1982, he and three others are suspected of having murdered eighteen women in Chicago. They drove around in a van, hunting for prostitutes to sacrifice in Gecht's apartment.

He had built an altar in the attic of his home in the city's Northwest Side, painting six red and black crosses on the wall and draping a red cloth over the altar. In the evening after his wife had gone to work, he and his friends would gather, kneeling around the altar while Gecht brought out the freshly-removed breasts of their victims. As he read from the Bible, each man masturbated into the breast and when that had been done, Gecht sliced it up and each man ate a piece.

One man – Tommy Kokoraleis – when asked by police what made him do such dreadful things, replied that Robin Gecht had a strange power over people and could make them do whatever he wanted. He sincerely believed that Gecht possessed a super-natural power and was, consequently, terrified of him.

The body behind the Moonlit Hotel was a mystery. No one had been reported missing. However, the discovery of a roll of dollar bills in one of her socks suggested that she was probably a prostitute. Fingerprints and dental records eventually identified her as twenty-one-year-old Linda Sutton and, indeed, she was a prostitute with a string of arrests on her rap sheet. She was also the mother of two children who were looked after by her mother.

Interestingly, although the body was in an advanced state of decomposition – hence the smell – the coroner established that she had only been dead for three days. The reason, the coroner suggested was that her breasts had been removed, permitting parasites to get into her body and devour it quickly.

It was a shocking case, but another followed very quickly. On 12 February 1982 a thirty-five-year-old cocktail waitress was found not far from her car. It appeared that she had run out of gas and looked for help. Instead, she was raped, tortured and mutilated – a breast had been removed.

Police withheld this vital piece of information, believing it could prove useful if they arrested a suspect.

A few days later a Hispanic woman was found dead. She had been raped and strangled but although her breasts had not been amputated, they were covered in bite marks. There was evidence too that her killer had masturbated over her dead body.

In May 1982, Lorry Ann Borowski was abducted from the car park of the place where she worked. She was raped a number of times and then a wire was wound round a breast and pulled tight to remove it. Finally, she was killed with a hatchet. Her body was dumped in the suburb of Clarendon Hills.

Two weeks later, on 29 May, as she was returning home from the restaurant owned by her family, Shui Mak was abducted. She had been in her brother's car, but they had argued and he had dropped her off to wait for a lift from some other family members that he thought were following behind them. Her body was discovered four months later, buried at a building site. It had been mutilated in the same way as the others.

The next victim, taken in June 1982, survived.

Angel York told investigators that she was abducted by two men in a red van and handcuffed in the back of the vehicle. They had raped her and horrifically forced her to cut her own breast with a knife. She described how this seemed to drive one man into a frenzy and he made further cuts with the knife before masturbating into her wound which was then duct-taped closed and she was tossed out into the street.

In August, however, another body turned up on the south bank of the Chicago River. Young prostitute Sandra Delaware had been tied up and her left breast had been removed. Around her throat was tied her bra.

Another two women disappeared. Carol Pappas was forty-two and Rosa Beck Davis, thirty, was a marketing executive. They found her body on 8 September 1982, hidden behind a stairway at an apartment building in North Lake Shore. She had been strangled with her sock and her face had been crushed with a hatchet. There were deep lacerations on her breasts and she seemed to have been numerous small puncture marks in her abdomen. It later emerged that, as well as a breast fetish, Gecht also enjoyed stabbing girls with pins, explaining the small puncture wounds in Davis's abdomen.

In October, twenty-year-old Beverly Washington had been mutilated, raped and left for dead but she lived and at last the police had a good description.

The driver of the van had been thin, white and looked about twenty-five years of age. His brown hair was greasy and he had a moustache. She vividly remembered his flannel shirt and square-toed boots. He forced her into the back of the van with a gun and ordered her to take off her clothes. He then handcuffed her and made her perform oral sex on him. Then, she was made to swallow a handful of pills. The last thing she saw as she lost consciousness was him standing over her with a cord in his hands.

She had been dumped, one breast severed and the other almost removed. She was found, however, before she died from loss of blood. She added to her description the fact that the van had tinted windows and a wooden divider inside. Hanging from the rearview mirror were feathers and a roach clip.

On 20 October, police officers routinely pulled over a red van. The driver had red hair and did not match the description given by Washington, but everything else about the vehicle was identical to the one in which she had been tortured.

The driver was Eddie Spreitzer and he told the officers that the van belonged to his boss, Robin Gecht. They took Spreitzer to Gecht's house and waited outside for him to emerge. They were lucky. Gecht matched the description to a tee, including the shirt and the boots.

Gecht acted as if he was completely innocent but when Beverly Washington identified him from a set of photos, detectives went to his house to question him. By this time, however, Gecht was already equipped with a lawyer.

Spreitzer and Gecht initially refused to cooperate but investigators believed that Spreitzer was the most likely of the two men to crack under interrogation. They were right. He produced a lengthy statement in which he admitted to driving the van in a drive-by shooting committed by Gecht. He also described incidents of abduction, Gecht picking up a black prostitute, taking her into an alley and removing her left breast with a knife. Sometimes, he told shocked detectives, Gecht would have sex with the amputated breast in the back of the van.

He also told about a time when Gecht had shot a woman in the head, chained her up and had thrown her in the river, weighed down by bowling balls. He had seen him batter a woman to death with a hammer and had been forced by Gecht to have sexual contact with one victim's wounds after her breasts had been removed.

Gecht, however, denied everything and when Spreitzer discovered that his boss was in an adjacent interrogation room, he became terrified and changed his story, blaming it all on his girlfriend's brother, Andrew Kokoraleis.

Kokoraleis confessed to his involvement and added more gruesome details to Spreitzer's story. He confessed to murdering Rose Beck Davis and Lorry Ann Borowski and added that he believed he had been involved in the deaths of around eighteen women.

Kokoraleis's brother Tommy was interviewed and he also turned out to be a member of the Ripper Crew.

Gecht was a frightening man. People spoke of his strange, magnetic power and one warned detectives never to look in his eyes. The jury was undeterred, however. Although there was not enough evidence to charge him with murder, he was found guilty of attempted murder, rape, deviate sexual assault, aggravated battery and armed violence. He was sentenced to one hundred and twenty years in prison.

Tommy Kokoraleis was sentenced to seventy years in prison for the murder of Lorry Ann Borowski and his brother Andrew was found guilty of the rape and murder of Rosa Beck Davis and sentenced to life. After a second trial for the murder of Lorry Ann Borowski, he was sentenced to death. On 23 September 1998, he became the last man to be executed in the state of Illinois.

Edward Spreitzer was also sentenced to death but in 2003 his sentence was commuted to life.

JOSEF FRITZL

It was an innocuous request. On 28 August 1984, Josef Fritzl asked his eighteen-year-old daughter, Elizabeth, to help him carry a new door downstairs to the basement beneath the three-storey house in which they lived in the tiny Lower Austrian town of Amstetten. Little did she know as they manoeuvred the door downstairs that she would not emerge from that basement until April 2008, almost twenty-five years later. During that time she would give birth to seven children whose father would be her father.

She had immediately obeyed her father. He was a stern man who dominated his household and made life difficult, not least because he regularly raped his daughter, having done so for the first time when she was just eleven years old. When they got downstairs, he handcuffed her and drugged her while he arranged things. He had been planning this for quite some time. In 1978, he had begun construction of a subterranean extension to the basement, exceeding the size permitted by planning officers. However, he built walls to conceal the full extent of the work and behind those walls lay a smaller room, fifteen feet square but only five and a half feet high. Elizabeth had already tried to escape. At the age of sixteen, she got away from Amstetten but was picked up by police in Vienna and returned to her parents. She was planning again to get away and this was what Josef Fritzl feared. Locking her up was the only way he could prevent it from happening.

Her mother Rosemarie knew nothing of her husband's plan and reported Elizabeth missing the following day. A month later Fritzl gave the police a letter that he had forced Elizabeth to write saying that she was staying with a friend and would not be coming back to her family. It was postmarked Braunau. Fritzl suggested that perhaps she had joined a religious sect and the police, happy to have a case off their books, went along with this suggestion.

Letters would arrive occasionally, warning her parents not to look for her and meanwhile, she was locked up in her tiny windowless room, alone for the first five years of her incarceration and raped repeatedly by her father on the bed that was the room's only piece of furniture.

Her first child was born in 1988, a girl she named Kerstin, and Stefan was born two years later. When Lisa was born in 1992, Fritzl smuggled her out of the basement prison cell and brought her upstairs. To anyone who wondered who the child was, he said that she was Elizabeth's and that she had abandoned her. The Fritzls adopted her but no one thought to check the truth of the story he had spun.

There were numerous visits from the childcare department of the local social services as more children appeared in the Fritzl household. Monika came upstairs in 1994 and when Elizabeth gave birth to twins in 1996, one of them, Alexander moved upstairs at the age of fifteen months. The other twin, Michael, had died three days after being born. Fritzl had callously disposed of the body in the household furnace. No one investigated the case very deeply and everyone was happy to believe that Josef Fritzl was a good family man who took in his irresponsible daughter's children and brought them up as his own.

His criminal record should have made social workers wary. Aged thirty-two, he had been convicted of rape in Linz and sentenced to eighteen months in prison. He had been suspected of indecent exposure as well as a couple of cases of assault locally. Another report says that he raped his wife's sister.

There is no denying he endured a brutal childhood that, although it was no excuse, must have had a deep psychological impact on the type of person he would later become. Born in Amstetten in 1935, he and his mother were abandoned by his father when he was still very young, leaving his mother to bring him up alone. She was a harsh disciplinarian and he often bore bruises from the savage beatings she gave him. It was a brutal time, the Nazis absorbing Austria into the Third Reich in 1938 and imposing their aggressively militaristic regime on the Austrians.

When the war ended, Fritzl got on with his life. He did fairly well, drove a Mercedes and kept his finances and the properties he owned in good order. In 1972, he had closed down a mail-order lingerie business that he had been trying to make a go of and invested in an inn and a campsite on a privately-owned campsite near Salzburg.

He had married Rosemarie, a kitchen assistant, when he was twenty-one and she was just seventeen. Fritzl dominated his wife just as much as he would later dominate his daughter. Not even his criminal acts or his sex tourism holidays in Thailand seem to have affected their marriage. He ridiculed her regularly, thinking it hilarious to tell people she was too fat to have sex. For her part, Rosemarie asked no questions about why he spent so much time in the basement – he told her he was working on mechanical drawings – and she was certainly never permitted to visit it. The frequent lodgers they took in through the years were warned that if they ever set foot in the basement, they would be out on the street immediately.

In 2002, Elizabeth gave birth to Felix who remained downstairs with his mother and Kerstin who was now fourteen years old and had never seen daylight. Elizabeth was now thirty-six years old and half her life had now been spent imprisoned in this tiny room.

During the day, he bought and sold property but at night he would spend hours in the basement, sometimes playing with the children and talking to Elizabeth when he was not raping her. Sometimes he even stayed the night.

Her prison had become more sophisticated over the years. He had installed locks on the doors that could only be opened by inputting the correct access code. He even ensured that if he died, she would be able to get out. The doors would automatically open once a specified period of time had passed.

He had also made life a little more bearable for his prisoners, bringing down a television, a video recorder, hotplates on which she could prepare meals for them and a fridge. The room, however, was still an oppressive, airless environment for three people to live in. The flickering pictures of the outside world on the television screen can only have added to the extraordinary torture to which they were being subjected.

By Christmas 2007, the strain of keeping up this elaborate pretence was beginning to take its toll on seventy-two-year-old Josef Fritzl. Coupled with that was the fact that Elizabeth was now forty-one-years old and had given birth to seven children. She was no longer the young, attractive woman he had locked up in 1984. He began to seek a way out for them all, coming up with a plan in which the cult that he had fooled people into believing she had become a member of all those years ago had finally let her go. She would return to the house and be reunited with her children.

Matters overtook him, however, when Kerstin became seriously ill. Elizabeth begged him to take her to hospital, but that, of course, was impossible. There would be questions asked for which he would have no answers. Unable to obtain the right medicines with which to treat her, he finally had no option but to take her to hospital when she fell unconscious in April 2008.

Hospital staff immediately became suspicious

and the police were called. A few days later, Elizabeth Fritzl stepped out of the room that had been her world for almost twenty-five years and into sunlight.

It was terrifying for the children who had been down there with her. Stefan, now eighteen and Felix, now six, were very afraid. They gazed in amazement at the moon for those first few days and were frightened out of their wits by the sounds of cars and police sirens.

Elizabeth met her children Monika, Alex and Lisa who had been taken upstairs. When she had last seen them, they had been babies. She also fell into the arms of her mother who wept and told her she was sorry and that she had no idea what was going on below her feet. Later, however, Elizabeth threw her mother out of the apartment she and her children were living in, suspecting that Rosemarie had, after all, been silently complicit in her husband's monstrous activities.

On 19 March 2009, Josef Fritzl was found guilty of all charges against him, including the murder of the twin Michael, rape, incest, kidnapping, false imprisonment and slavery. Elizabeth, who had given her evidence via video during the trial, slipped into the courtroom a few days before the end of proceedings, anxious to be there to ensure that her father was held accountable for his dreadful acts. It was the only time during the entire process that Josef Fritzl showed any emotion. When he saw her and she looked back at him, he broke down and wept. He had pleaded not guilty but after that look, he changed his plea to guilty.

He was sentenced to life imprisonment without the possibility of parole and is currently serving his sentence in Garsten Abbey, a former monastery in Upper Austria that has been converted into a prison. Fritzl is held in the section of the prison for the criminally insane.

NATASCHA KAMPUSCH

He had been beating her regularly for two years, often delivering two hundred blows a week to her young body. She fought back with a kind of passive resistance, punching herself in the face before he got a chance to do it. It became so bad that she tried to kill herself, attempting to strangle herself with items of her clothing, slitting her wrists with a needle and on one occasion setting fire to the cellar in which she was held prisoner.

And then, on Wednesday, 23 August 2006, she staggered into the house of an astonished elderly neighbour, and breathlessly announced to her, 'I am Natascha Kampusch!' She had been held captive for eight and a half years.

On 2 March 1998, ten-year-old Natascha was returning to school after a holiday in Hungary with her father, Ludwig Koch. He and her mother Brigitta Sirny had separated when she was a baby and relations between them were still chilly. They had rowed yet again when he had brought Natascha home the previous day and the girl woke up in a bad mood that she took out on her mother, refusing to say goodbye to her that morning. Little did she know that she would not see her again until she was eighteen years old.

As she walked through Donaustadt, the large district in the northeast of Vienna where she lived, she disappeared, grabbed by a pair of hands as she walked past a white Mercedes van and bundled into the van. It seemed to drive around for hours before coming to a halt outside a nondescript house. She did not know that she was only twelve miles away from her house. Wrapped in a blanket, she was taken inside, led through a doorway in his garage, concealed behind a cupboard, and down into a tiny cell. It had a steel door and was soundproofed to prevent her screams from being heard. This five square metre space would be her home for the next eight and a half years and her captor, Wolfgang Priklopil would have full control of every aspect of it – even the very air she breathed, the supply of which he could increase or decrease as he wished.

When it was realized that Natascha was missing, the police were informed and a massive search was launched. A twelve-year-old boy came forward and said that he had witnessed the girl being abducted by two men in a white van. Police officers stopped almost eight hundred white vans and questioned their drivers. One of them was her abductor but he was able to provide a convincing alibi for the time in question, telling them that he had been alone that morning and had been using his van to transport rubble from construction work he was doing at his house. No one bothered to follow up his story anyway, just one of the many errors made by the police in this case.

The witness had been wrong in saying that there had been two abductors. In fact, only one man was involved – Wolfgang Priklopil, a thirty-five-year-old communications technician whose house was located about an hour from Vienna in the town of Strasshof an der Nordbahn, near Gänserndorf.

There were numerous theories posited at the time for Natascha's abduction. Some commentators suggested she might have been taken by a child pornography ring while others said that she had been taken so that her organs could be used, noting the considerable sums of money for which organs changed hands. It was said that she would already have been transported out of Austria, a task that would have been rendered very easy by the fact that she was still carrying her passport after her Hungarian holiday with her father.

Rumours also spread that her mother was

involved in the abduction, even that she had sold her daughter. This version of events gained currency when it was revealed that Birgitta Sirny had had what were described as 'highly sexualized' photographs of Natascha taken when the girl was just five years old. Naturally, Birgitta vehemently denied all such allegations.

Her childhood had, however, been difficult, the tensions between her estranged parents rising to the surface each time they were in each other's company. Bizarrely, some later suggested that she might even have been provided with a better upbringing by Priklopil than she would have received from her mother. Given that he sexually abused her and beat her on a regular basis, this is, of course, nonsense.

The first six months of her captivity were spent in her cell but gradually Priklopil would allow her to go upstairs in the house. Every night she was sent back downstairs to sleep, however. She also remained there while he was at work.

As time went on, however, he granted her more freedom, even allowing her to go out in the garden occasionally. A business partner of Priklopil said after she escaped, that he had met Natascha on one occasion when he had visited the house to talk about borrowing a trailer.

She was mainly allowed upstairs to cook and clean for him but on those occasions, he made her go about the house half-naked, believing she would not try to escape if she was wearing next to nothing. Priklopil had no friends, to speak of, but his mother visited the house now and then. She did observe some changes. There were two pillows on the bed and plants in the living room. There was also the smell of cooking in the kitchen and Wolfgang, she knew, never cooked. She wondered if her son had at last found a girlfriend, but thought no more about it.

He had to be extraordinarily careful not to be caught out throughout those years, of course, dumping rubbish far from his house, having carefully sifted it all to make sure there was nothing that would compromise him and expose his secret.

Natascha, meanwhile, was fighting her captivity by soaking up every piece of information she could. Priklopil had provided her with some luxuries, one of which was a radio. It helped her to endure the long days in her cell when her captor was at work. He also let her read newspapers although he would read them first and cut out any stories that he considered unsuitable. He also let her watch television, but only after he had recorded the programmes on to videotape.

She was educating herself and gradually changing the nature of their relationship. He had told her that she was still in captivity because her parents had refused to pay a ransom.

'Your parents don't love you at all,' he would tell her. 'They don't want you back; they're glad to be rid of you.'

But her growing intellect and understanding of her situation enabled her to begin to win small victories. Life became more normal and she often ate breakfast with him. They even exchanged gifts on birthdays. After her eighteenth birthday, he trusted her enough to take her on shopping expeditions with him, forcing her to walk ahead of him and although she stared into the eyes of people she passed, willing them to see the face that had been on the posters her father had distributed when she was first kidnapped, she always returned to the house with him. Once, remarkably, he even took her skiing for a few hours at a ski resort not far from Vienna.

Of course, questions have been asked why she did not escape, and she has tried to explain that he threatened to kill her the moment she made a wrong move when they were out. He warned her that the doors and windows of his house were booby-trapped with explosives and that even if she did succeed in getting out of the house and tried to raise the alarm with one of his neighbours, he would kill her and the neighbours.

But, although she was finally seeing something of the world outside, she was still virtually a slave. At night he would take her to bed with him, tying her to him so that she could not escape when he was asleep.

Finally, she seized her opportunity.

That Wednesday in August, Priklopil had ordered her to clean his BMW 850i that was parked in the garden of the house. She switched on the vacuum cleaner to hoover the vehicle's carpets and just at that moment he received a call on his mobile phone. He walked away from the car so that he could hear better and when his back was turned she turned and ran, the noise of the machine covering her footsteps. She ran through neighbours' gardens and when she encountered someone screamed at them for help. They just stared at her as if she was mad, however. Finally, she staggered into the house of the elderly woman who finally called the police.

When Priklopil discovered that she was gone, he leapt into his car and drove off. He drove around aimlessly, panic rising in his chest. Finally, he called his business partner and lied to him that he was on the run from the police following a drink driving offence. His friend met him and took him to Vienna's Wien Praterstern railway station.

Priklopil had always told Natascha that he would never allow himself to be taken alive and he was true to his word. At around nine o'clock that evening, he stepped in front of an approaching train and was killed.

Natascha became one of the most famous people on the planet when she was released. She also became well-off when she was awarded £450,000 by the Austrian Criminal Injuries Compensation Board and the government provided her with an apartment in Vienna. In 2008, she became a star of television when she launched her own television chat show, *Natascha Meets*....

However, some worry that she has not truly escaped from that basement cell. She carries a photograph of Priklopil's candle-lit coffin in her purse and washes and irons items of clothing she wore during her captivity, as if they were holy relics. Or perhaps she is trying to wash herself clean after the events of those years and the clothes are merely the physical manifestation of her feeling of being, somehow, dirty.

THE ABDUCTION OF ELIZABETH SMART

Lois and Ed Smart frequently hired homeless men to do odd jobs at their house in the Federal Heights area of Salt Lake City. So, when she encountered a man calling himself Emmanuel begging, she offered him half a day's work raking leaves and doing some small repairs to the roof of her house. He was polite, relatively clean, given his lifestyle and he spoke well in a soft voice. He told her his mission in life was to be a minister for the homeless.

Emmanuel was happy to accept the offer of work. He arrived at the Smart home by bus and worked for about five hours at the end of which Ed Smart paid him and he went on his way.

On the night of 4 June 2002, however, Emmanuel was back. The house was in darkness. The Smarts had been out to an award ceremony at their daughter Elizabeth's school and as they got ready for bed, Ed made sure that all the doors were locked. He did not turn on the alarm, however. They had had a few problems with one of the kids getting up in the middle of the night and setting it off, waking the whole house as well as the neighbours.

Emmanuel, whose real name was Brian David Mitchell, broke in that night and went to the bedroom shared by fourteen-year-old Elizabeth Smart and her nine-year-old sister, Mary Katherine. Mary pretended to be asleep as Mitchell abducted her sister at knifepoint. He told Elizabeth as he roused her out of her bed that if she remained quiet she would not get hurt. When she asked him why he was doing it, he muttered something like 'for ransom'.

Mitchell spoke in a calm and even polite tone that Mary was sure she recognized, but she could not quite place it. Only months later would it come back to her. She suddenly remembered the quietly-spoken homeless man who had worked on the roof.

When she thought they had left the bedroom, Mary hopped out of bed to go and tell her parents. But in the corridor she saw the man and her sister, looking into her brothers' bedroom. She crept quietly back into her room and crawled into bed. She was worried that if he heard her, he would take her too. She waited until she was sure it was safe and then sneaked into the corridor and into her parents' room. It was four in the morning.

At first they thought Mary must have been having

a nightmare but Ed got up to make sure everything was alright. To his horror, he could find no sign of Elizabeth. It was when they noticed that a screen window downstairs had been sliced open with a knife that they contacted the police. As well as neighbours, family and friends.

People arrived immediately and the neighbourhood was searched for the girl. Still, there was no sign of her. A massive search was launched as soon as it was light and Ed appeared on television appealing to the kidnapper to return his daughter.

In the next few days, two thousand volunteers were sent out each day to look for her. Information was put out on the Internet and flyers were distributed. Dogs and helicopters were drafted in but as the days passed the task seemed increasingly futile.

Police had nothing to go on but Mary's eyewitness account but she had not seen the man's face. There were no fingerprints and not DNA samples. They interviewed hundreds of potential suspects but could link none of them to the abduction.

The milkman in the Smarts' neighbourhood provided a useful clue. He had been in the neighbourhood at around seven on the evening of 3 June, just a few hours before the abduction. He told investigators that he had noticed a green car cruising slowly along Kristianna Circle. He overtook the car in his milk truck and forgot about it until he saw it again and began to think the green car was actually now following him. Fearing that the man might be about to rob him, he wrote down its licence number and called the police.

The following weekend, there was a vigil for Elizabeth at Liberty Park in Salt Lake City. Police officers patrolled the car park, checking number plates, hoping to find the one provided by the milkman. One officer noticed a green Saturn sedan with the number 266HJH which was not exactly the number they had been told to look out for, but was close.

They staked out the car, waiting for its owner to return. When he did come back, two officers approached him, but as they did so, he put his foot hard on the accelerator and sped off. Later that day, the plates were found, abandoned by the side of a road. Fingerprints found on them matched a man named Bret Michael Edmunds, wanted for assaulting a police officer and someone who had done work in the Smarts' neighbourhood. He was finally found ten days later in a hospital in Martinsburg, Virginia where he was being treated for a serious liver ailment. He was questioned and his car was searched. Nothing incriminating was said or found and they eliminated him from the list of suspects.

They focused on another prime suspect, Richard Ricci who had been arrested since the abduction for breaking into houses in exactly the way the abductor had broken into the Smarts' house. Like Emmanuel, he had done some work for the Smarts and was on parole for the 1983 murder of a police officer. Shortly after, however, Ricci died of a brain Hemorrhage, closing down that line of enquiry and leaving the police with nothing. Even a $250,000 reward did not seem to be helping.

On the night of the kidnapping, Mitchell had made Elizabeth walk four miles up into Dry Creek Canyon, outside Salt lake City where he had constructed a concealed shelter consisting of a twenty-foot trench dug in the ground covered with a lean-to. He had been living there with Wanda Barzee.

Mitchell came from a troubled background. At the age of sixteen, he had been caught exposing himself to another child and was sent to live with his grandmother, but he discovered drugs and alcohol and eventually dropped out of school. Married at nineteen, he fathered two children but the marriage failed and he fled with his children to New Hampshire.

In 1980, he was back in Utah, devoting his life to the Church of Jesus Christ of Latter Day Saints. He married again and had another two children but this marriage also failed as his religious views became ever more extreme and his wife began to become frightened by his obsession with Satan. The church elders also began to tire of him and he was asked to rein in his wild depictions of the devil during services. In 1984 his second wife divorced him, accusing him of abusing two of her children from a previous marriage.

Mitchell married Wanda Barzee the day that his divorce came through. Six years older than him, she was a divorcee with six children who soon tired of Mitchell's brand of religion and moved out. By this time he was claiming to have conversations with angels and to be a prophet. Wanda worshipped him and adopted the name 'God Adorneth'. Meanwhile, the Mormon church excommunicated him for 'promoting bizarre teachings and lifestyle'.

In the streets of Salt Lake City, dressed in flowing white robes, they begged for money. It was while doing this that he had encountered Lois Smart.

When they arrived at the encampment, Mitchell made Elizabeth remove her red pyjamas and gave her white robes like his and his wife's to wear. He tied a cable round her leg and tethered her to a tree.

He wanted to perform a ceremony that would make Elizabeth his wife. Wanda was completely in favour of this. Polygamy had long divided the Mormon church, but Mitchell was in favour, believing that it was God's will.

They remained in Dry Creek Canyon until 8 August. By then, they were occasionally accompanied by Elizabeth when they went on a begging trip into Salt lake City. On those days, Barzee and Elizabeth would wear veils that covered the lower halves of their faces. By this time, however, Elizabeth was not showing any signs of being held against her will.

It was in October that Mary Smart had her 'eureka' moment and remembered where she had heard the voice before. Investigators were sceptical and still thought that Richard Ricci had been the abductor. They checked their files for anyone answering to the name Emmanuel but found nothing. What they did not know was that they had arrested Brian Mitchell the previous month for shoplifting but the officer had written his name down as 'Immanuel'. When a drawing that had been made of the man she had described was shown on *Larry King Live* and *America's Most Wanted*, Brian Mitchell's family recognized it immediately and informed the police.

Meanwhile, Mitchell had taken his two 'wives' to Lakeside, California, about twenty-five miles east of San Diego. He was keen to take another wife and had set his sights on the twelve-year-old daughter of a Church of Latter Day Saints official who lived nearby. He was foiled by burglar alarms, however, when he tried to break into the house later that winter.

He was arrested in February, 2003 after breaking into a school and was held over the weekend while at their makeshift camp in some woods, Barzee was becoming frantic. She prayed for hours in the woods for him to return, leaving Elizabeth back at the camp alone. Oddly, she did not try to escape.

Mitchell was sentenced to probation for the break-in and fined $250.

On 1 March, Elizabeth's disappearance was featured on *America's Most Wanted* and police began to receive reports of sightings. They were seen in San Diego and then in Las Vegas where they were begging in front of a Burger King outlet. By this time, they had discarded their robes and looked like run-of-the-mill transients. They were questioned by police after complaints by staff at the restaurant, but were allowed to go on their way. The following day, they were forty miles south of Salt lake City in Sandy, Utah, Elizabeth wearing a grey wig and large sunglasses to hide her face. However, the appearance on *America's Most Wanted* had done the trick. Two women phoned the police reporting the presence of Mitchell in Sandy.

When they were approached by a police officer, Mitchell claimed that they were the Marshall family from Miami. He added that they had no need for ID as they were messengers from God.

The officers called for back-up and managed to separate Elizabeth from Barzee and Mitchell. She insisted when questioned that she was not Elizabeth Smart but she was unable to properly answer questions about the other two who had claimed to be her parents. When other officers arrived and showed her a picture of herself from before her abduction, her eyes filled with tears. Again they asked her if she was Elizabeth Smart. She answered enigmatically, 'If thou sayest, I sayeth'.

Mitchell and Barzee were arrested and when he was asked his address, he answered, 'heaven on earth'. Asked for an emergency contact, he said 'God'.

Mitchell and Barzee were charged with a catalogue of crimes including aggravated kidnapping, aggravated burglary and aggravated sexual assault.

However, in January 2004, they were both found mentally unfit to stand trial. He had been ejected from several hearings for singing the hymn *Repent for the Kingdom of Heaven is at Hand* and had become increasingly delusional following his arrest.

Finally, Wanda Barzee was judged mentally competent to stand trial in 2009. She was found guilty and sentenced to fifteen years in prison.

Mitchell was finally found sane enough to be tried in 2010. The jury rejected his plea of insanity and after deliberating for only five hours, they found him guilty. He will be sentenced sometime in 2011.

PART FOUR

RITUAL MURDERS AND SATANIC KILLINGS

THE MURDER OF
DR HOWARD APPLEDORF

Murder scenes are, of course, by their very nature, not nice places but this one was particularly nasty. Howard Appledorf, one of America's best-known nutritionists, was lying dead on his back on his living-room sofa, bound and wrapped in a sheepskin rug. Some of his stomach was exposed where his shirt had ridden up and a cigarette was incongruously stuck in it where it had been stubbed out on his flesh. His ankles were fastened together with a belt, a tie bound his knees and a canvas bag covered his head, held on by a necktie knotted around his throat. There were also two towels tied around his neck. Removing the bag, investigators saw that one necktie had been used to gag him and another to blindfold him.

There were four plates in the room, three of which contained the crumbs of some sandwiches. The fourth had a handwritten note on it reading, 'HOWARD, I wish you could join us'. The place was a mess. Drawers had been emptied, clothes strewn across the floor and food and rubbish had been scattered around. On the walls, the perpetrators had scrawled in red ink the words 'murder' and 'redrum', which is 'murder' backwards and which had been written on a wall in the film *The Shining* in which Jack Nicholson had starred. Also written there was, 'HOWARD, we love you dearly, the Slez sisters'.

On the floor was found a notepad on which a strange message had been written. It said:

> *I realize murder is a felony crime, but I want whoever finds this body to know that I am criminally insayne [sic], and have no control over what I do. I know I won't [illegible] be caught for this crime because I have [illegible] of getting away, but I am very sorry that this is how HOWARD APPLEDORF had to go. I didn't mean it. Help me, X.*

It was hard to say what the motive for it was. It could have been part of a cult ritual, it might have been a burglary gone wrong or it could even have been a revenge killing. One thing was sure. It had been brutal and agonising death by asphyxiation.

Dr Howard Appledorf had come to national attention after claiming that junk food was alright to eat, that fast food could constitute a balanced meal, providing lots of protein, vitmins and minerals. He became a regular on chat shows and in newspapers. Naturally, fast food operations such as McDonald's and Kentucky Fried Chicken loved him and paid for his services as a fast food champion.

Appledorf had earned his spurs, however. He had a Ph.D from the prestigious Massachusetts Institute of Technology and had authored a number of books on nutrition. He had also been honoured for his research into vitamin metabolism and its relation to endocrine function. At the time of his murder, he was teaching at the University of Florida where his charismatic lecture style drew large audiences of students.

He had a big secret, however. He was gay. Many of his friends and associates were totally ignorant of this but a number suspected as much. It was when he was away from his home, at conferences or on holiday that he stepped out of the closet. He spent a lot of time in San Francisco, at the time the centre of the gay world, and in the words of a waiter with whom he enjoyed a brief relationship, 'he really let loose there'.

In the days before his murder, he had been mixed up in a legal tussle with three young men – Gary Bown, twenty-one, Paul Everson, nineteen and

Shane Kennedy, fifteen – who worked together as a team of hustlers.

Appledorf met Bown while attending a conference in San Francisco. He paid him $200 for two nights of sex in June 1982 and then bought him clothes and gave him another couple of hundred dollars before returning to Florida. On 14 August, he sent Bown $100 in New York and $25 in Orlando a week later. That day that the trio turned up at his condominium in Gainesville.

They stayed for two nights but before leaving on of them helped himself to a cheque from his chequebook. Everson forged Appledorf's signature and tried to cash it over the counter at a bank for $900. When the bank cashier became suspicious, Everson gave her a phone number and told her to call it to confirm that it was genuine. She alerted the police who trace the number and when she called it, they were waiting to arrest the other two members of the trio, one of whom was pretending on the phone to be Dr Appledorf.

Shortly after, probably fearful of being exposed, Appledorf requested that the charges be dropped on condition that the trio left Gainesville. The charges were duly dropped and on 2 September, Dr Appledorf flew to New York to deliver a lecture, having a new lock put on his door prior to his departure.

Bown, Everson and Kennedy did not leave Gainesville as agreed. Instead, they returned to Howard's condo where they broke in through the back door. They went through his things, strewing his belongings around the house and ate his food and watched his television. They found two gold rings which they exchanged for money at the nearest pawnshop. On Friday 3 September, Bown called the university to ask when the doctor would be back. He was told Appledorf was due back the following Tuesday.

That Tuesday, the three had bought subway sandwiches which they were eating in front of the television when Appledorf arrived back home. Shocked to find them there, he asked them what they thought they were doing. The trio told him they needed money to be able to get back to New York. When he told them he did not have any, things turned nasty. At one point, Appledorf is reported to have struck the youngest, Shane Kennedy, on the face, in reaction to which Everson picked up a metal frying pan and hit the doctor on the head with it. Kennedy, meanwhile, had gone outside, terrified by what was transpiring. He was not present during the killing.

They tied Appledorf up and Everson, finding his credit card, demanded the PIN number. He then went to the nearest ATM and withdrew $200.

Back at the house, they moved Appledorf on to the couch and while Bown smoked a cigarette, Everson sat on the doctor's chest and bounced up and down. As Everson did this, Bown picked up the frying pan again and began beating Appledorf on the head with it, only stopping when the handle broke. At that point Kennedy came back in and extinguished his cigarette on Appledorf's stomach. Appledorf did not respond to it. He was already dead.

The three then went round the room, writing the notes and scrawling messages on the walls to make it seem like a ritual murder or one committed by a madman. They then climbed into Appledorf's blue Pontiac Firebird and drove to New York.

Bown, Everson and Kennedy were immediately suspected, of course, and investigations were carried out in the area of New York's East 53rd Street, known as a hang-out for homosexual prostitutes. The Firebird was found and officers waited for the three to return to it. Sure enough, Bown appeared and climbed in, but realizing he was being watched by police officers, he took off on a terrifying 100 mph chase through the city's streets. He was eventually stopped by a road block and Everson and Kennedy were picked up shortly after.

They were all from difficult backgrounds. Gary Bown was born to a teenage mother in Long Beach California and his early life was blighted by domestic violence. As a teenager, he suffered from depression and tried to kill himself several times, once by trying to set himself on fire. He spent time in juvenile facilities for burglary during which he had his first homosexual experience with one of his counsellors. He became a homosexual prostitute, wearing mascara and shorts so tight that his buttocks were visible. It was in the course of this work that he met Howard Appledorf.

The backgrounds of the other two were little different. Paul Everson was a persistent truant and was constantly at war with his father, sometimes coming to blows. His rap sheet as a teenager included arrests for breaking and entering, possession of a stolen credit card, check forgery, trespassing, and unauthorized use of a motor vehicle. He liked dressing in drag and like Bown became a rent boy.

Shane Kennedy ran away from home in Connecticut aged fourteen. Living with his father and his new wife after his parents' divorce, he had been harshly disciplined for the smallest misdemeanours and he was bullied at school because he seemed effeminate. He met Bown and Everson in New York and became a prostitute.

Bown and Everson pleaded guilty in exchange for avoiding the death penalty and, the murder charge against him having been dropped, Shane Kennedy was sentenced to four years in prison for burglary, robbery and grand theft of a car belonging to the victim. Kennedy would, only days after his release be committed to a mental hospital after stalking fashion designer Todd Oldham, having sent him bizarre love notes, erotic art and condoms and having loitered near the designer's SoHo office.

THE SATANIC KILLING
OF ELYSE PAHLER

It was a murder that stunned the small coastal Californian town of Arroyo Grande, near to San Luis Opispo, and sent shockwaves through the entertainment industry. A fifteen-year-old girl, Elyse Pahler was apparently sacrificed to the devil by three teenagers who believed that by delivering 'virgin meat' to him they would be granted success for the death metal band Hatred that they had formed. They hoped to become as successful as their favourite band, the phenomenally successful Slayer who were counted in the so-called 'Big Four' of thrash metal bands along with Megadeth, Anthrax and Metallica.

Slayer's songs covered the waterfront of death metal, the lyrics dealing with the genre's customary subject matter – death, violence, Satanism, necrophilia, rape, torture and the sacrifice of virgins. They could actually have been said to have invented death metal, slipping into it from thrash metal, the ultra-fast heavy metal music that adults find impossible to fathom.

The three boys, sixteen-year-old Royce Casey, fifteen-year-old Jacob W. Delashmutt and fourteen-year-old Joseph Fiorella, looked the part with their lank, greasy hair and grungy, baggy clothes. They smoked marijuana and swallowed methamphetamines as they bobbed their heads to the music they loved at each other's houses. They especially liked the song *Necrophiliac* from their hit 1985 album *Hell Awaits*. The song is about killing a virgin and performing necrophilia on her corpse. It includes the verse:

I feel the urge, the growing need
To fuck this sinful corpse
My tasks complete the bitch's soul
Lies raped in demonic lust

What the boys failed to understand was that bands like Slayer do not actually champion the things about which they are singing on their albums. The lyrics contain irony and are fictional. Sadly, for Casey, Delashmutt and Firella they were real and they believed that they were receiving instructions on how to achieve their ambitions.

Alongside their interest in death metal, the boys were fascinated by the occult. Fiorella had an extensive collection of books that stood on shelves that lined the walls of his black-painted bedroom. He especially enjoyed the works of the notorious British black magician, 'The Great Beast', Aleister Crowley.

The three surfed the Internet to learn about organizations such as Anton LaVey's Church of Satan that is dedicated to the acceptance of the carnal self. They read LaVey's books, *The Satanic Rituals* and *The Satanic Bible* and a film called *River's Edge* also held a fascination for them. Starring Keanu Reaves and Dennis Hopper, it tells the story of a teenager who murders his girlfriend and shows her body to his friends who argue about whether they should report it to the police. The boys knew the screenplay by heart, especially lines such as 'I get into a fight and I go fucking crazy. Everything goes black and I fucking explode, like it's the end of the world.' The soundtrack featured a number of Slayer tracks.

On the evening of 22 July 1995, pretty blonde fifteen-year-old Elyse Pahler received a phone call from the three boys whom she knew from high school. They invited her to meet up with them to smoke some weed and maybe drop some acid. Later that night, she said goodnight to her parents,

David Pahler, a contractor and his wife Lisanne, pretending to go to bed. She slipped out of the house and met Fiorella, Casey and Delashmutt at the eucalyptus grove known as Nipomo Mesa about a mile from her home. It was an area already designated a natural devil's altar by the three boys and they had selected it as the ideal place to carry out the wicked plan they had devised.

As they sat smoking marijuana and getting lost in the warm night air, Delashmutt stood up and walked behind Elyse's back. He removed his belt from around his waist and looped it around her neck, pulling it tight. Casey then held her down as Fiorella pulled a hunting knife from a sheath and plunged it into her neck repeatedly. He passed it to Delashmutt and then it was Casey's turn. She was stabbed at least twelve times but as a forensic pathologist later told the court, none of the individual wounds was actually fatal. She slowly and agonizingly bled to death and as she did so, she cried out for her mother and prayed to God for help. As she lay there, Casey became tired of the noise. He stamped on the back of her neck to silence her.

The three now took it in turns to have sex with her dead body, living out their ultimate fantasy, as depicted in *River's Edge* and sung about by Slayer.

When asked later by an investigator why they had done it, Casey answered that, 'It was to receive power from the devil to help them play the guitar better'.

They had planned the murder meticulously for the past month and some months afterwards, Casey wrote in a journal:

> I'm fighting on the other side now. Allied with the darkened souls, Satan's arised and shall conquer and reign ... in the Bible it says that in the end Lucifer will bring out his best in everything, music, love, murder... All the psycho serial killers and rapists don't know that if they would just build an altar of sacrifice and kill the person on the altar and then [have repeated sex] with the corpse. Virgin meat is the ultimate sacrifice. He told investigators that Elyse Pahler, being blond and a virgin was the perfect sacrifice.

They had almost killed her before, although on that occasion another teenager named Williams was also involved. They had enticed Elyse from her house and walked with her to a spot on the Mesa where there was a steep ravine. One of the boys pretended to slip down the ravine in a ruse to get Elyse to go to the bottom and Fiorella threw Williams a knife but as the others urged him to do it, he froze. Casey later said that Elyse must have believed they were just fooling around and thought nothing of the incident.

Naturally, the police searched for her, but once it became known that she had been a fairly troubled teenager who had been expelled from school for drinking and had later had to attend a drug rehabilitation unit, they concluded that hers was probably just another incident of a kid running away from home to seek her thrills elsewhere. The case was soon forgotten about.

The three boys returned to her corpse on many occasions in the months following the murder, laughing hysterically until the tears rolled down their cheeks. However, eight months after the crime, Royce Casey walked into a police station and confessed. He came forward partly because of his recent religious conversion, but also because he feared that Fiorella and Delashmutt were going to kill again. They had told him that 'she wouldn't be the only one. There would be others'. He even feared that he might be their next victim because he had tried to stay away from them. As he said, there was a lyric from a Slayer song that explained why he should have been afraid: 'If you're not with us, you may no longer exist'.

The other two were arrested and, like Casey, pleaded guilty to murder. They were sentenced to twenty-six years to life in prison.

The case naturally created a media storm and questions were asked about the influence of music such as Slayer's on young people. Elyse Pahler's parents filed a lawsuit against Slayer that claimed that their music had been responsible for their daughter's murder.

The music industry waited with baited breath for the ruling by a judge in 2001. However, he said that although Slayer's lyrics may have been offensive, they had not incited the three boys to murder. 'Slayer lyrics are repulsive and profane,' he wrote in his fourteen-page decision, 'but they do not direct or instruct listeners to commit the acts that resulted in the vicious torture-murder of Elyse Pahler.' He also ruled that the music was not harmful to children, as alleged by Mr and Mrs Pahler.

HEAVEN'S GATE

Comet Hale-Bopp, which was visible to the naked eye for eighteen months in 1996 and 1997, was not just the most widely observed comet of the twentieth century; it was also the signal to an American religious group that called itself Heaven's Gate that their spaceship was coming and it was time for them to leave their earthly bodies and move on to the 'next level'.

Heaven's Gate had been established by Marshall Herff Applewhite and Bonnie Lu Trousdale Nettles in 1972. Applewhite had been born into a religious family in 1931. His father was a Presbyterian minister but after initially intending to follow in his father's footsteps, he was encouraged instead to develop his considerable music talents. He became a college music teacher in 1956 and married and had two children. In 1970, he was fired from his teaching job at the University of St. Thomas in Minnesota, university authorities citing 'health problems of an emotional nature'. It is suggested, however, that the real reason was an affair with a male student.

In his early forties, Applewhite, suffering from depression and hearing voices, admitted himself to a

Houston psychiatric hospital. There he met a forty-four-year-old nurse named Bonnie Nettles. She was a member of the Theosophical Society and held esoteric views. They had a lot in common, a shared interest in UFOs, astrology and science fiction and she convinced Applewhite that they were earthly incarnations of aliens. Their mission she convinced him, was to save as many humans as possible when the world ended. Just as he had left behind his family, she walked out on her four children and they set out to gather followers who could be saved.

Before they could begin their mission proper, Applewhite was arrested and spent four months in prison in Harlingen, Texas, for credit card fraud.

In 1975, they headed for California, the state most likely to provide them with likeminded people. They launched Human Individual Metamorphosis and twenty-five people signed up. They canvassed for members further afield and at a meeting in Waldport, Oregon, they recruited another twenty followers who abandoned their lives to join them, one couple even leaving their ten-year-old daughter behind.

Their doctrine was similar to that of many other cults with a strong basis in paranoia and fear. They told people that at the end-time they would be beaten and persecuted by their enemies and their bodies would lie out in the open for three and a half days. However, they would then rise and disappear into a cloud and from there they would ascend to a higher level to be with God. They interpreted the word 'cloud' that appeared in the Bible, as being a spaceship and they were expecting to be able to get on board. It would be the only way to escape from the Luciferians – evil aliens who enslaved human beings through worldly things like jobs, sex and families. Believe the message and be saved, was what they were preaching.

One of the ways they had succeeded in enlisting the people from Waldport was by announcing an exact date for the arrival of a UFO. They gathered together and waited on the day but, of course, there was no sign of an alien encounter. Applewhite was apologetic and he at least had the decency to invite people to leave if they wanted to. Although many did leave, a lot stayed, having given up everything and being left with nowhere else to go. Undaunted, Applewhite and Nettles persevered and soon membership had grown to ninety-three. The search for the 'next level' continued.

Members now developed a uniform look and dress code. Applewhite asked them to cut their hair short and to wear the same unisex clothing. They had to aspire to be genderless, sexless beings. Sex was banned and privacy was not permitted. They cut themselves off entirely from society, believing that their work was being distorted by the media and outsiders.

Applewhite encouraged what he called 'crew-mindedness', a way of thinking and acting as one, skills that would be needed, he said on the spaceship. He told them they were all related. He was their father and nettles was their grandfather. He called himself 'Do' and she was named 'Ti'. The members added the letters – 'ody' to their Christian names, often dropping the vowels. Therefore, the Heaven's Gate member named Vern would become 'Vrnody'.

Numbers fell by the end of 1976 from a high of two hundred to only eighty and as the years passed, finances became difficult. They sold 'spaceship rides' for $433 and were delighted when they received a legacy of £300,000.

To make matters worse, Ti/Nettles contracted cancer and died in 1985 and, in contradiction of what Applewhite had promised, failed to resurrect. He explained it away by saying she had gone on ahead to prepare everything for them. He added that when the mothership finally arrived, she would be piloting it.

In 1993, Applewhite placed an ad in USA Today announcing the end of the world. He told the American people that the American people would soon be 'spaded under' and that they had just one last chance to escape. He told them that he was the alien who had been inside the body of Jesus Christ but that two millennia ago the souls had not been ready. He had come back to earth as Marshall Applewhite in order to take those with him who were ready. The advert was under the name by which the group was now calling itself – Total Overcomers Anonymous.

Three years later, in 1996, they moved to their last location – 18241 Colina Norte in the quiet commuter town of Rancho Santa Fe in San Diego County, California. Filled with large, expensive houses and with only one shopping street, Rancho Santa Fe was the highest income community in the country.

They earned money from a web design company they called Higher Source and they promoted their beliefs on the internet. They had by this time changed their name again. They were now Heaven's Gate.

The organizational structure of Heaven's Gate has been described as resembling that of a medieval monastic order. They lived communally, members giving up all their material possessions and living a highly ascetic existence. There were absolutely no indulgences and certainly no sexual contact. Six male members, including Do/Applewhite, even underwent voluntary castration in order to ensure their ascetic lifestyle.

Some members went out to work. For three months before the fateful day, three of them worked for a small San Diego company that developed computer-based instruction for the US Army. It was later reported that although they were polite and friendly, they mostly kept themselves. When they quit, shortly before taking part in the mass suicide, they told their supervisor that they had completed their mission.

Hale-Bopp had last visited the earth in 2020 BC, and was considered then to be an indication of the arrival of a great teacher. This latest visit was, therefore, heralded with great anticipation by the New Age community and by Do, in particular. He told his followers that Hale-Bopp was the sign for which they had been waiting.

One comet-observer claimed that he had photographs that showed an object in the wake of Hale-Bopp and that it looked like an alien spacecraft. This particular observer told a radio show host that he had actually looked inside the spacecraft with his telescope and had seen alien life forms. Heaven's Gate were frantic with anticipation. They went as a group to see the film *Star Wars* and they attended a conference on UFOs. They also took out insurance policies against alien impregnation and abduction.

They also bought a high-powered telescope to try to see the spacecraft. They explained this to a puzzled store manager who was even more confused when they returned the telescope complaining that they had failed to see the spaceship with it.

On the evening of Friday, 21 March, the thirty-nine members of Heaven's Gate all went to a chain restaurant named Marie Callender's where they ordered thirty-nine identical meals of salad, pot pies and cheesecake. It was their final meal on earth. The following day Hale-Bopp would reach its closest point to the Earth and they would be departing for the 'next level'.

That morning, everyone dressed in identical black long-sleeved shirts, black sweat-pants and black and white Nike trainers. On their left arms they wore armbands that bore the legend 'Heaven's Gate Away Team', a reference to the group of crewmen in the TV show *Star Trek: The Next Generation* who left the mothership to undertake planetary missions.

They each packed a small overnight bag with

clothing, lip balm and spiral notebooks. These were placed at the foot of their beds.

Each put three quarters and a five dollar bill in his or her pocket – the amount they always took with them when they left the house. It was enough to make a phone call or pay for a taxi home.

There were three teams. The first fifteen ate pudding or apple sauce into which had been mixed the barbiturate Phenobarbital, washing it down with vodka. They then lay down on their beds with plastic bags over their heads until they became unconscious. Those left alive at this point removed the bags and covered each of their colleagues, now dead, with a purple shroud.

The following day, the next fifteen did the same, with another seven doing the same on Monday. The final two who were both women tidied up and then took the poison.

Meanwhile, videotapes had been sent out to former members who, realizing what had happened from the messages on the tapes, alerted the police. Officers broke into the house, realizing from the stench of human decay that something terrible had happened.

The members of Heaven's Gate had moved on at last to the 'next level'.

THE SOLAR TEMPLE

The note said, 'It is with unfathomable love, pure joy and no regret that we leave this world. Men, do not cry for our fate, but cry for your own.'

It had been left by a member of the Order of the Solar Temple, a secret society, or cult, that was based upon the modern myth of the continuing existence of the medieval Christian military order, the Knights Templars. Between 1994 and 1997, seventy-four members of this cult killed themselves in three separate incidents in Switzerland and Canada. They did it because by doing so, they could move on to a better place, a new level of existence. To the members of the Solar Temple, that move would lead them to the planet they knew as Sirius.

The Knights Templar was a chivalric order that had come into existence in the middle ages and existed for two centuries, from 1129 when it was officially endorsed by the Catholic Church until 1312 when it was officially disbanded by Pope Clement V. Its leader at that time, Jacques de Molay was burned at the stake as a heretic but legends concerning its secrets and mysteries have grown around it in the centuries since.

In 1984 the order was re-born in a modern form when Belgian Luc Jouret and a French jeweller, Joseph di Mambro founded the International Chivalric Organization of the Solar Tradition, more commonly known as the Order of the Solar Temple.

Di Mambro was born in rural southern France in 1924 and trained to be a clockmaker and jeweller. Fascinated by occultism from an early age, he joined the Ancient and Mystical Order of the Rosae Crucis (AMORC) and in the late 1950s became head of an AMORC lodge in Nimes. He remained a Rosicrucian until 1969.

In 1970, he gave up his career to become a lecturer in New Age issues and in the next few years founded several New Age Organizations, moving to Geneva where he began to present himself as a representative of the Great White Brotherhood, the group of beings that Occultists believe were crucial in the development of the human race. He said he was an incarnation of several notable figures such as Moses and the Egyptian Pharaoh, Akhenaton. It impressed many who were happy to make donations to his organizations.

In the early 1980s, the popular New Age and holistic health speaker, Luc Jouret gave a talk at a meeting of one of Di Mambro's organizations, the

Golden Way. Born in the Belgian Congo in 1947, Jouret was a member of another occult group, the Renewed Order of the Temple. The two men immediately recognized that they had a great deal in common, Di Mambro seeing in Jouret the prophet for whom he had been waiting, an impressive and persuasive man who convinced people that he was the reincarnation of a fourteenth-century Knight Templar and the third reincarnation of Christ. Best of all, he had an astonishing skill for getting money out of wealthy people.

Soon, the Solar temple had grown out of the membership of the Golden Way. Amongst its aims were establishing 'correct notions of authority and power in the world', an affirmation of the primacy of the spiritual over the temporal, assisting humanity through a great 'transition', preparing for the Second Coming of Jesus as a solar god-king, and furthering a unification of all Christian churches and Islam.

In 1982, Di Mambro fathered a child, a daughter named Emmanuelle. He described his children as the harbingers of the new age, but Emmanuelle, he claimed, was the 'new messiah', a cosmic being who would lead in the coming new age. She was prevented from having contact with anyone but her immediate family.

By 1989, the Solar Temple boasted a membership of around 500 and there were Solar Temple lodges in Morin Heights and Sainte-Anne-de-la-Pérade, Quebec, Canada, as well as in Australia, Switzerland, Martinique and other countries. Jouret was most interested in attracting wealthy and influential members, and several rich Europeans were reputed to be secret members of the group. As a result, he and Di Mambro were becoming extremely wealthy. It has been estimated that they had something in the region of $93 million in their coffers by this time.

As with such organizations, the Solar Temple was organized into a hierarchical structure, the top thirty-three members of which were known as the Elders of the Rosy Cross. Beneath that was the core community and below that were the 'clubs', the section of the organization that was occupied with the recruitment of new members.

The Temple's activities were a mix of early Protestant Christianity and New Age philosophy using variously adapted Freemason rituals. Jouret preached that when members of the Solar Temple left their bodies, they would undertake 'death voyages' that would take them to Sirius where they would continue in a higher form of spiritual being. Death was just an illusion, he claimed. He also prophesied that the world would end in a terrible ecological disaster and some Temple members would be selected to undertake the journey to Sirius. The only way they would escape, he added would be through fire.

As time went on, Jouret became increasingly erratic in his behaviour. Before leading one of the organization's rituals, he insisted on having sex with a female member, in order, he claimed, to give him 'spiritual strength'.

As the 1990s dawned, the Solar Temple began to experience problems and some began to question Di Mambro's authority. A member who left in 1991 filed a lawsuit against the organization, claiming it was a cult.

Meanwhile, Jouret, becoming increasingly paranoid, ordered Temple members to start stockpiling guns in anticipation of the chaos that was sure to erupt around the time of the end of the world. When he was arrested in Canada in 1993 attempting to purchase illegal weapons, the resulting publicity did a huge amount of damage both to his reputation and to the organization. Members began to lose confidence in their leaders and, worse still, contributions began to dwindle. His arrest also had the unfortunate consequence of attracting the unwelcome attention of the authorities. As it unravelled, things began to turn nasty.

Tony Dutoit had been a Solar Temple member and he and his wife Nicky had been ordered by Jouret not to have a child. When Nicky became pregnant, therefore, the couple fled to Canada where their son Christopher-Emmanuel was born. Di Mambro was furious and started referring to the baby as the Antichrist. He was further angered when Dutoit began making allegations publicly about the Solar Temple. He talked about how Jouret made the Holy Grail and spiritual beings appear to believers, but that it was all done using lasers. Di Mambro resolved to put an end to Dutoit's insinuations and shortly before the mass suicide of October 1994, Dutoit and his wife and new-born child were found brutally murdered in their burned-out home in Morin Heights, Quebec. Dutoit had been stabbed fifty times while Nicky had been stabbed four times in the throat, eight times in the back and once in each breast. The baby's body was in a black plastic bag on top of which lay a bloody wooden stake that had been used to stab him six times. In the ashes of the house another two charred bodies were found. They belonged to the family's murderers who appeared to have killed themselves after dispatching the Dutoit family. Warrants were issued for the arrest of Di Mambro and Jouret.

Solar Temple members increasingly resentful of Jouret's autocratic leadership style, voted him out of office as Grand Master. This caused turmoil in the European community and Di Mambro was furious. But he also had problems. He was ill with kidney failure and was suffering from cancer. He was about to be investigated for money-laundering and his daughter Emmanuelle had found out about the chicanery with the lasers and was denouncing her father to other members who began to ask for their money back. She was also tired of being shielded from the outside world and wanted to be among children of her own age.

Di Mambro and Jouret interpreted all this negativity simply as the sign that it was time to move on to the next level. Preparations began and members were urged to go to 'arks of safety' from which they could move together to the next stage of consciousness.

On 5 October 1994, the senior members of the Solar Temple ate a grim 'Last Supper' before unleashing the violence.

A fire broke out in a farmhouse at the village of Cheiry. When firemen arrived to put out the blaze, they discovered a man – later learned to be the owner of the farm, seventy-three-year-old Albert Giacobino – lying on a bed with a plastic bag over his head. It initially appeared to be a suicide but on closer examination, it was found that he had been shot in the head.

Police discovered a number of incendiary devices and when they went into what they thought was the garage, they discovered that it was actually a kind of meeting hall. As they looked around, they found that one of the walls of this room was moveable. They pulled it aside and were greeted with a scene of abject horror. The room, with crimson carpet, high mirrors and red satin draperies contained eighteen dead bodies, dressed in white, gold, red and black clothing and capes. They were organized in a circle, like the spokes of a wheel. In the middle was a triangular altar and empty champagne bottles were scattered around them. Many had plastic bags over their heads. In a room next door lay another three corpses.

Most of them had been shot in the head and some bore bruises, as if they had been beaten.

Meanwhile, in Granges-sur-Salvan, another Swiss village about a hundred miles from Cheiry, three ski chalets were burning. Police found twenty-five corpses inside, including three teenagers and four children. Many had been shot in the head, some as many as eight times while others had been stabbed or poisoned.

It would be learned from autopsies that fifteen had been voluntary suicides but that thirty more had been killed after being lured into the ceremony. Seven, it was deduced, had simply been executed.

But it was not over. A little more than a year later, on 23 December 1995, sixteen bodies were found in a burned-out chalet in the Swiss Alps. The corpses lay in a star pattern, their feet pointing inwards. As in the incidents of the previous year, the victims had been shot, stabbed or poisoned.

Two years later, five more Solar Temple adherents died in a fire at St. Casmir in Quebec. The corpses of four of the dead were discovered lying in the shape of a cross while the mother of the owner of the property, Didier Queze, lay on a sofa upstairs, a plastic bag over her head. Outside in a workshop, Queze's terrified children were found. They had persuaded their parents that they should be allowed to live.

As for the two leaders of the Solar temple, it was initially believed that they had organized the carnage in Canada and Switzerland before disappearing with the vast sums of money they had made. However, it soon came to light that their bodies were actually amongst the dead.

They had believed, after all.

ROD FERRELL AND THE VAMPIRE KILLERS

'I had decided to take the darker path, the evil path. I found that more exciting. If it wouldn't have been the Wendorfs, at the rate I was going, it would have been somebody, if not more people.'

On 2 February 1998, the teenage boy who said the above, seventeen-year-old Rod Ferrell, pled guilty to beating to death a Eustis, Florida, couple with a crowbar. The victims of this brutal slaying, forty-nine-year-old Richard Wendorf and his common-law wife, fifty-three-year-old Naomi Ruth Queen died in their home on 25 November 1996.

The 'darker path' selected by Ferrell started out almost from birth. Born to seventeen-year-old parents, Sondra Gibson and Rick Ferrell in 1980, he was introduced to occult ritual at a very early age. It was not an ideal situation. The young couple married just nine days after the birth of their son, but it was short-lived. Rick left Sondra after a few weeks, filed for divorce and enlisted in the military. Rod would never see him again.

His mother re-married and the family moved frequently before Sondra eventually left him in the small southern Baptist town of Murray, Kentucky with her parents and moved to Michigan with her husband. It was her intention to return to Murray to be with her son, but when her second husband informed her that they were never moving back, she divorced him and returned to her hometown.

Even life with his grandparents was an ordeal for Rod. They lived on a trailer park on the outskirts of town and he claims to have been raped at the age of five by his grandfather.

As he grew, Rod turned into a troubled and difficult teenager. He also claims to have turned into a vampire. He spent nights in the local cemetery, cut himself so that he and others could drink his blood and claimed to be a five hundred-year-old vampire named 'Vespago'. He grew his dark hair long, wore a long black trenchcoat and carried a cane. When he stayed home from school, he occupied himself painting skulls and skeletons in vivid colours and devouring every piece of reading material on vampires that he could find. He attempted to change his name to Lestat, the anti-hero of the Anne Rice book *Interview With the Vampire* and started telling people that he could not go out in daylight.

At school, his work inevitably suffered. He skipped class, flagrantly breached school rules and was insolent to teachers and other school officials. There was little help for him at home. His mother let him stay out all night, ignored his truancy from school and turned a blind eye to the drugs he increasingly began to take. He spent a great deal of his time playing the game, 'Vampire: The Masquerade' a live action role-playing game which involves vampires living in a modern gothic-punk world.

He was 'crossed over' into the vampire world by a young friend, Stephen Murray who, in September 1996 attacked him, although Ferrell refused treatment at a local hospital. Murray was convicted for the attack. Shortly after, thirty-five-year-old Sondra Gibson, Rod's mother, was charged with soliciting a minor – Murray's fourteen-year-old brother. She wrote love letters to the boy, begging him:

to become a vampire, a part of the family… you will then come for me and cross me over and I will be your bride for eternity and you can be my sire.

Heather Wendorf had met Ferrell when he lived in Florida and the two had remained in touch when his family moved on. She had purple hair, wore fishnet stockings and a dog chain around her neck. Like Ferrell, she was obsessed by the occult, claiming, like him, to drink blood and maintaining that she had been a demon in a past life. She and others were part of a group led by Ferrell that included nineteen-year-old Dana Cooper, sixteen-year-old Scott Anderson and sixteen-year-old Sarah Remington who also used the aliases Charity Keesee and Shea Remington.

The gang members who lived in Kentucky mostly hung out at a place that became known locally as the 'Vampire Hotel'. For several decades the ruins of an old hotel situated in the remote Land Between the Lakes National Recreation Area had been a magnet for teenagers and college students searching for an isolated location for parties and fraternity ceremonies, far from the prying and judgemental eyes of grown-ups. Its Gothic architecture and eerie atmosphere made it an ideal place for Ferrell and his vampire-loving friends to indulge their fantasies. Although the structure has mostly been destroyed, graffiti remains as a reminder of what used to go on there. Daubed on the pieces of wall that still stand are skulls, pentagrams, mystic symbols and phrases such as 'Follow me to death' and 'Those who came to this place fear not even evil' as well as references to the antichrist. It was in this place, Rod Ferrell claims, that in October, 1995, he became involved in a human blood-drinking ceremony with some unidentified adults. He claims that they made him one of the 'undead' which gave him power over any living being.

The gang started creating havoc in October 1994 when they broke into a local animal shelter. They stamped one puppy to death and pulled the hind legs off another. Ferrell took Scott Anderson to a cemetery, cut his arm and drank his blood.

Police suspected that vampirism was rife in Kentucky at the time. They even believed rumours of rival gangs of vampires, each of whom initiated local youths. In one story, a car with a faulty tail-light was stopped by police three days before Halloween on a secluded road between Murray and the nearby town of Mayfield. Inside were four people dressed entirely in black with their faces painted white. There was a fifth passenger, a young girl who was dressed normally but wore a blindfold over her eyes. When they were questioned, they laughed and told the officer that they were on their way to a fancy dress party. There was nothing suspicious and the officer merely checked the ID of the driver, a man named Kile Bayton.

A few days later, however, a message arrived from the Tennessee police saying that a fifteen-year-old girl, Susan Cates, had been reported missing. Her description was a match for the girl in Bayton's car. Furthermore, letters had been found at her home from Dean Frank, a Murray resident who was a friend of Kile Bayton. The letters talked about blood rituals and human sacrifices and told her about the powers she could have if she 'crossed over' to become a vampire.

Susan Cates was never found and Bayton denied ever having met her. There are many who suspect, however, that she died in an initiation ritual that went wrong at the Vampyre Hotel.

Sondra Gibson was believed to be at the root of her son's vampire fantasies. She was rumoured to lead one of the vampire groups that sprang up and encouraged teenagers to become involved in The Masquerade. Part of the rules state that a vampire who spots a rival vampire must attack and it has been claimed by friends of Rod Ferrell that he became convinced that Heather Wendorf's parents were vampires from another group and that they were trying to turn Heather against him. She complained endlessly to Ferrell about them, describing life with them as 'hell'. She told him she wanted to get away, but first he would have to kill her parents.

With Scott Anderson, Dana Cooper and Charity Keesee, Ferrel drove to Eustis in Florida. They met Heather near her house and he sent her and the other two girls off to meet another gang member, Jeanine LeClaire. Ferrell and Anderson armed themselves with a couple of heavy pieces of wood and cautiously approached the Wendorf house. Finding the garage door unlocked, they entered that way. Seeing a crowbar, Ferrell decided that would make a much better weapon. He picked it up and they entered the house.

In the living room, Richard Wendorf was snoozing on the sofa while his partner Naomi was having a shower. Ferrell crept across the room, raised the crowbar above the head of the sleeping man and brought it crashing down on his head with all his might. He hit him repeatedly – 'Boom, across the temple, on the head. I just beat him until he died,' as he later told police officers.

Suddenly Naomi walked in from the kitchen, a cup of coffee in her hand and was confronted by a blood-soaked Ferrell, a bloody crowbar in his hand. She threw the coffee at him but he leapt on her and the two of them fell struggling to the floor. He brought the crowbar down on her head and killed her with another few crushing blows.

It is claimed that as Heather's parents lay dead, Ferrell and Anderson drank their blood. They then searched the house for credit cards and car keys, discovering the keys to the Wendorfs' Ford Explorer. They took the car and met up with the others.

They drove both cars to Sanford where they swapped the vehicles' number plates. Leaving the other car behind, they piled into the Explorer and set off along Interstate 10 in the direction of New Orleans. Their reason for going there has been speculated about. Some say they planned to visit Anne Rice, the author of *Interview With a Vampire*. Others suggest that there was an amusement arcade there that Ferrell loved.

In Baton Rouge, Charity Keesee was persuaded to telephone her mother to ask if she could send them money. Her mother was suspicious, however, and worried about her daughter. She told them to go to a Howard Johnson's Motel where she would arrange for a room for the night. However, as soon as she put the phone down, she called the police who were waiting for the group when they pulled up at the motel.

Rod Ferrell pleaded guilty to the two murders, armed burglary and armed robbery, insisting in his statement that the others were innocent apart from

Scott Anderson who was an accomplice. He was sentenced to death, a sentence later reduced to life imprisonment without the possibility of parole.

Scott Anderson was found guilty of first-degree murder and sentenced to life. Charity Keesee and Dana Cooper were convicted of third-degree murder and sentenced to ten and a half years in prison.

Heather Wendorf was not charged with any crime.

BEASTS OF SATAN

The relationship between heavy metal – especially some its sub-genres such as death metal and black metal – is well documented and there are a number of cases where crime and the music of bands whose songs show an interest in the occult are connected in some way. Some say that such music should be banned. Following the horrific revelations in the Beasts of Satan case, Italian priest Don Aldo Buonaito called for death metal to be banned, saying, 'If music makes itself an instrument of nefarious deeds and death it should be stopped.' Others claim that it encourages violence, suicide and murder and, in fact, there have been a number of court cases in which people have tried to put the blame for a crime on to the music of a particular band. The most notable was probably the suit that was brought against the American band Slayer because of the part their music was alleged to have played in the brutal killing of Elyse Pahler in Arroyo Grande, California, in 1995. This case was dismissed as was a second and it has always been virtually impossible to prove that music is the spur for murder. As the father of one of the perpetrators of the Elyse Pahler murder said, 'The music is destructive but that's not why Elyse was murdered. She was murdered because Joe [Fiorella] was obsessed with killing her.'

In the case of the 'Beasts of Satan', the same can be said. The three murders that members of this Italian metal group committed had little to do with the music. But as someone once said, you can enjoy horror films without being a Satanist.

One night in January 1998, nineteen-year-old shop assistant Chiara Marino and her sixteen-year-old boyfriend, Fabio Tollis, lead singer in a heavy metal band called Beasts of Satan, were enjoying a normal Saturday night in the Midnight Pub, the centre of Milan's heavy metal scene. They drank beer and listened to the music they loved. That night, however, would be their last. They failed to return home and it would be six years before their bodies would be found.

Beasts of Satan was a black metal band. This type of music is an extreme sub-genre of heavy metal, notable for its ultra-fast tempos, shrieked vocals, highly distorted guitars and unconventional song structures. It is raw and uncompromising both in its musical style and in its lyrical content and its aggressively anti-Christian and misanthropic stance has raised the ire of many. Songs are replete with Satanic references, ritual sacrifice and the occult. But it is music that remains resolutely underground and is unashamed of its outsider stance.

The man behind the murders was Andrea Volpe. He convinced his fellow band members that Chira Marino was actually the embodiment of the Virgin Mary, this even though her room at home was decorated with black candles and the skulls of goats. Nonetheless, she had to die and an attempt to burn her to death in her car a few weeks before had failed.

That January night, she and Tollis were driven to woods near to the village of Somma Lombardo, north of Milan where a drug-fuelled Satanic ritual followed. Chiara was the one who was supposed to die, but Tollis tried to prevent the others from going through with it and for his trouble was killed by a blow to the head with a hammer.

They were buried side by side in a hole six feet deep and the murderers, Volpe, Nicola Sapone and Mario Maccione urinated into the grave after they had thrown the bodies of the teenagers into it. Reportedly, another sect member, a twenty-six-year-old woman, danced on their graves after they had been filled in, laughing and shouting, 'Zombies!

Now you are both zombies! Try to get out of this hole if you dare!'

When Tollis and Marino failed to return home, the authorities concluded that they had simply run away together. However, Fabio's father, Michele Tollis, refused to accept this. Just a few hours before he was killed, Nicola Sapone, one of the killers, forced Fabio to telephone home and tell his father that he would not be coming back home that night because he preferred sleeping with his girlfriend. Michele was puzzled by this call and believed something was not right about it. Knowing his son spent his Saturday nights there, he called the Midnight, hoping to speak to him. But it was too late. Fabio and Chiara had already left with their friends for Somma Lombardio.

While it seemed that the police had washed its hands of his son's disappearance, Michele Tollis launched an investigation of his own. He discovered just how heavily involved Fabio and Chiara had become in Satanism and the occult, influenced, no doubt, by their love of black metal and death metal. He even travelled to heavy metal music festivals across Europe, distributing leaflets and pictures of his son and his missing girlfriend in the hope that someone would come forward and tell him they had been seen. But there was more horror to come.

In January 2004, Andrea Volpe and his eighteen-year-old girlfriend, Elisabetta Ballarin, invited twenty-seven-year-old shop assistant, Mariangela Pezzotta, to dinner at a remote chalet. High on drugs and alcohol, the pair shot Mariangela in the face after a violent struggle because they believed she knew too much about the other two murders and there was a risk that she would go to the police. They buried her in a shallow grave, even though she was still breathing. They called Nicola Sapone for help and when he arrived, he finished the girl off with a spade, complaining to them, 'You can't even kill a person!'

Some hours later, Volpe and Ballarin, high on cocaine and heroin, tried to get rid of Mariangela's car by pushing it into a nearby river, but as they made their way to the river, they were involved in a car crash and were arrested.

When Michele Tollis heard on the television news about the murder of Mariangela Pezzotta, and that a young man named Andrea Volpe had been arrested, he sat up and took notice. He knew that his son had played in a death metal band with Volpe. He immediately called the police and at a meeting presented them with the files he had put together during the previous six years. Investigators began quizzing Volpe about the murders of Fabio Tollis and Chiara Marino. He eventually confessed and led them to where the bodies were buried.

Mario Maccione, who had been a schoolfriend of Fabio, confessed to having bludgeoned him with a hammer and further revealed that the boys had been part of a wider Satanic sect called the Beasts of Satan. It emerged that the band's drummer, Andrea Bontade, who had committed suicide, had been terrorized by the others into doing it because he refused to join them in the murders at Somma Lombardo. On a September night in 1998, he had consumed a large quantity of alcohol and had then killed himself by lying down and letting his car roll over him.

On 22 February 2005, Andrea Volpe and Pietro Guerrieri were sentenced in Busto Arsizio to thirty and sixteen years in prison, respectively, Volpe's sentence a full ten years longer than the one demanded by prosecutors. Mario Maccione, who had also confessed, was acquitted due to his minor role in the murders.

Of the other members of the group, Nicola Sapone, who was its leader and was suspected of being behind the killings, was sent to prison for life.

Paolo Leoni, Marco Zampollo, Eros Monterosso and Elisabetta Ballarin, received sentences of between twenty-four and twenty-six years.

These crimes horrified Italy and brought home to the Italian people just how attractive Satanism and the occult was becoming to young Italians. Many were attracted by the kind of views expressed by Andreas Volpe in the diary he kept:

We are wicked individuals. We plague the people and
we play with their lives. We know no pity. Pitiless,
we will eliminate and cleanse, donating the ash of our
enemies to he who sits on the throne.

CHILDREN OF THUNDER

At six feet five, dressed entirely in black, with shoulder-length brown hair and pony tail, he had it all. Tall, handsome and charismatic, people listened to what he said and believed it. He believed that he was a prophet, an instrument for peace, love and understanding in the world who could channel the words of God and use them to achieve his goals. He would often ask people to be quiet so that he could hear God speak and is once reported to have run outside in pouring rain and raised his hands into the air like aerials so that he could hear a message from on high. He often started sentences with 'Spirit says', conveying the words of the Lord to the person standing in front of him. He ominously said, 'If people aren't loyal to me, I'm just going to have to kill them.'

Glenn Taylor Helzer and his younger brother Justin were former Mormons who aided by another Mormon, Dawn Godman, embarked upon a killing spree in which five people were brutally murdered. They killed for money that would help them launch a religious group that they believed would spread 'joy, peace and love' throughout the world. The deadly trio of vicious killers were convinced they had God on their side. They called themselves the 'Children of Thunder.'

To know them when they were growing up, however, in the small town of Martinez, just under an hour's drive north of san Francisco, it would have been unimaginable that one day they would become killers. Their parents were devout Mormons and the boys enjoyed a relatively normal childhood. They were nice kids; Taylor the elder of the two, was more outgoing and Justin quieter and more withdrawn.

They graduated from high school and like all Mormons went off to do two years of missionary work, Taylor travelling to Brazil while Justin worked in Texas. On their return, Taylor found a job as a stockbroker at the firm of Morgan Stanley Dean Witter in San Francisco. Justin, meanwhile, earned a living as a cable installer.

Taylor met a woman whom he married in 1993, and they had two daughters. By 1996, however, he was bored with marriage and also seemed to be bored with being a good Mormon. At his trial, his wife intimated that he had a yearning to try a 'normal life' by which she meant a non-Mormon life. He threw himself into it with abandon, drinking, smoking and going to be with other women. His marriage was over and he was excommunicated by the church on account of his wayward behaviour.

He had also started to devise his own belief system and frequently argued with one of his cousins about it while the two were high on drugs. He believed that good and evil and right and wrong did not exist and that society was restricted by its beliefs in these values. Work began to suffer and eventually Taylor was given sick-leave after suffering a nervous breakdown.

Dawn Godman, the third member of the trio was brought up in the small town of Sutter Creek that lay beneath the Sierra Mountains in California. Married at eighteen, she lost one son, but had a second who lived. Her marriage foundered, however, and her husband was granted custody of the boy. By that time, she was living in her car and had tried to kill herself with an overdose of pills.

She arrived in Martinez to live with a relative and began attending the Mormon church there where she met the Helzer boys, somewhat appropriately at a murder-mystery event on Memorial Day, 1999. The Helzer brothers who always dressed in black stood out amongst the other Mormons and she started dating Justin although it has been reported that, like many women, she was far more interested in his older brother.

Taylor offered her spiritual guidance after persuading her to enroll in a self-awareness seminar. He believed he could do a better job and had shortly convinced her that she was a prophet of God. To keep his disciples – Justin and Dawn – in line, he composed the 'Twelve Principles of Magic', a set of rules to be observed that included the lines, 'I am already perfect and therefore can do no wrong' and I gain control by losing control'.

In the Mormon temple in Oakland he explained his plan to launch a self-help group that would defeat Satan. Furthermore, he added, he would one day take over the Mormon church, even if he had to organize the assassination of its leaders.

The problem was, of course, that he required money to establish his self-help group. But he had a plan. He was still acting as stockbroker to a number of clients from his days at Morgan Stanley Dean Witter. He would kill one of those clients, having extorted the necessary money from them.

When he asked Godman if she was prepared to kill for the Lord, she replied that it would be a blessing. The self-help group was to be known as 'Impact America' and as well as the plan to kill a client, Taylor devised other methods of extracting money from people's bank accounts to fund it. He planned a company called Intimacy that would provide wealthy businessmen with drugs and prostitutes. They even tried to recruit women for the job, distributing leaflets at clubs and parties. Another scheme involved importing underage girls from Brazil to seduce businessmen who were married and could therefore be blackmailed. He also had a plan to recruit Brazilian orphans who would be trained to assassinate the leaders of the Mormon church. Taylor would then step in and take over. He truly believed this was prophesied in the Book of Mormon, the church's holy book.

Ultimately, however, the plan to kill a client proved to be the most feasible but they needed another person who would be able to launder the money once they had obtained it. They would, of course, be expendable and after the money was safe, he or she would have to die.

In spring, 2000, Taylor met twenty-two-year-old Selina Bishop, daughter of famous blues guitarist Elvin Bishop, and decided she fitted the bill. For her part, she fell head over heels in love with Taylor although her friends and family were uncertain about this enigmatic character about whom she knew very little, not even his last name or where he lived. In fact, he told her his name was Jordan.

Taylor dreamed up the perfect ruse to fool Bishop into thinking she was helping him. He told her that he was about to inherit money from his grandmother but that his ex-wife was trying to get her hands on it. He asked her to open bank accounts into which the money could be deposited to hide it from the former Mrs. Helzer.

The first target that Taylor selected from his list of clients was not home when Taylor and Justin called. He was lucky; his absence saved his life. They moved on to the second on their list – eighty-five-year-old Ivan Stineman and his seventy-eight-year-old wife, Annette. Over the years, he had become good friends with the Stinemans. They trusted his judgement and he had even gone rafting one summer with them and their grown-up daughter.

On Sunday 30 July 2000, Taylor and Justin arrived at the Stineman house dressed in suits – black, of course – and carrying briefcases in which they had shackles to immobilize the elderly couple and a quantity of the 'date rape' drug, Rohypnol. They tied the couple up and drove them to the house they were renting.

A short while later, the Concord branch of Morgan

Stanley Dean Witter received a call from Annette Stineman saying that she wanted to liquidate all of her and her husband's investments.

Taylor had apparently thought that an overdose of Rohypnol would kill the Stinemans but it failed to work. Instead, Justin had to smash Ivan's head on the floor of the bathroom and Taylor slit Annette's throat with a hunting knife. The following day, they dismembered the bodies with a power saw, Justin doing the slicing while Taylor meditated. In a macabre gesture, Taylor, Justin and Godman then kneeled beside the body parts and Taylor said a prayer, thanking the Stinemans for 'being willing to sacrifice their lives for a greater cause.'

They had adopted some dogs to whom they had hoped to feed the body parts but when the dogs failed to show much interest in the flesh, they stuffed it into sports bags, weighed down with rocks and threw them into the Mokelumne River.

There was a bizarre sight next morning at a bank in Walnut Creek when Godman, wearing a gold cowboy hat and riding in a wheelchair, rolled in and asked to deposit two cheques totalling $100,000 in Selina Bishop's bank account. Bishop, she explained, was about to have open-heart surgery and this money, provided by her grandparents, had to be deposited in the account as soon as possible so that she could undergo the procedure that would save her life.

The night before Taylor and Selina were due to take a trip to Yosemite Park, they were at his rented home. Taylor was giving Selina a massage on the floor when Justin walked into the room and slammed a hammer into her skull. She was still alive when Taylor carried her into the same bathroom in which the Stinemans had died. He finished her off with his hunting knife. It is reported that just before he did it, he said to her, 'Spirit says you get to know this isn't a dream.'

Selina's mother was next. Selina had told Justine Villarin too much, Taylor believed. She knew where he lived and about the bank accounts. In the early hours of the following morning, he drove to her house where he found her in bed with 54 year-old James Gamble, a customer at the bar where she worked as a waitress. Taylor shot them both at point-blank range with a 9mm Beretta pistol.

The following morning, 4 August, the police were alerted after the Stinemans' daughter reported that her parents were not answering her telephone calls and neighbours had reported that newspapers were piling up at their front door. Then, when Justine

Villarin failed to turn up for work and there was no answer at her door, a missing person's report was also issued for her.

Meanwhile, the sports bags began to bob to the surface of the Mokelumne River. Nine bags were eventually discovered containing the mixed body parts of the Helzer's three victims. It would take more than a week to piece the victims' bodies together properly.

On Sunday, 6 August, the Stinemans' Chevrolet Lumina minivan was found in Oakland and inside were found the fingerprints of Taylor and Justin Helzer. There was further evidence in film from a surveillance camera that showed a vehicle like Justin Helzer's pick-up on a bridge over the San Joaquin River. It was towing a trailer carrying jet skis. It was the brothers on their way to dump the sports bags.

The following day, sheriff's deputies arrived at the Helzer house where they found the three killers as well as a ecstasy, hallucinogenic mushrooms and drug equipment. Although they failed to find Taylor's gun, they arrested them for possessing drugs. Suddenly, however, Taylor made a break for freedom, running into the garden and leaping the fence. Forcing his way into a neighbour's house, he changed into the frightened woman's husband's clothes and, having snipped off his pony tail, ran out with a knife and a pair of scissors as weapons. A few blocks away, they ran him down and pushed him into a cruiser. He immediately dived through the back window and escaped again, but again was re-captured.

Dawn Godman testified against the brothers in order to avoid the death penalty. She was sentenced to thirty-eight years to life in prison.

Justin pleaded not guilty by reason of insanity but on 4 August 2004 was sentenced to death for three of the murders and life for the other two. He had already told the court he wanted to die.

On 15 December of the same year, Taylor Helzer was given five death sentences.

ADAM — THE 'THAMES TORSO BOY'

On September 21, 2001, a man walking across London's Tower Bridge spotted an orange object floating in the waters of the Thames below. On closer inspection, he saw, to his horror, that it appeared to be a body, the orange being an item of clothing. The Metropolitan Police were alerted and sent their marine search unit to the scene. A short while later, the torso of what appeared to be a five-year-old black boy wearing orange shorts was recovered a little further downstream. Another two turns of the tide and it would have been well on its way to the North Sea.

The torso was just that. It had been decapitated and its limbs had all been amputated. As shock at the discovery spread around the country and the world, police realized immediately that they were dealing with one of the most extraordinary cases in their history. They soon began to realize that they were probably dealing for the first time ever with an example of medicine or *muti* murder, most common in southern Africa.

Muti is a term for traditional medicine in southern Africa, which is practiced as far north as Lake Tanganyika. The word itself is derived from the Zulu word for tree, although it appears in many languages of the region, and the medicine makes use of various natural products, many derived from trees. In Afrikaans, it is used to describe medicines that appear to have 'miraculous' properties, that provide immediate and dramatic healing.

In a perverted form of *muti*, medicine murders are sometimes carried out. A human being is killed in order to obtain body parts that can be used in medicine. This cannot really be described as ritual sacrifice for religious reasons.

Medicine murder has taken place in South Africa, Lesotho and Swaziland since the 1800s, especially during hard times when the economy is failing or there is political unrest.

The way it is done has changed over time, however. The perpetrators are usually men, although women have occasionally been convicted for involvement in a *muti* murder. The best known is probably restaurateur Philippa Mdluli who was hanged in Swaziland in 1983 for commissioning a medicine murder. She persuaded one of her employees to give her his five-year-old daughter who was killed a short while after. Her body parts were removed and served in Mdluli's restaurant where the bodies of little girls were considered a great delicacy by patrons.

Normally, a traditional healer or *inyanga* or *nanga* is commissioned by an individual or by a group of several people to help them by creating medicine or *muti* that will strengthen their personality or their personal force, enabling them to succeed in business, politics or whatever they are interested in. A human victim is selected who could be either young or old, male or female. Occasionally, the victim is purchased for a sum of money. The victim is taken to a remote location.

The objective is to mutilate the victim while he or she is conscious. It is believed that the anguished screams will make the subsequent medicine more powerful and although the objective is not to actually kill the person, it is fairly inevitable that he or she will die from the terrible wounds inflicted.

The body parts in which the nanga is interested are mostly soft tissue – eyelids, lips, scrota and labia. However, in many instances, as in the case of the boy found in the Thames, entire limbs are also sometimes taken.

These body parts are then mixed with medicinal

plants and cooked to produce what practitioners believe to be a powerful medicine. Sometimes it is drunk, but more often than not it is merely carried around or rubbed onto items to frighten enemies.

A fourteen-year-old girl, Segametsi Mogomotsi was famously murdered for her body parts in Mochudi, Botswana in 1994. Police did manage to recover some of the body parts but they were destroyed before they could be analysed, leading many to believe that the authorities were complicit in the case. The case led to student riots and Scotland Yard were eventually invited to help as a neutral force.

Human skulls are buried in the foundations of new buildings to bring the occupants good fortune, body parts are buried on farms to ensure good harvests and severed hands are built into shop entrances to draw customers. An investigation found that to buy a testicle costs £80, a kidney £200, and a heart £4,000. Brains and genitals sell for up to £4,000 and the organs of white people are seen as more valuable as whites are more successful in business.

In the case of the Thames Torso Boy, or Adam, as he was named by Metropolitan Police investigators, there was little to go on. It was decided, however, that the best way to find out what had happened to him and who had done it, was to find out where he was from. Genetic tests indicated that he was almost certainly of West African origin, probably from Nigeria or one of its neighbours, Togo or Benin.

Analysis of his stomach contents and bone chemistry was undertaken and that showed categorically that he could not have been brought up in London. They began to deduce that he had been brought to London for the explicit purpose of being killed for muti. The British food in his stomach and the pollen in his lungs confirmed the notion that he had been in Britain for only around seventy-two hours.

Also in his stomach was a mixture of seeds and nuts that suggested that he had been fed a magic potion before his death. Of particular note was the presence of a carabar bean which is closely associated with Voodoo and is indigenous to West Africa. Anyone swallowing carabar beans suffers a rapid and dramatic rise in blood pressure which is quickly followed by paralysis. In Nigeria it is believed that this bean possesses the power to reveal whether a person is a witch or not.

West Africa was also signalled as his home in the fact that he was circumcized. In southern Africa circumcision is carried out as a symbol of the passage from youth to manhood, but in West Africa a boy is circumcized shortly after birth. Even the fact that his genitals were left on his body points to West Africa. While the genitals are often seen as powerful medicine in muti, in West Africa it is thought that the real power lies in the blood.

Police began to think that Adam had probably been sacrificed to one of the 400 Orisha or ancestor gods of the Yoruba people of West Africa who are found mainly in Nigeria. The Yoruba river goddess, Oshun, is particularly associated with the colour orange which was the colour of the shorts that Adam was wearing. These shorts were put on to Adam's torso twenty-four hours after he was killed and the body was then stored for a further twenty-four hours before being thrown into the river.

The cuts where the head and limbs were sliced from the body displayed the work of an expert using extremely sharp knives. The flesh around the limbs and neck was cut down to the bone and then a single blow from an implement probably resembling a meat cleaver severed them. The boy would undoubtedly have been laid out horizontally during this procedure so that the blood could carefully be drained from the body. Blood, too, was used to make powerful medicine. It is likely that the man who had carried out the killing had been brought to Britain specifically for that task, given the level of expertise that seems to have been displayed.

Thirty-two-year-old Joyce Asaguede, originally from Sierra Leone, was arrested in her Glasgow tower-block flat in connection with the killing a year after the body was found. She had been boasting that she knew all about human sacrifice and when her flat was searched, clothes were found that had come from the same German shop as the shorts that Adam had been wearing. A DNA test, however, proved that Adam was not her son, and she denied all knowledge of the murder. She was eventually deported to Nigeria after making a bogus asylum application.

Meanwhile, in 2003, her husband thirty-seven-year-old Sam Onogigovie, also believed to be connected to the case was picked up in Dublin and extradited to Germany to face human trafficking offences.

The case of the Thames Torso Boy remains unsolved.

CHILD WITCHES OF NIGERIA

Christianity reached Nigeria in the nineteenth century and there are said to be more churches per square mile in the Niger Delta than any place on earth. Of course, the vast majority of the country's sixty million Christians are perfectly moderate in their worship and their views of the world. However, an influx of Pentecostals during the last fifty years has led to the adoption by some churches of extremist views. To combat the poor treatment of children and the abuse that many suffer because they are thought to be witches, the Nigerian government passed a Child Rights Act five years ago. However, not every state in Nigeria has adopted it.

Nigeria is a wealthy country, its riches coming from its plentiful supplies of oil and gas. It is a wealth, however, that bypasses most Nigerians who live in abject poverty and the ignorance and suspicion that it breeds.

In the small Niger Delta state of Akwa Ibom, this is particularly the case and in the name of Christianity – or a perverted form of it – possibly thousands of children are enduring horrific abuse and many are even murdered. Witchcraft is blamed for everything in that part of the world, whether it is divorce, disease, accidents or the loss of a job. Pastors rail against it from the pulpits of countless churches with names such as New Testament Assembly, Church of God Mission, Mount Zion Gospel, Glory of God and the Brotherhood of the Cross. They make a healthy living from it, too, carrying out exorcisms or 'deliverances' for around £170 in a land where people often earn no more than £1 a day.

In recent years, the pastors have turned the spotlight on children, declaring certain of them to be witches and unleashing panic and terror amongst their parents and their neighbouring villagers. Villagers turn on the children en masse, burning them, slashing them, chaining them to trees, burying them alive or merely beating them and chasing them into the bush where they starve to death. In cases where the parents do not want to lose their child, their neighbours are liable to attack him or her in the street.

Some manage to scrape together the money needed for a 'deliverance' – sometimes as much as three or four months' wages for them – but when it has been done, the pastor will often warn them that he might need to do it again in the future.

One young girl tells of how when she was seven years of age her mother was told by the pastor when her youngest brother died, that it had happened because her daughter was a witch. Later, three men came to the house and beat the girl in front of her parents. They then took her to the church for a 'deliverance'. A day later, she was taken into the bush by her mother who picked poisonous berries, made them into a drink and forced her daughter to drink it. Her mother told her that if that failed to kill her she would suffer a barbed-wire hanging. Finally, when the drink had failed to kill her, her mother threw boiling water and caustic soda over her and she was dumped in a field, screaming in pain, by her father. She survived and after staying close to the house for a while, she wandered into the bush but was eventually taken in by an organization that shelters children accused of being witches.

An eight-year-old boy named Gerry was declared to be a witch by a 'prophetess' at a prayer meeting. After the meeting had dispersed, his father siphoned off petrol from his motorbike and poured it over his son's face before setting fire to it.

Sixteen-year-old Nwaeka was punished for being declared a witch by barbarically having a three-inch nail driven into the top of her skull. Another had five nails hammered into his head while a twelve-year-old named Udo was beaten and slashed by villagers with machetes after he was abandoned by his mother for allegedly being a witch.

The mother of seven-year-old Magrose dug a pit in the bush and tried to bury her child alive. Thirteen-year-old Ekemini Abia was tied to a tree after being declared a witch. The rope cut into her ankles during the week in which they left her there and she can now barely walk.

One girl, nine-year-old Rita, told her mother that she had had a dream in which there was lots to eat and drink. From that, her mother deduced that she must be a witch because witches fly to their covens at night while their bodies sleep. She had shared food with her four-year-old brother Prince. Therefore, as that is one of the ways in which witchcraft is believed to be spread, both children were abandoned.

Around five thousand children are estimated to have been abandoned in the area since 1998 and many bodies turn up in the rivers where they have been drowned or in the forests where they have been abandoned. Countless more are just never found.

The pastors claim to base everything they say on the Bible and, of course, the good book does contain its fair share of exorcisms, Satanic possessions and dramatic miracles. There are references to killing witches in Exodus, Deuteronomy and Galatians. Of course, the more witches a pastor can declare, the better known and richer he is going to be. It is beneficial, therefore, to his church to declare children to be witches.

But, even when a child-witch has been abandoned or killed, the curse remains on the parents and they still have to pay a pastor to exorcise them.

One of the most influential evangelical preachers is Helen Ukpabio who is the self-styled prophetess of the 150-branch Liberty Gospel Church. She made a film that was widely distributed called End of the Wicked. It details how children become possessed and contains footage of them being inducted into covens, eating human flesh and bringing death and disease to their families. She published a bestselling book that told mothers how to identify if their child was a witch.

This scourge is not unique to Nigeria, however. In Angola, orphaned children are often accused of being witches by relatives in order to justify not providing for them; in the Congo, there are 25,000 children living on the streets, sixty per cent of whom were thrown out of their homes following allegations of witchcraft. Around 15,000 children are currently branded as witches in the Nigerian states of Akwa Ibom and Cross River.

TRACEY WIGGINGTON AND LISA PTASCHINSKI

Brisbane in Queensland, Australia, was for the twenty years between 1968 and 1987 under the control of the uncompromisingly conservative government of Sir Joh Bjelke-Petersen. It had been a time of police brutality, union-busting and clamping down on anyone who dared to be different. Bjelke-Petersen's regime was eventually brought down by an investigation into police and political corruption.

Strange then, that after such a harshly repressive time, one of Australia's – if not the world's – most bizarre murders, involving lesbians and vampirism, should be committed there.

On Friday nights, forty-seven-year-old council road paver and father of five Edward Clyde Baldock drank and played darts at the Scottish Caledonian Club. Friday, 20 October 1989 was no different to any other. He was drinking with the lads and would stagger home after last orders. It would be the last Friday night drink he would enjoy.

A few weeks earlier, at Brisbane's most notorious club, the Lesbian bar, Club Lewmors, the full moon seemed to be having an affect on four young women with an unhealthy interest in the occult.

Kim Jervis, a twenty-three-year-old photo processor was there with her girlfriend, Tracey Waugh, an unemployed secretary, also twenty-three years old. Jervis was dressed in the conventional black and purple garb of the Goth, her face caked in black and white make-up. She was heavily tattooed and on her wrists, neck and on her fingers she wore occult jewellery that bore pentagrams and other magic symbols.

Beside her sat the much quieter Waugh, but anyone would have seemed quiet compared to the woman who sat across the table from them. Tracey Wiggington was a six feet tall, seventeen stone, twenty-four-year-old student sheet-metal worker. They had met Wiggington two months earlier when she had just arrived in town, and a mutual interest in Satanism and witchcraft had confirmed their friendship.

That night, Kim Jervis had brought along another friend to meet Wiggington. Lisa Ptaschinski, at twenty-four-years of age, was another large woman who had tried an unhappy marriage before she decided she was gay. She suffered from depression, however, and had been admitted to hospital eighty-two times in the past five years after apparent suicide attempts. She had tried every way to kill herself, including a heroin overdose and swallowing razor blades.

Tracey Wiggington and Lisa Ptaschinski were attracted to one another immediately and were soon deep in conversation about witchcraft and their favourite horror films. They discovered that they had a great deal in common and left the club together that night.

'She has a strange fascination,' Ptaschinski said later of her new lover. '… She dominated me more than anyone has in my life. She had some kind of inner power.' This was a phenomenon remarked upon by others. Waugh would later describe her 'mind power', the ability to make people do what she wanted.

That first night, Ptaschinski began to find out about Wiggington's bizarre lifestyle. After they had made love, Wiggington declared that she was hungry. She told her companion, however, that she did not eat normal food. She drank animals' blood that she got from local butcher's shops. She invited Ptaschinski to wrap a tourniquet around her arm to raise a vein before making a small cut on her wrist and sucking her blood. Ptaschinski was keen to make her new lover happy and would oblige in this bizarre way a further three times.

Wiggington's vampirism also extended to staying out of daylight and avoiding mirrors, according to her other friends, Jervis and Waugh.

The four friends got together on 18 October at Kim Jervis's flat in the Brisbane suburb of Clayfield. Tracey Wiggington had a plan she wanted to share with them. She told them that the Devil wanted her to become a being she named 'the Destroyer' and to do this she had to kill someone and drink his or her blood. To achieve this, she suggested, Tracey Waugh and Lisa should pretend to be prostitutes and lure a victim – it was irrelevant if it was a man or a woman – into a secluded part of a park and there she and Kim Jervis would drink his or her blood. Afterwards, they would take the body to a cemetery, find a newly dug grave and put the corpse in it, covering it up again with soil. The following day when the coffin for that particular grave arrived, it would be lowered into the hole, covering their crime.

All agreed that it was a good plan and that they were unlikely to be found out. Wiggington showed them the small butterfly knife she planned to use to kill the victim. Jervis bought an identical blade the following day.

On the evening of October 20, as Edward Baldock downed pints of beer at the Scottish Caledonian Club, the four women convened once again at Club Lewmors. They drank champagne to celebrate their plan, something the manager of the club found strange. She had been serving regulars Jervis and Waugh for several years and they had never before ordered champagne.

At 11.30, they left the club and took to the streets.

A little over half an hour later, Edward Baldock staggered out of the Scottish Caledonian Club. As he began his laborious journey home, weaving along the street, a green car passed him. It was driven by Tracey Wiggington who had been driving through the Botanic Gardens and New Farm Park since leaving Club Lewmors, looking for a likely victim. Seeing Baldock, she stopped the car and she and Kim Jervis got out and asked him if he was looking for a good time. Baldock evidently was, for he clambered enthusiastically into the back seat of the car. Lisa Ptaschinski took over the driving, heading for Orleigh park in Brisbane's West End. At the deserted South Brisbane Sailing Club building, she stopped the car.

Wiggington got out of the car with Baldock and

they walked down towards the river. A few minutes later, however, a breathless Wiggington returned to the car looking for help. Baldock was proving too strong for her. Ptaschinski, ever eager to please her lover, borrowed Jervis's knife and accompanied Wiggington down to the river.

She found Baldock seated on the sand at the edge of the river, completely naked apart from his socks. The two women crept up behind him but at the critical moment, Lisa found herself unable to stab him. She collapsed at the feet of the drunk, almost hysterical.

Wiggington was furious but took her own knife from her pocket. Confused, Baldock asked her what she was doing just before she thrust the small blade into his body. She then sliced him first on one side of his neck and then the other. She continued to plunge the knife into him before seizing hold of his hair, pulling back his head and plunging the blade into the front of his throat. Astonishingly, however, he was still alive.

She kept stabbing, desperate for him to die and then sat down and waited for the life to flow out of him. She had almost decapitated him by this time.

Wiggington ordered Ptaschinski back to the car while she drank Baldock's blood. She then washed herself in the river before returning to the others. They could smell the blood on her breath.

Back at Jervis's flat, however, Wiggington discovered, to her horror, that she had lost her credit card. She forced Ptaschinski to drive her back to the scene of the murder to look for it.

It was nowhere to be found, however. What they did not know was that, drunk as he was, Baldock had the presence of mind to realize that there was a chance these girls were bent on robbing him. When Wiggington had returned to the car to get help, he had hidden his wallet behind the metal swing doors of the sailing club. As he did so, however, he spied a credit card lying on the ground. It was a Commonwealth Bank card and as he banked there, he presumed it must have been his and that it had fallen out of his wallet. He hid it inside his shoe that was beside his pile of clothes.

Wiggington and Ptaschinski searched frantically, but failed to find the card, not thinking for one moment to look in Baldock's shoe. They decided she must have lost it somewhere else and got back into the car to drive back to the flat.

They drove along the road that ran beside the river, but were stopped by a police car that was out looking for stolen cars and drunk drivers. The two girls, having left Jervis's flat in a hurry, had forgotten to bring their documentation with them. Their details were taken and Ptaschinski was breathalysed before the officers let them drive on. She was instructed to present her driving licence at the police station the following day.

Back at the flat, they were terrified. It seemed certain that when Baldock's body was discovered, the police would connect their vehicle with the murder. They began to concoct alibis.

The body was found early next morning and the lost credit card was retrieved from Baldock's shoe. Before long, as Wiggington had dreaded, the green car that was stopped in the early hours was identified as belonging to the same person whose name was on the credit card.

She had already visited the Sailing Club once that morning, finding the crime scene taped off and a crowd of onlookers watching investigators do their painstaking work. At one o'clock she returned, this time to talk to detectives. She told them that she and Kim Jervis had been in Orleigh Park the previous day and then as she stumbled over her version of events, blurted out that she had been there the previous night and had found the body but had been too frightened to report it. At no time, however, was she able to explain what her credit card was doing in the dead man's shoe.

She soon confessed, as did Lisa Ptaschinski who handed herself in at Ipswich police station.

Tracey Wigginton pleaded guilty and in January 1991 was sentenced to life imprisonment for the murder of Edward Baldock, with a minimum time of thirteen years to be served. She remains incarcerated at Brisbane's Women's Jail despite four parole applications.

The other three pleaded not guilty. Ptaschinski, however, was sentenced to life, while Kim Jervis was sentenced to eighteen years. Tracey Waugh was acquitted.

NICO CLAUX: THE 'VAMPIRE OF PARIS'

Following the arrest on 15 November 1994, of Nico Claux outside the Moulin Rouge cabaret in Paris on suspicion of shooting to death thirty-four-year-old Thierry Bissonnier the previous month, police officers began a search of his apartment at 9 Rue Coustou. In the words of Claux himself, what they found surprised and horrified them:

> *Throughout my apartment, bone fragments and human teeth were scattered about like loose change; vertebras and leg bones hung from the ceiling like morbid mobiles, and hundreds of videocassettes, mostly slasher and hardcore S&M flicks, filled my shelves. One can only imagine what went through the minds of the investigators as they looked around my living quarters. On one wall hung a bullet-riddled target, while across the room sat a TV set with jars of human ashes resting on top of it. Several bondage magazines were piled in a far corner, and nearby my backpack was found, which contained handcuffs, surgical instruments and duct tape. In addition to my tastes and choice of décor,*

> *investigators also discovered several stolen blood bags*
> *inside of my refrigerator.*

They also found a .22 calibre handgun under Claux' bed. Ballistics tests proved that this was the gun that had been used to kill Thierry Bissonnier. However, the grisly contents of the flat worried detectives. Did they have a serial killer on their hands?

When questioned, Claux told them that the bones and body parts came from a number of Parisian cemeteries that he had robbed. The bags of blood discovered in his refrigerator, came, he explained from his job as a mortuary assistant. He told them that he had harboured a life-long ambition to become a cannibal and his job had given him the opportunity, finally, to achieve that ambition. When he had stitched bodies after autopsies had been carried out on them, he would cut strips of meat from the ribs and eat them. Sometimes, he brought the meat back to Rue Coustou, he said, and cooked it before eating it.

Claux' fascination with death came from his past. He was born in 1972 in the African state of Cameroon where his father, a French citizen, worked for a bank. In 1977, when he was aged five, the family moved to London and then to Paris a couple of years later.

As a child, he had been introverted and withdrawn which made it difficult for him to make friends. He was, consequently, very lonely, spending much of his time alone in his room. Around this time his interest in death and the occult began to develop and he devoured countless books on vampires and werewolves.

What appears to have been the seminal moment of Nico Claux' young life happened when he was aged ten. He was having an argument with his grandfather when the elderly man collapsed and died in front of him from a cerebral embolism. He felt that his family, especially his mother, whose father the dead man was, blamed him for the death. For him, however, it added to his fascination with death and the ceremony that surrounds it.

When he was twelve, his father's job took the family to Lisbon in Portugal. Once again, however, during the four years he lived there, he failed to make friends and interact socially. At sixteen, he was back in Paris, living with his father.

Between 1990 and 1993, he told investigators, he spent all of his time in the cemeteries of Paris, his favourites being Pere Lachaise, Montmartre and Passy. He was fascinated by mausoleums, peering in through their windows. Eventually, it was simply not enough to be looking in from the outside. He began to break into them, prising open their rusty locks with a crowbar or climbing through a window. He described how once he was inside one of these houses of the dead, he felt 'like an emperor reigning in Hell'. Often, he would break into a mausoleum during the day and remain there until it was dark enough for him to explore the cemetery, opening coffins and mutilating corpses, without fear of interruption.

Gradually, however, this was not enough for him. He really wanted to dig up a corpse and mutilate it. He assembled a kit for this work, consisting of a crowbar, a pair of pliers, a screwdriver, black candles and a pair of surgical gloves. Carrying it in a backpack, he set out one day for Passy Cemetery in the western part of Paris. Passy is a huge, nineteenth century graveyard filled with the grand mausoleums that Claux loved so much. He had already selected one particular grave – a small mausoleum the last resting place of a family of Russian immigrants. He had already broken the lock a few days earlier and all it took was a kick to open it. He stepped inside and climbed down some steps into the crypt.

He carefully removed one of the coffins from its stone casing. It was very heavy and it took some time.

It was fairly new and he was anticipating finding a fresh corpse. He unscrewed the lid before prising it off with the crowbar. A terrible stench assaulted his nostrils and he saw the cadaver of an old woman. He stared into the empty eye sockets and experienced, he said, a feeling 'like I was falling into a whirlwind'. He lost control at that point and began frenziedly to stab the corpse with the screwdriver.

It was the first of many graves that he would desecrate in the next few years.

When he was twenty, he enlisted in the French army, hoping that it might provide him with a career. He was trained as a gunsmith but he was soon bored and after serving a year, he left. His next career choice seemed more appropriate to his particular interest – he would become a mortician.

His application to the only local college that taught embalming was rejected and, instead, in 1993, he found a job at the Saint Vincent-de-Paul children's hospital in Paris. He was assigned the job of mortuary attendant, allowing him to maintain his contact with dead bodies.

Later that year, he left the hospital and began to work as mortuary attendant and stretcher-bearer at Saint Joseph Hospital. It was here that he really developed his taste for human flesh. He was able to indulge his fantasy after the autopsy when he was left alone with the body to stitch it up. He described its taste as 'like tartare steak or carpaccio' and expressed a preference for eating the meat raw, describing the big muscles of the thighs as the best.

His job also involved delivering bags of blood to the operating theatre from the hospital's blood bank. There were always surplus bags which he hid in his locker until he went home. There, he let it cool in the fridge and when it reached the desired temperature, he mixed it with powdered proteins or human ashes and drank it.

Finally, however, even this was not enough for him. He wanted to be responsible for another's death and it was irrelevant to him who his victim was, whether male, female, black, white, old or young.

On 4 October 1994, he spent the morning searching the streets for a victim, but was unable to find one. He was aware that a lot of gay men used Minitel, an early French version of the Internet to chat dates to each other and organize dates. It was perfect for him because there was no possibility of conversations on Minitel being traced back to him. He decided, therefore, that it might provide him with the opportunity he sought. He logged on at home and before long was engaged in conversation with restaurateur and part-time classical musician Thierry Bissonier who expressed an interest in bondage and sado-masochistic sex. Claux told him he was into the same things and Bissonnier gave him his address. Claux hid his gun under his jacket and set out for Bissonnier's apartment.

He shot Bissonnier almost immediately on arriving in the apartment, the bullet entering through the right eye and lodging in his brain. As he lay on the ground, Claux pumped four more bullets into him, one in the chest and three more in the head.

When, fifteen minutes later, he had still not died, Claux smashed his skull with a concrete plant pot. He then sat down and munched some biscuits as Bissonnier died on the floor in front of him. He grabbed a few items, wiped away any fingerprints he might have left and went home. He later said that he did not perform necrophilia on the corpse because he feared catching AIDS. Bissonnier's body was discovered three days later.

Claux was caught after trying to purchase a camcorder with a cheque in the name of Thierry Bissonnier. The shopkeeper thought that the signature on the cheque was different to the one on the driving licence he was using as ID. He also noticed that the photograph on the driving licence had been tampered with. Claux realized he had been found out and fled, leaving the documents, including a photograph of himself on the driving licence, behind. A month later he was arrested and charged with murder, armed robbery, attempted fraud, use of forged documentation and use of a stolen cheque.

For two years after his arrest, Claux was subjected to a barrage of tests and examinations to determine whether he was sane enough to be tried. Eventually, he was revealed to be suffering from a borderline psychotic personality disorder but was judged sane enough to stand trial.

Needless to say, he was found guilty of all charges and sentenced to twelve years in prison.

Nico Claux was released from prison in March, 2002 and, after living in Sweden and England, now lives in Paris with a girlfriend, earning a living as an artist and profiting from his celebrity status as the Vampire of Paris.

NATASHA CORNETT AND THE LILLELID MURDERS

Pikeville, Kentucky, was not a town to be a teenager in. It was a town where nothing much happened and that had seen better times. In fact, the best thing about it in the minds of the young people who been born and brought up there was the road out.

Eighteen-year-old Natasha Wallen had other problems, however. Her medical insurance had run out and she had been released from Charter Ridge behavioural Center in Lexington, Kentucky where they had diagnosed her as suffering from bipolar disorder.

Life had already dealt some harsh blows to the youngster. Her mother, Madonna, had been sexually abused as a child and, as is so often the case, the cycle of abuse continued as an adult. She had entered into a series of doomed relationships with men who abused her and she had even shot one of them in self-defence. Madonna unsuccessfully tried to kill herself when Natasha was just ten years old by swallowing a bottle of pills. Natasha's response was to becoming increasingly difficult. She developed eating disorders and began to hang out in the town's drug scene, regularly using marijuana, LSD, PCP and ecstasy.

As a teenager, with her grandmother's encouragement, she began to develop an interest in the paranormal and the occult. She dressed as a Goth, wearing dark clothing and heavy make-up. She also took pleasure in spelling her name backwards – 'Ah Satan'. She cut herself with razors and knives and started drinking her own blood.

She also indulged in petty crime, being arrested a couple of times for theft and forgery. Violence was never far away and on one occasion police were called when she threatened her mother. Aged seventeen, she married Steve Cornett, a local boy that she had been dating for some time. The marriage foundered after a year, however, and he left her.

Her circle of friends came from similar, dysfunctional backgrounds. Eighteen-year-old Crystal Sturgill had suffered sexual abuse at the hands of her stepfather but when she complained about it, her family took his side and called her a liar. Seventeen-year-old Karen Howell drank heavily, like Natasha and also like her, took drugs. She was, in all likelihood, also bipolar, as her violent mood swings suggested. Also in common with Natasha, she was fascinated by vampires and she, too, cut herself and drank her blood. The two girls also drank each other's blood as well as that of their boyfriends.

School was a nightmare for these three girls. All three dressed as Goths and stood out from their schoolmates. They were bullied and called names. When they complained to teachers they were merely told that it was their own fault for drawing attention to themselves by dressing in the way they did.

The boys in the group were little better. Twenty-one-year-old Joseph Risner came from a family in which drugs were a part of everyday life. His parents had openly used marijuana, LSD and cocaine in front of him and he had himself started to use them at the age of nine. He had suffered sexual abuse at the hands of babysitters as early as twelve years of age. He had fared badly, too with authority, being convicted for his part in a fatal accident and having been discharged from the US Army after being caught smoking marijuana.

Jason Bryant, at fifteen, the youngest member of the group, but already had a conviction for car theft, while nineteen-year-old Edward Mullins was just the opposite. He had never been in trouble with the police and was an active church-goer.

These six disenchanted and hate-filled young

people seethed with anger at the town around them, the people of Pikeville, the teachers at school and those in authority who showed disdain for the way they looked and the thoughts they had. By April 1997, they had had enough. They decided it was time to leave the small-mindedness of Pikeville behind, once and for all.

On 5 April, they drove out of town in Joseph Risner's mother's blue Chevrolet Citation. Karen Howell had stolen a gun from her father as well as $500 and with another gun borrowed from a friend, they decided to make for New Orleans where Natasha Cornett had once briefly lived. The horror-story writer Anne Rice lived there and they thought they might possibly go and visit her.

Risner was violating a probation order by leaving town and this fact was reported to the police by Jason Bryant's father who had argued with his son about leaving Pikeville. The fact that the police would be looking for their car plus the difficulty of fitting six people into the Citation made them decide to find another vehicle.

That night they arrived at a rest stop on Highway 81 near the town of Greenville.

Also at the rest stop were Vidar Lillelid and his wife Delfina. Vidar had emigrated to the United

States from Norway and had married Delfina in 1989. They had initially settled in Miami, but, deciding it was not a place conducive to bringing up kids, moved to Knoxville, Tennessee where Vidar found work as a bellboy in a hotel. Delfina stayed home to home-school their daughter, Tabitha.

The couple had become Jehovah's Witnesses and on that April day were on their way home from a religious convention with their son and daughter. As Jehovah's Witnesses, they saw it as their duty to proselytize – to spread the word of the Lord and seeing a group of half a dozen young people at the rest stop – Natasha Cornett and her friends – decided to go and talk to them. A pleasant enough conversation seemed to ensue, according to the other people who had stopped for a rest. Then, the family and the teenagers left together, some of the teenagers climbing into the Lillelids' van with them.

It had not been apparent at the time, however, that Joseph Risner had pulled out his gun and ordered the shocked family into the van. As he did so, Vidar pleaded with the gun-wielding youngster to just take him, to leave his wife and children behind. He offered them the contents of his wallets and the keys to his vehicle but Delfina and the children would be able to recognize them. It would mean leaving witnesses behind and that was impossible. They drove off in the two vehicles.

They ordered Vidar Lillelid to turn off into the unpaved, tree-lined Payne Hollow Lane but there is some confusion as to what occurred next as the gangs' individual stories differ. Although Risner had the gun and, as the oldest, seemed to be the leader of the group, it was Bryant who is said to have pulled the trigger. Bryant, however, claims it was Risner. Cornett and Howell claim to have begged for the children's lives but gunpowder residue on Howell's clothing would suggest that she was heavily involved. Gunpowder residue also found on Edward Mullins' clothing would also suggest that his claims to have remained in the vehicle with Crystal Sturgill throughout to be false.

The terrified Lillelid family was ordered to stand in a ditch at the side of the road and seventeen shots were fired at them. Vidar and Delfina died and their two-year-old son was shot in the right eye and in the body and survived. When they were found, six-year-old Tabitha was alive but she died in hospital from the major head wound that had been inflicted on her. The gang left the Citation behind and as they drove away, callously drove over the bodies of Vidar and Delfina. Risner later claimed that this was an accident but the others in the vehicle countered this claim, saying that he drove over them deliberately.

They drove to the Mexican border but because some of them were not eighteen, they were denied entry into Mexico. By this time, however, the Lillelid family had been found after someone had reported hearing gunfire in the vicinity of Payne Hollow Lane and it was obvious from the Citation left behind who had been responsible. Warrants were issued for their arrests and they were picked up a short while later. In the car police found a wounded Bryant. He claimed that he had been shot by Risner, but the others told police that he had accidentally shot himself.

The media made much of the group's Satanic connections and Natasha's frightening Goth look did nothing to reduce the frenzy that erupted. There were suggestions that the killings had been some kind of ritual sacrifice and that Cornett had been ordered to do it by voices she heard in her head. Even the District Attorney, Charles Bell, said that he believed that demonic forces had been at work that day and that the Lillelids had been sacrificed to the devil.

All six members of the group were sentenced to life imprisonment without parole. At least they would never be going back to Pikeville again.

ADOLFO DE JESÚS CONSTANZO

In Little Havana in Miami where Adolfo de Jesús Constanzo was born in 1962, they said that his fifteen-year-old mother, Aurora, was a witch. If she fell out with someone, headless goats or chickens were likely to turn up shortly after on his or her doorstep. She was a Cuban immigrant who had given birth to three children, each by a different father, but the death of her second husband had left her comparatively well-off.

Aurora was an adherent of the Santeria cult, a religion that mixed together various belief systems and that had originated amongst the Yoruba tribe in West Africa and came to the Caribbean with slaves taken there to work on the sugar plantations. Amongst its rituals, it featured a trance for communicating with ancestors and deities as well as animal sacrifice and sacred drumming.

At the age of nine, Aurora initiated her son Adolfo in the art and practice of Santeria, sending him to Puerto Rico and Haiti to be trained in Voodoo. Later, when he was fourteen, he was instructed in the religion of Palo Mayombe, another religion that had developed amongst Africans, in this case the Bantu African slaves from Central Africa. 'Palo' means 'stick' in Spanish and sticks were used in the preparation of altars or receptacles that were called 'Nganga', 'el caldero' or 'la prenda' that are crucial to the religion. This cauldron is filled with sacred earth, human remains, bones and other items and each Nganga is dedicated to a specific spirit.

For Adolfo, however, his training was made more interesting by the involvement of the man training him with local drug dealers. He had become very wealthy through his work for these people and Adolfo began to make his own plans to do something similar.

By 1983, Constanzo had pledged himself to Kadiempembe, his religion's version of Satan. He decided to devote himself to the worship of evil for profit. His final initiation included ritual scarring, his mentor carving mystic symbols into Constanzo's flesh. 'My soul is dead,' he declared, as the ritual reached its climax. 'I have no god.'

He was a handsome and charismatic young man and at the age of twenty-one, was selected for a modeling assignment in Mexico City. Already displaying bisexual tendencies by this time, in Mexico City he hooked up with three men –

Martin Quintana Rodriguez, Omar Orea Ochoa and homosexual psychic Jorge Montes who became not just his servants but also his lovers. He was, even at this time, building a reputation as a sorcerer and they were the first recruits to the extraordinary cult that he had begun to create.

Adolfo was providing services such as tarot readings and ritual cleansings and, like his mentor, he began to work for drug dealers. He promised them that he had the power to make them invisible and invulnerable but, of course, services such as these came at a steep price. One pre-eminent drug-dealing family, the powerful Calzadas, proved particularly lucrative for him. He made himself an essential part of their business, persuading them that it was his magic that was keeping them in business.

However, his services were not exclusive to those on the wrong side of the law. He also worked for many people from the upper echelons of Mexican society – doctors, property developers, models and musicians. He was also consulted by high-ranking police officials, including Salvador Garcia who was head of the Mexico City drug squad and Florentino Ventura, officer in charge of the Mexican branch of Interpol.

Through such contacts, Constanzo became a

very wealthy young man. He lived in an expensive townhouse in an upmarket Mexico City suburb and drove any one of a fleet of luxury cars, including an expensive, top-of–the-range Mercedes.

Constanzo and his colleagues were now raiding cemeteries for bones and human body parts to feed his Nganga. Increasingly, however, Constanzo became interested in human sacrifice as a means of filling it. He claimed that it was a vital part of his magic.

Twenty-three people are thought to have been ritually slaughtered by him and his followers, but that number is believed to be merely a conservative estimate of the true number. He was clever enough to select victims who would not be missed – runaways, drug-dealers, transvestites and poor peasants about whom the authorities did not care.

Constanzo was becoming increasingly powerful and eventually he demanded a partnership in the Calzada drug cartel that was headed by Guillermo Calzada. When his request was denied, he exacted terrible vengeance on the family. Within a month Giullermo and six other Calzada family members had disappeared. Their mutilated bodies were found minus body parts – brains, fingers, sexual organs, toes, ears and hearts.

Sara Aldrete was a twenty-two-year-old six foot one inch tall student at Texas Southmost College in Brownsville, Texas, who Constanzo wooed away from her boyfriend, Brownsville drug smuggler, Gilberto Sosa, in July 1987. He initiated her into his cult and shortly afterwards appointed her as his second-in-command. She ran things while he was away on his frequent trips smuggling marijuana into the United States. He named her 'la Madrina' Spanish for 'godmother'.

Almost a year later, Constanzo established a new headquarters at Rancho Santa Elena, about twenty miles from the city of Matamuros in the Mexican state of Tamaulipas. It would become the notorious site for most of his killing, a place of brutal, sadistic, ritual horror where many would lose their lives.

His first victims there, on 28 May 1988, were drug dealer Hector de la Fuente and farmer Moises Castillo, both shot dead. In Mexico City, meanwhile, the gruesomely dismembered remains of transvestite, Ramon Esquivel, were found on a street corner.

The Nganga was being satisfied.

It was satisfied, too, when Constanzo performed a human sacrifice to secure the release of kidnapped drug dealer, Ovidio Hernandez and his two-year-old son. The kidnappers were terrified by the prospect of having the mighty sorcerer working his magic against them. They released their captives. Ovidio, naturally, became a follower and when Constanzo told him that he needed a human sacrifice, the drug dealer killed his own cousin and handed his corpse over to the sorcerer.

His deathlust knew no bounds and his own followers were not exempt. When one of his own, Jorge Gomez, breached one of the cult's rules by snorting cocaine, he was sacrificed to the Nganga. This deathlust would bring about his ultimate downfall, however.

Not only did he want people to die, he wanted them to suffer and when one of his victims died without begging for his life or pleading for mercy, Constanzo was furious. In his rage, he demanded that his followers bring him an American to be sacrificed. It was a tantrum he would live to regret.

Matamoros, just across the Rio Grande from Brownsville, with its prostitution, sex shows and abundant supply of booze and drugs, had become a popular destination for students who wanted to let their hair down. In the first three months of 1989, sixty people had gone missing in the town, but that did not put off twenty-one-year-old Mark

Kilroy, a student at the University of Texas who was holidaying there with some friends. In the early hours of 14 March, he disappeared on the streets of Matamoros.

Unlike the other disappearances, this one generated a huge storm of interest. Kilroy's uncle worked for the US Customs Service and a reward of $15,000 was immediately offered for information. Every crook in Matamoros was hauled in for questioning but no one was able to shed light on the mystery.

A huge manhunt was launched in the area and roadblocks were set up to check traffic on the surrounding roads. A member of Constanzo's cult, Serafin Hernandez, driving with another cult member, David Martinez, came upon one such roadblock, but believing himself to have been made invisible by Constanzo, drove right past it.

Police cars took off in pursuit and when they stopped his car, he got out and invited the officers to shoot him, because he also believed that the sorcerer had cast a spell making him bullet-proof.

The officers learned that the two men had come from Rancho Santa Elena and took them back there. A search of the property revealed drugs and firearms and the Nganga with its contents of spiders, blood, scorpions, a dead cat, a turtle shell, bones, deer antlers and a human brain simmering away. They started to dig and uncovered fifteen corpses.

Constanzo and his closest associates had vanished and, as a massive manhunt was launched, reports came in that he had been sighted as far away as Chicago. He was much closer than that, however. He had traveled to Mexico City and was holed up in an apartment with Sara Aldrete, Martin Quintana Rodriguez and professional hitman Alvaro de Leon Valdez who went by the nickname El Duby.

Aldrete could see that there was nowhere left to run and, in an effort to save herself, tossed a handwritten note out of the apartment window.

It read:

Please call the judicial police and tell them that in this building are those that they are seeking. Give them the address, fourth floor. Tell them that a woman is being held hostage. I beg for this, because what I want most is to talk – or they're going to kill the girl.

The note was found by a passerby who, thinking it was a joke, failed to pass it on to the authorities.

All was not well in the apartment, however, and on 6 May a loud argument broke out. Gunshots followed and terrified neighbours called the police. As they began to surround the building, Constanzo appeared at the window and opened fire on them with a Uzi machine gun. For the next forty-five minutes, the air was filled with gun-smoke as a vicious gun battle ensued.

Realizing there was no way out, Constanzo handed his gun to El Duby and ordered him to shoot him and Rodriguez. At first El Duby refused to do it, but Constanzo slapped him on the face and warned him that if he did not do as he was ordered, he would personally ensure that he would suffer in the afterlife. Constanzo and Rodriguez embraced and the terrified gunman pulled the trigger, raking them with bullets.

Aldrete and El Duby were arrested and she was given a six-year prison sentence for criminal association and sixty years for murder. El Duby was sentenced to thirty years.

American authorities have announced that if she is ever released from prison, she will immediately be arrested and tried for the murder of Mark Kilroy.

THE ZEBRA MURDERS

They were a unit known as the Death Angels, a special unit of the black Muslim organization, the Nation of Islam. Each of them had been specially selected and was informed that he was expected to kill nine white men, five white women or four white children. By doing so, each would earn the right to enter Paradise and a pair of black wings would be affixed to their photographs which were pinned on the wall of an upstairs room of the Nation of Islam's Black Self-Help Moving and Storage warehouse on Market Street in San Francisco where they met. By April 1974, they had killed fourteen people and wounded a number of others.

The first murder took place on 19 October 1973 when thirty-year-old mining engineer Richard Hague and his twenty-eight-year-old journalist wife, Quita, both white, were walking near their house after dinner in Telegraph Hill in San Francisco. Ahead of them, they saw two well-dressed young black men standing on either side of the pavement. As they walked past one of them suddenly reached out and seized Richard by the arm. His wife started to run away, but when she saw one of the men point a gun threateningly at her husband's chest, she stopped running and went back. It was a mistake because if she had not run back, they would probably have let her husband go as she had got a good look at them and would have been able to identify them.

The men pushed the couple into the back of a white van parked at the kerb nearby. Inside, they tied their wrists together with wire and laid them on the floor face down. One of them put his hand up Quita's sweatshirt but when Richard objected he was struck savagely across the face with a tyre wrench. His jaw was smashed by the blow.

They drove for a while until they arrived in San Francisco's deserted warehouse district. The van stopped and Quita was dragged struggling from the vehicle. They threw her to the ground where she pleaded for her life. It was to no avail. One of the men produced a machete, swung it above his head and brought it down on her neck again and again until she was almost decapitated.

Richard was dragged semi-conscious from the van and the man with the machete hacked at his face and body with it, injuring him horrifically but miraculously failing to kill him. They drove off, believing him to be dead.

A short while later, a couple were driving through the industrial section of the city when a man staggered out of the darkness towards them. When they stopped, the driver got out of his car to see what he could do to help. When the other man turned round, he was horrified. He was grotesquely mutilated, his skin hanging in blood-covered tatters from his skull. But he lived.

The Zebra Killers had claimed their first victim and had taken the first step on their bloody road to Paradise.

Ten days later, on 29 October, twenty-eight-year-old Frances Rose was slowly approaching the gate to the University of California at Berkeley extension centre in her gold Mustang when a man appeared in front of her car. He had his hand up, signalling her to stop and when she did so, he leaned through the window and asked for a lift. She was immediately suspicious, however, and instead of letting him in, she floored the accelerator. Before the car sped off, however, the man threw open the passenger door and sprayed bullets into the interior, killing Frances with shots to the chest, neck and face.

Their next victim had a little more luck.

On 9 November, Robert Stoeckman, a twenty-six-year-old Pacific Gas & Electric clerk, was attacked by a black man with a gun at a company stockyard on Amy Street. The man, a thirty-five-year-old ex-con named Leroy Doctor, asked him for directions and then thanked Stoeckman when he provided them.

Later, as he left the yard, Stoeckman was surprised to find Doctor waiting outside for him. He grabbed Stoeckman and pushed him behind a fence, pulling out a gun and pointing it at his mouth. Just as Doctor pulled the trigger, Stoeckman moved his head to the side and he felt the bullet graze his neck as it flew past.

Stoeckman staggered a couple of steps and crumpled to the ground. He then realized he was not badly hurt, jumped up and grabbed the gun. He wrestled it from Doctor's hand, sending it spinning across the ground. Both men scrambled for the weapon but Stoeckman got there first. As Doctor came at him, he shot him. Leroy Doctor was later convicted of assault with a deadly weapon.

A fortnight later, on Sunday, 25 November, popular fifty-three-year-old Jordanian immigrant grocery storekeeper, Saleem 'Sammy' Erkat was working in his store on Larkin Street when a tall black man carrying a briefcase and wearing a raincoat entered. The man pulled a gun from the case and held it to

Sammy's head, ordering him into the store-room at the rear of the shop. There, he pulled the trigger, killing the father of four instantly.

Paul Dancic was a twenty-six-year-old junkie who had just been released from prison for possession and was looking for a fix. He stepped up to a phone booth on Haight Street to call a dealer whose number he had obtained but as he did so, a black man approached him from behind and shouted to him. As Dancik turned the man fired three bullets into his chest. Dancik had had his last fix.

Politician Arthur Agnos, a future mayor of San Francisco, had been at a meeting in Potrero Hill on the evening of 13 December. After the meeting, he was talking to a couple of women outside when a black man approached them. He suddenly pulled a gun and shot Agnos twice in the back, seriously wounding him but failing to kill him.

On the same night thirty-one-year-old Marietta DiGirolamo was out looking for her boyfriend who was late coming home. As she walked up the street, she was pushed into a shop doorway by a black man with a gun. He killed her with two bullets to the chest.

On 20 December, twenty-year-old student Angela Roselli survived three bullets fired by a well-dressed black man as she parked her car in The Haight. Sadly, however, that same night eighty-one-year-old janitor, Ilario Bertuccio did not. He was walking home from work when a man walking towards him on the pavement pulled a gun and pumped four bullets into him. He fell to the ground dead.

Three days before Christmas another two whites were shot dead – nineteen-year-old Neal Moynihan who had been out Christmas shopping, shot in the face, neck and heart and fifty-year-old Mildred Hosler, killed by the same man five minutes later.

His place in Paradise was rapidly becoming a certainty.

The police were baffled. These killings had no apparent motives. There had been no rape, no robbery and no arguments or fights beforehand. Furthermore, there seemed to be nothing to link the victims. All that they could glean from victims who survived was that the men who had shot them appeared to almost be in a trance as they pulled the trigger.

And, of course, the victims were all white and the killers were all black.

Meanwhile, the white inhabitants of San Francisco were terrified to go out in case they became the next statistic in this wave of senseless violence.

When the police chief announced that the 'Z'

radio frequency was being reserved exclusively for all communications regarding the case, at least they got a name to pin on the perpetrators. They started to call them the 'Zebra Killers'.

As suddenly as it had started, however, it stopped. But the hiatus lasted only five weeks. Then in the course of one horrific day – Monday, 28 January 1974 – five people were shot. Forty-five-year-old Jane Holly was shot dead as she spun her clothes in a laundromat. Her killer was seen by witnesses leaving the scene in a 1969 Cadillac. Tana Smith, a thirty-two-year-old unmarried secretary was shot by a black man at the intersection of Geary Boulevard and Divisadero Street. She died shortly after. Vincent Wollin died on his sixty-ninth birthday ten minutes after Tana Smith had been killed, shot by a young black man at the corner of Fulton and Divisadero Streets. Just fifteen minutes later eighty-four-year-old John Bambic was shot at point-blank range as he rummaged through a rubbish bin. He was seen briefly struggling with his assailant, a black man, before he fell dead to the ground. Finally, the only victim to survive the horror of that night, twenty-three-year-old Roxanne Macmillan was walking from her car to her apartment when a black man approached her saying 'hello'. As she turned to see who it was, he shot her once in the back and once in the side. Although she lived, Roxanne would spend the rest of her life in a wheelchair.

February and March passed without incident but it started again on the evening of 1 April as two Salvation Army cadets, twenty-one-year-old Linda Story and nineteen-year-old Thomas Rainwater, were leaving the Salvation Army Training Center, heading for a snack at the Mayfair market a few blocks away. Not far from the market, they were overtaken by a black man who suddenly spun round. To their horror, they saw that he had a gun in his hand and was pointing it at them. As they turned and started to run, he fired, hitting each of them in the back. Linda lived but Thomas died from his injuries. Two police officers, not far away in a patrol car, arrived on the scene seconds after the incident and narrowly missed capturing the killer. They found shell casings from a .32, the same calibre weapon used in all the other incidents.

On Easter Sunday, two boys were wounded as they waited at a bus stop and then on 16 April, twenty-three-year-old Nelson T. Shields IV, handsome son of a wealthy Du Pont executive was killed while he sat in a car one evening in the Ingleside district waiting for a friend. More .32 cartridges were found and a black man was seen running up the street.

The case was now seriously affecting the city's tourist industry and the streets were deserted after dark.

Police presented a sketch of a black man they believed to be the killer and officers stopped hundreds of young black men and questioned them to the extent that the mayor was accused of persecuting the black community.

Of more success, however, was the offer of a reward of $30,000. Anthony Harris who worked at Black Self-Help came forward and provided police with information about the Death Angels, even furnishing them with information about a murder they knew nothing about.

On 1 May, police officers carried out raids at addresses across the city. The Death Angels were picked up one by one, J.C.X. Simon being picked up at Apartment 2, at 844 Grove Street and Larry Green arrested in Apartment 7 of the same building. Another two suspects were picked up at Black Self Help and a total of seven altogether were in custody by the end of that morning.

There was indignation from black leaders about the notion of a death squad in the Nation of Islam and Anthony Harris was described as 'a crackpot'.

The Zebra Killers' trial was the longest in Californian criminal history to-date. Three and a half million words of testimony were recorded and evidence was heard from 181 witnesses. Anthony Harris was in the witness box for twelve gruelling days.

However, it took the jury just eighteen hours to find all four defendants guilty of first-degree murder and conspiracy to commit first degree murder. Each was sent to jail for life.

THE WEST MEMPHIS THREE

In the 1980s and 1990s there was an extraordinary moral panic in the United States and around the world about Satanic ritual abuse. There were reports of physical and sexual abuse carried out in the context of the occult or Satanic ritual and some claimed that there was a worldwide conspiracy that involved the wealthy and the powerful in abduction of children for sacrifice, pornography or prostitution.

The panic was influenced by the testimony of children and adults obtained using now largely discredited therapeutic and interrogation techniques and was disseminated through television talk-shows, conferences and books. Children claimed to have seen witches fly, to have travelled in a hot air balloon, to have taken part in orgies at car washes and airports, to have been flushed down toilets and into secret rooms where they were abused before being cleaned up and returned to their parents. Assault by a figure dressed as a clown featured in one testimony as did being forced to drink urine and being tied to a tree naked. However, no real evidence was ever found to confirm that any of these incidents actually took place.

It was against this background that the mutilated bodies of three eight-year-old boys – Steven Branch, James Moore and Christopher Byers – were found on the afternoon of 6 May 1993. Word spread that they had been cut with a knife, raped and at least one of them showed signs of having his genitals cut.

The boys had last been seen together between 5.30 and 6 pm the previous evening. School had ended at 3 pm and Steven Branch went home but went out again shortly after. When Christopher Byers' stepfather, John Byers, arrived home at 3.10 his son was not there. Christopher usually had to wait for his brother Ryan to come home at 3.30 to get into the house as he was not allowed a key.

When Ryan came home, John and he went off and in the meantime Christopher returned home and broke in. John Byers gave him a beating with his belt for it when he caught up with him.

At 6 pm, James Moore's mother saw him cycling with Steven and Christopher, Chris seated on the back of Steven's bike. She tried to call her son but he rode off without hearing her.

When John Byers discovered on his return home at 6.30 that Chris was once again not home, he was furious and he, Chris's mother Melissa and Ryan drove around the area looking for him. They found not a trace of him and, becoming worried, informed the police that he was missing. He was told to give it until eight o'clock before making it official. At eight a police officer came to the house and fifteen minutes later, Diana Moore, James's mother told them that she had seen the three boys earlier.

Although darkness had now fallen, John Byers went out to the Robin Hood Hills area with Mrs. Moore, Melissa Byers and Ryan, where the boys had last been spotted and began to search for them. As the night wore on, the search party grew in size.

At 11 pm, John Byers called the sheriff to ask that a search and rescue team be detailed to help but the sheriff told him they would have to wait until the following morning.

As the search continued into the night, Byers and a friend, Tony Hudson checked the Mid-Continent building which was being rebuilt after collapsing in a storm. When they got there, they saw a black van parked nearby. It was locked and they assumed it belonged to one of the construction workers. But there was no sign of the boys. They went home with the intention of resuming the search the following morning.

The search started at first light but at 1.45 they received the news they had been dreading. A body had been found. It was in a creek near the Blue Beacon Truck Wash and was removed by police officers an hour later. A second body was found shortly after about twenty-five feet away from the first. The third was found nearby.

The officers at the scene concluded that the boys had been raped but this was disproved by the autopsy, although the coroner did not discount the possibility that they may have been sexually assaulted.

James Moore had drowned in two feet of water in a drainage ditch after receiving multiple injuries to his entire body. He was naked and his wrists were tied to his ankles with his own shoelaces. There was no evidence of any sexual assault having taken place.

Steven Branch had died in the same way, again having been savagely beaten beforehand. He was bound in the same way and, unlike James who had probably been unconscious during much of the attack on him, his hands and arms did bear defensive wounds. The coroner concluded that he may have suffered sexual assault despite the fact that there was no supporting evidence.

The attack on Chris Byers had been the most savage of the three and he did suffer sexual injuries. His penis, scrotal sac and testes had been cut off and there were a number of stab wounds to the genital area. He had wounds on his buttocks and had multiple injuries to the head and body. He did not drown as he was already dead when he was put in the water. Again, although there was no evidence of rape, the coroner concluded that it was a possibility.

There was no sign of a weapon at the murder scene and the boys' clothing and bicycles had been thrown into the water, removing any evidence they might have provided. The clothing was pinned down by sticks which the police failed to collect at the time, instead claiming that two sticks found in the woods six months later were the ones used. An imprint of a tennis shoe was found on a part of the bank which had been deliberately cleared.

The following day, the notion of ritual or cultish sacrifice was introduced for the first time in a conversation between Lieutenant James Sudbury of the West Memphis Police Department and Steve Jones, a Juvenile Officer for Crittenden County in Arkansas. Jones told the other man that he knew someone in the area who was interested in such things and that he believed was capable of such an act – nineteen-year-old Damien Echols.

The two men went to Echols' West Memphis home where they interviewed the boy, following up with another interview a few days later at the police station. When asked whether one of the boys had been more savagely beaten than the others, Echols replied that one had had his genitals removed, information that the police officers believed only the killer would know. However, knowledge of this fact was circulating freely around the local area. The interview completed, Echols was allowed to leave without being charged.

Damien Echols was born Michael Wayne Hutcheson in 1974 and spent the first years of his life on the move, his father's work forcing the family to constantly re-locate. Following his parents' divorce, his mother re-married and he was adopted by her new husband, West Memphis man Jack Echols. Life did not improve, however, and Damien fought constantly with his mother, while at school his work began to suffer.

He stood out from his schoolmates, always dressing in dark clothing, especially a long black coat that he wore in all weathers. He experimented with religion for a while and changed his name to Damien, borrowing the name from Father Damien, a 19th century Catholic priest, although many thought he had taken it from the character Damien in the horror movie *The Omen*.

Damien became depressed but began to find

solace in the study of Paganism. He tried to commit suicide a number of times, trying and failing to hang himself, drown himself and overdose on drugs.

At the age of seventeen, he and his girlfriend ran away and broke into an abandoned house where they planned to spend the night. The police were called, however, and Damien was arrested. He underwent psychological tests and was sent to Charter Hospital in Maumelle where he was diagnosed as manic-depressive and prescribed the anti-depressant Trofanil. At this point, he met chief Juvenile Probation Officer Jerry Driver, a man who was convinced that Satanic cults were behind a great deal of the criminal activity in the area.

When he left hospital, life got worse. His mother divorced Jack Echols and remarried Damien's biological father and moved with her son to Portland, Oregon. Damien, meanwhile, began to drink heavily and on one occasion tried once more to kill himself. Hospitalized again, doctors could find nothing to make him feel better. He returned to Arkansas where he stayed with an old school friend.

Although the authorities had been notified of his various moves – he was on probation and had to keep them informed – he was arrested one day by Jerry Driver who claimed that he had violated his probation. He was sent back to Charter Hospital for two weeks and soon after his parents returned to West Memphis.

In the investigation into the murders, a West Memphis woman, Vicky Hutcheson became important. Her son Aaron claimed that the boys had been murdered at a place known as 'the playhouse'. He then claimed to have witnessed the murders and that they had been committed by Satanists who spoke Spanish. Although 'the playhouse' did not seem to exist and his statements were wildly inconsistent, he was unable to identify Baldwin Echols as the killers.

Hutcheson also told police that two weeks after the murders, she went to a meeting of a witches' coven with Misskelley and Echols where Echols openly boasted of killing the boys. This evidence was discounted.

As police investigated the murders, they became convinced that a boy named Jessie Misskelley had been involved. Brought in for questioning on 3 June 1993, he confessed to having been present when Damien Echols and James Baldwin killed the three boys. Furthermore, he admitted to being a member of a Satanic cult that met in the woods and staged orgies as well as initiation rites that included killing and eating dogs. His statement contained many inaccuracies, including what Damien had been wearing on the day and he changed the time of the murders a number of times, sometimes after prompting by investigators.

When Baldwin and Echols were arrested, police seized various items from their homes – a red robe that belonged to Baldwin's mother and two notebooks from Damien's home that appeared to contain Satanic or cult writings in them. Fibres were found that were claimed to match the victims' clothing although these, like much in this case, were disputed. A knife was found in a lake behind Jason Baldwin's house and although there was no evidence that Jason or Damien had ever owned it, it became a major piece of evidence.

Other suspects were never really considered seriously. There had been a report of a black man in the rest room of the Mr Bojangles Restaurant near Robin Hood Hills that night. He was 'dazed and covered with blood and mud' according to the manager. It later became a significant observation when of two human hairs found on one of the dead boys' clothes, one was negroid in origin.

John Byers was interviewed by police after he had been seen giving a knife to a member of a film crew.

Blood was found on the knife that matched Chris Byers' blood type but no more tests were carried out and it was forgotten.

Curiously, the tennis shoe print found at the scene did not match any shoes owned by any of the accused but police chose to ignore this in their focus on proving that Misskelley, Baldwin and Echols were the perpetrators.

Jessie Misskelley was found guilty and sentenced to life plus forty years in prison. James Baldwin was sentenced to life and Damien Echols was sentenced to death. The appeals process grinds slowly on as Damien Echols waits for death by lethal injection in the Varner Unit of the Arkansas Department of Correction.